Saint Oliver Plunkett

Journey to Sainthood

by
Tommy Burns

Foreword b
Archbishop Eamc

The Canonisation Picture, hung from the balcony of St. Peter's Basilica in Rome, during the Canonisation Ceremony in 1975. It is now located at the National Shrine in Drogheda. See description in Appendix V.

Published by the Author
Drogheda, Ireland.

ISBN 978-1-78280-285-3

Copyright © 2019 Thomas M. Burns. All rights reserved.
Revised edition 2019 - First printed 2014
pontana@eircom.net

All rights reserved. No part of this publication may be reproduced, distributed, or transmitted in any form or
by any means, including photocopying, recording, or other electronic or mechanical methods, without the
prior written permission of the publisher, except in the case of brief quotations embodied in critical reviews
and certain other non-commercial uses permitted by copyright law. For permission requests, the publisher
may be contacted by email: pontana@eircom.net

Printed by Anglo Printers, Mell, Drogheda, Co. Louth, Ireland

ACKNOWLEDGMENTS

The author would like to thank all those who willingly offered help or advice for this publication and to all those persons, libraries or religious communities/institutes who offered resources, all of which was greatly appreciated. A special word of thanks is due to the Siena Sisters, Drogheda, the Medical Missionaries of Mary, Drogheda and the Dominican Sisters, Cabra for supplying pictures and other material.

A large proportion of the text was gleaned from St. Oliver's two hundred and thirty letters, all of which are printed with commentary in what should be a first source of reference for any study of St. Oliver, namely, Mgr. John Hanly's: 'The Letters of Saint Oliver Plunkett' Dublin, 1979. The nuggets of information from his publication are so numerous that I have not included many of their references, however their origins in 'The Letters' may be taken as read. I wish to thank Mgr. Hanly for his ever willing help and gracious consent in allowing me this latitude.

My intention for this volume was to write a concise biography while including a large number of interesting facts from multiple sources about St. Oliver's life and times. For those who wish to undertake further study on the subject, Fr. Emmanuel Curtis in his biography of Archbishop Oliver gives a sizeable bibliography of books, articles and manuscripts at the back of his book. A list of the sixty-three known biographies of St. Oliver is printed for the first time in Appendix VII of this publication. If taken together, they provide a pretty comprehensive index of sources of information about our saint and hero, Oliver Plunkett.

CONTENTS

FOREWORD BY ARCHBISHOP EAMON MARTIN

On Divine Mercy Sunday 2014, Pope Francis celebrated Mass for the Canonisation of two great saints of our time: Pope St John XXIII and Pope St John Paul II. In his homily, the Holy Father reflected on the 'glorious wounds of the risen Jesus' and commented that the two new saints were 'not afraid to look upon the wounds of Jesus, to touch his torn hands and his pierced side'. The two new saints were priests and bishops who had lived through tragic events of the twentieth century, but who were not overwhelmed by them. 'The wounds of Jesus are a test of faith', he said, continuing: 'For them, God was more powerful; faith was more powerful – faith in Jesus Christ the Redeemer of man and the Lord of history; the mercy of God, shown by those five wounds, was more powerful'. Therefore they were able to courageously bear witness before the Church and the world to God's goodness and mercy and in so doing, bring new life and hope to the Church. This, Pope Francis believes is what characterises a true saint. He summed it up perfectly towards the end of his homily when he said:

'Let us not forget that it is the saints who give direction and growth to the Church'.

It is wonderful to think that, back in 1975, the young Cardinal Karol Wojtyla from Krakow, just happened to be present in Rome at the canonisation of our own St Oliver Plunkett – he was leading a pilgrimage from Poland to Rome at the time. Four years later, on 29 September 1979, as Pope John Paul II, he knelt at Killineer, just outside Drogheda, to venerate the Relic of the Head of St Oliver Plunkett.

Like our two new saints, St Oliver lived through the tragic events of another century but was not overwhelmed by them. He was not afraid to look upon the wounds of Jesus. His faith in God was more powerful than anything the cruelty of the world at that time could throw at him. He courageously bore witness to the love and mercy of God, and, in everything he did, he gave much needed direction and growth to the Church of his time.

In this volume, Tommy Burns takes a fresh look at the journey to sainthood of St Oliver Plunkett. Much has been written about the saint down the years, but it is always important to return to the stories of the lives of the saints, because new lessons, new inspiration and new hope can always be found there.

Through a careful study of the letters of St Oliver, Tommy brings us new insights into the experiences which shaped the saint's life and which can continue to inspire the Church in Ireland on its journey of renewal. A number of these insights resonate strongly with the message of Pope Francis in his exhortation, Evangelii Gaudium (The Gospel of Joy). Pope Francis is convinced that the Church of today must evaluate all that it is doing in the light of mission: 'I dream of a missionary option, that is, a missionary impulse capable of transforming everything, so that the Church's customs, ways of doing things, times and schedules, language and structures can be suitably channelled for the evangelisation of today's world, rather than her self-preservation (EG 27)'. St Oliver Plunkett, Journey to Sainthood, reminds us of how central to St Oliver's life and motivation was the call to mission. In many ways the Church in Ireland in the mid-seventeenth century was in pieces – the legacy of violence, turmoil and ecclesiastical indiscipline of the preceding decades meant that Oliver, as the new Archbishop of Armagh, had a huge challenge ahead of him. But he was not overwhelmed. His approach was to fearlessly go out to the peripheries, to visit, encourage, bring new hope and direction to the Church of his time.

I expect also that St Oliver would agree wholeheartedly with Pope Francis' consistent reminders that the Church should not forget the poor. In these challenging words from Evangelii Gaudium Pope Francis says:

'I prefer a Church which is bruised, hurting and dirty because it has been out on the streets, rather than a Church which is unhealthy from being confined and from clinging to its own security (EG 49)'. St Oliver was a man of great charity – his pawning of two silver candlesticks and a silver cup to help feed the poor during the famine of 1674 is well known. But he also strove to tackle the root causes of poverty in his day – the taking of land, the actions of the Tories, the basic need for education. His own income was paltry – perhaps fifty pounds a year – and much of this he used to help the needy or fund his many projects. He knew what it was like to be hungry, in debt, to rely on the providence of God and the help of benefactors. He once said 'The Bishop of Waterford and I would greedily gobble down a piece of oaten bread'. This plea for help from the Church in Rome says it all: 'If I should die tomorrow, who would pay my debts? I would not have a halfpenny to take care of my burial or have Masses said, nor would I have thought that after so many labours I should be reduced to living from hand to mouth. I commend myself to your kindness to help me.' Archbishop Oliver might have spared himself if he had chosen an easier life, but this was not his style. Instead he continued to go out to the peripheries, journeying the length and breadth of his Archdiocese and further afield to rally the pastors and people of Ireland to renewal.

As we move towards the fortieth anniversary of the canonisation of St Oliver Plunkett, another theme from his life is apposite for the Church in Ireland today. It is the call to communion. A few years ago the Catholic Church in Ireland had the honour of hosting the Fiftieth International Eucharistic Congress with the theme: Eucharist, Communion with Christ and with one another. The Congress was a time of great grace for our country and many people have commented on the renewal of hope and humble confidence that it has helped to generate after the terrible trauma of recent decades. If we are to build on this we will need to continue to build communion across the Church in Ireland, communion between the faithful of the Church and the pastors of the Church, communion between priests and people, people and bishops, bishops and priests. We cannot forget those who have been hurt or scandalised or left feeling traumatised or excluded by all that has happened among us. We might turn for inspiration in faith and prayer to St Oliver Plunkett who was faced with a serious lack of communion in the Church in Ireland of his time. However his approach was to witness to unity and peace within the Church, to encourage those who were faithful and, where necessary, to gently but firmly confront any sources of division or disharmony. His experience of studying and living in Rome had given him a deep sense of loyalty to the Holy See, and he was anxious to bring healing and communion in everything that he did. He wrote: 'The Holy See is the chief physician, I am the under-physician and to me is entrusted a great number of patients... the will to cure this illness is not enough for us under-physicians; the proto-physician must put his hands on it.'

It is no accident that St Oliver Plunkett, a man with such a sense of communion, charity and peace, should have been chosen as the Patron Saint of Peace and Reconciliation in Ireland. The prayer movement for peace in Northern Ireland which began in 1997 was a powerful driver for healing and reconciliation and provided a firm foundation for the peace talks which slowly but surely bore fruit in the Good Friday Agreement and peace process. This volume is replete with examples of where St Oliver sought to sow seeds of charity and reconciliation in an Ireland which was tense, fragile and hostile. His efforts had mixed results during his own day, and his violent martyrdom was itself testimony to the fact that evil is not easily overcome. However the inspiring witness of St Oliver lives on and it is important that we continue to seek his intercession. The legacy of our own bitter conflict still lurks beneath the surface and is easily inflamed by careless words. The wounds left by the terrible atrocities are still raw and easily opened. Suspicion and blaming continues, combined with a lack of understanding of each other's stories. Failure to reach agreement on parading, flags and how to remember the past slows up our progress towards a brighter future. There are also, however, many positive shoots of hope and new beginning – the powerfully symbolic visits of Queen Elizabeth and President Higgins between Ireland and England; communities coming together to listen, commemorate and ask forgiveness; schools engaging in sharing and cooperation; Christians of different traditions joining to ensure that the voice of faith is being heard in the public square, particularly on critical issues like the protection of life.

St Oliver Plunkett would want us to redouble our efforts towards ongoing peace and reconciliation in Ireland and to this end the St Oliver Plunkett Committee for Peace and Reconciliation continues to make his name and his peace-making efforts known throughout the country. In his unforgettable speech to the people of Ireland at Drogheda in 1979, Pope St John Paul II had no doubt that St Oliver is for ever an outstanding example of the love of Christ for all people. He said: 'As bishop (St Oliver) preached a message of pardon and peace. He was indeed the defender of the oppressed and the advocate of justice, but he would never condone violence. For men of violence, his word was the word of the Apostle Peter: 'Never pay back one wrong with another' (I Pet 3:9). As a martyr for the faith, he sealed by his death the same message of peace and reconciliation that he had preached during his life. In his heart there was no rancour, for his strength was the love of Jesus, the love of the Good Shepherd who gives his life for his flock. His dying words were words of forgiveness for his enemies'.

As you read St Oliver Plunkett, Journey to Sainthood, I invite you to reflect on these powerful words of Pope St John Paul II. They will help you to realise that in the life of St Oliver we have a saint for today, a saint of our own who offers much food to nourish our personal prayer, conversion and renewal and much inspiration for the renewal of the Church in Ireland in the coming years. In thanking Tommy Burns and all those who have contributed to the publication of this volume, I return once more to the message of Pope Francis at the canonisations on Divine Mercy Sunday this year: 'Let us not forget that it is the saints who give direction and growth to the Church'.

1. EARLY LIFE IN IRELAND 1625 - 1647

St. Oliver was born a member of the influential Plunkett clan in Loughcrew, Oldcastle Co. Meath on All Saints day, 1st November 1625. A certain amount of debate has existed about the date of his birth; earlier biographers giving it as 1st of November 1629, but since an ancient reference[1] was discovered in the Bodleian Library, which stated that Oliver Plunkett was born on the 1st November 1625, biographers since the 1930's are almost unanimous on the 1625 date. These include Hanly, Ó Fiaich, Curtis, Forristal, Concannon, Stokes and more than a dozen others.

The Plunkett family belonged to a respected clan of pre-Norman origin, whose first recorded settlement in Ireland was near the mouth of the river Boyne, at Beaulieu[2] just outside Drogheda. This is documented by the death of a John Plunkett in 1082, a date which would place Oliver's ancestors in Ireland, almost one hundred years before the Norman invasion.

Although the Loughcrew Plunketts belonged to one of the lesser branches of the Plunkett clan, nevertheless they had excellent family connections. Oliver's father, John Plunkett, was the Baron of Loughcrew and his mother Thomasina, was a member of the well-connected Earls of Roscommon family, a daughter of Henry Dillon of Kentstown and a grand-daughter[3] of Sir Lucas Dillon. Indeed, it was through Oliver's mother and the Dillon family that the Plunkett's of Loughcrew had an even closer family bond with more senior branches of the Plunkett family, notably the Earl of Fingall at Killeen and the Plunkett's of Dunsany castle. Oliver was also connected by birth with the Plunkett's of County Louth, notably the Baron of Louth, the first nobleman of the Archdiocese of Armagh. These strong family ties would prove useful to Oliver later on in his apostolate, when appointed Archbishop of Armagh and Primate of Ireland.

His father's estate comprised a sizeable two hundred and fifty hectares[4] of fine land in and around Loughcrew, along with a tower house, church and a corn mill. The church would undoubtedly have been used by the local population for Sundays and holy days and as it was attached to his home, it must have left a strong spiritual impression on the young Oliver. One can easily imagine the young Oliver, regularly attending and in all probability serving at Holy Mass on a regular basis in the family church. There was a strong cultural tradition of fosterage in Gaelic Ireland and it is quite probable that Oliver was fostered for a time as a young boy. His home at Loughcrew was barely two kilometres from Sliabh na Calliagh, the highest point in county Meath and location of Loughcrew megalithic burial grounds from which stunning views can be had in all directions. Dating back over five thousand years it contains important megalithic art works and is of considerable historical significance; the monument is one of the four major passage tombs in Ireland today. As a young boy, Oliver would have known the site well

Loughcrew Church and Tower House
During the hot summer of 2018, traces of a late medieval house became clearly visible in the dry ground nearby, almost certainly the boyhood home of St. Oliver

along with the stories and folklore of the chariot races which had been held between Loughcrew and Royal Tara. Poems attributed to Oliver are in Appendix II.

Oliver had an elder brother Edward and three sisters, Katherine, Anne and Mary. By all accounts it was a happy family setting and in letters written many years later, he wrote lovingly of his family including his nephews and nieces. As a young boy, Oliver was tutored by a first cousin of his mother, Fr. Patrick Plunkett, a brother to Sir Nicholas Plunkett and also of the Earl of Fingall. Fr. Patrick, titular Abbot of St. Mary's Cistercian Abbey in Dublin, later became the Bishop of Ardagh in 1647 and subsequently the Bishop of Meath in 1669. Fr. Patrick Plunkett would have resided in Killeen Castle and in nearby parishes such as Kilcloon. Oliver would have stayed with him at Killeen and at other locations in the locality for extended periods of time during his education. Fr. Patrick took Oliver under his wing at the tender age of six and educated him until his sixteenth year. A hard working and merciful priest, he left a life-long impression on Oliver, who for the rest of his life, held his tutor in the highest of esteem.

Following on from broken promises and the threat of further plantations, the Ulster rising took place in 1641. Many thousands of people were killed as a result of the battles and atrocities committed by both sides; some reports mention that up to twelve thousand people had been killed during these years. The town of Armagh was burned along with its Cathedral, as were many smaller towns and their churches. In the battle of Benburb, near Armagh in 1646, the Irish, led by Eoin

Killeen Church

8

Roe O'Neill defeated the Scots in a horrific encounter. This was the precursor to the invasion by Oliver Cromwell to Ireland barely three years later.

The atrocities although very real and horrible, were usually wildly exaggerated and this added to the alarm and terror throughout the land. The rumour had been relayed throughout England, that hundreds of thousands of settlers in Ireland had been murdered during the uprising, even though the total number of

Ruined Church at Loughcrew

settlers in Ireland at the time was much smaller than this number. It has been estimated, that the total population of Ireland was slightly more than one million people at the time. England was then ruled by Cromwell after the civil war and King Charles I was soon to be executed.

The Confederation of Kilkenny had begun in 1642 and Fr. Patrick Plunkett, as a Lord Abbot took his place among the peers and he played a prominent part in the proceedings. He rebuilt part of St. Mary's Abbey and lived there for a time with a small community of monks. In 1633 he was[5] elected first President of the Irish Cistercians. His brother, Sir Nicholas Plunkett, one of the foremost lawyers of the time, was elected as a member of the Supreme Council and was later selected as Speaker. Oliver must have moved in this influential circle over a protracted period as many years later at his trial, he stated: "These thirty-six years past, I was not at Limerick, Duncannon or Wexford." This account would place Oliver in these locations in the same time frame as some important events were unfolding in the lifetime of the Confederation during the 1640's. In all probability, Abbot Patrick must have furthered both the education and life experiences of the young Oliver by employing his young cousin as a secretary and companion, during those most interesting of times. Many of Abbot Patrick's Cistercian influences would have rubbed off on his young and impressionable student, such as prayer in ones work, simple and frugal lifestyle, hard work, obedience, humility, hospitality and poverty. Before reaching the end of this biography, the reader will undoubtedly agree that Oliver possessed all of these charisms in super-abundance.

Oliver wished to become a priest and he was selected along with four other young men to travel to Rome, where it was hoped they could all enter the Irish College, which had been founded barely twenty years earlier as a seminary for the Irish mission. The young men were obliged to wait however, before an opportunity to travel presented itself. Setting off for the continent to be educated or to become a priest was a serious business and demanded considerable planning and preparation, particularly as Ireland was in upheaval during this time. Mainland Europe was also much troubled during this era, as it was still in the grip of the thirty years war and it was therefore important for the wellbeing of the young men, that they should travel with someone trustworthy who would be familiar with the continent, its languages and customs.

Reminder, as previously stated in the 'acknowledgements,' the nuggets of information from Mgr. John Hanly's, 'The Letters of Saint Oliver Plunkett,' Dublin, 1979, hereafter referred to as Hanly 'The Letters,' are peppered throughout this publication and only some of the more important references are included. I thank Mgr. Hanly for his gracious help and consent.

[1] Concannon Helena 'Blessed Oliver Plunket' Dublin 1935. p. xxi ref. Bodleian Library, Ashmolean, MS., 436, f.119

[2] Walsh Rev. Paul 'Blessed Oliver Plunket - Historical Studies' League of Prayer Dublin 1937. p.21

[3] Curtis, Fr. Emmanuel 'Blessed Oliver Plunkett' Dublin 1963. p.14

[4] Civil Survey for Meath. Vol. V pp.264-72

[5] Phillipson Rev. Dom Wulstan 'Blessed Oliver Plunket - Historical Studies' Dublin 1937. p.154

2. Don Oliverio's Journey to Rome 1647

Abbot Patrick Plunkett[1] wrote later: "I sent him to Rome to pursue his studies at the fountain-head of truth." Fr. Peter Francis Scarampi from Italy had attended the Confederation as envoy of the Pope. Fr. Scarampi was a holy, devout priest and having declined the honour of becoming the first Papal Nuncio to Ireland, was planning his return to Rome. It was decided that the select group of five young students should accompany him on his journey which was planned for late 1646. From that moment, Fr. Scarampi took Oliver under his wing and besides providing for him later in Rome, was constantly on the lookout for his welfare. Undoubtedly, both Fr. Scarampi and Fr. Patrick Plunkett were destined to have the greatest spiritual influence on the young Oliver. Hard working, they showed great charity and mercy for the poor and it was certainly their model which Oliver would follow in an exemplary fashion for the rest of his life. Fr. Scarampi had been replaced by Papal Nuncio, Archbishop John Rinuccini over a year earlier. Both Fr. Scarampi and Archbishop Rinuccini had sided with the Gaelic element of the Confederation. As things started to fall apart in the Confederation, the new Nuncio had an increasingly difficult time with the Anglo Irish grouping, issuing unpopular censures upon them until he was eventually forced to return to Italy.

Fr. Peter Francis Scarampi

Oliver and his party had to wait several months in Waterford for a boat and for favourable wind before they finally set sail in February 1647. As the papal envoy to the Confederation since 1643, Fr. Peter Francis Scarampi held an influential position and was obviously so highly regarded by Gaelic Ireland that a playing band

and a multitude of people marched with him and his party to the quayside in Waterford on the day of departure. There also to wish him 'bon voyage' were assembled the leading members of the Confederation of Kilkenny, the Government of Gaelic Ireland of the time. And so it came to pass that Oliver, or Don Oliverio as he was then under the patronage of Fr. Scarampi, was waved off by thousands of people, including leading churchmen and many influential personages of the day as he left Ireland. Such a greeting would not be the case some twenty three years later, when Oliver would return to Ireland as the Archbishop of Armagh and Primate of Ireland. Then, he would find it necessary to travel in disguise as a Captain William Browne, complete with sword, wig and pair of pistols, during a period when the government of the day would have spies actively on the look-out for him.

As far as English law was concerned, it was forbidden for young men to travel to the continent to enter seminaries, or indeed to return home as priests. Setting sail for the continent, the little group had therefore become felons as soon as they had left Ireland's shore. Journeys in those days were always an adventure and this one turned out to be both exciting and dangerous. While out at sea, they were chased for twenty-four hours[2] by two English privateer warships who were rapidly gaining on them. Although licenced to operate by the English government, these were in essence pirates, who opportunistically preyed on vulnerable vessels of enemy nations. Very much on this list, were the vessels travelling between Ireland and continental Europe. Particularly vulnerable, were vessels from Gaelic Ireland, which was largely controlled by the Confederation of Kilkenny, with the notable exception of some northern counties and a number of the larger towns and cities.

Chased by the larger, faster vessels, Fr. Scarampi and the little group knelt and prayed earnestly for deliverance and promised to go on a pilgrimage to Assisi if they could escape their pursuers. They knew that jail or perhaps death was the likely consequences for them if captured. Shortly afterwards, a terrible storm blew up which lasted for two whole days and greatly endangered their boat. One peril having been replaced by another, their bobbing boat was soon at the mercy of the tempestuous wind and waves. When the storm finally subsided the warships were nowhere to be seen. In thanksgiving, Fr. Scarampi renamed the ship 'St. Francis' and they finally landed after some time at Ostend in Flanders, having been blown many miles off their original course.

Narrowly escaping the grave dangers of pirates and shipwreck, their troubles were not yet over as they were soon abducted by a gang of robbers in the Ardennes region of Belgium. Robbed and imprisoned, they were only released after a ransom was paid. A Good Samaritan may have paid the ransom and the little group was finally allowed to proceed on their way. They stopped off in Paris and headed further south through France to avoid a war torn Germany before progressing on their journey into Italy. It must have been an exhilarating experience for them, to see many of the famous landmarks on the continent for the first time. As they continued on their journey they would surely have had the odd sing song and many a laugh, while at the same time looking forward with eager anticipation to journeys end and the sights of the eternal city of Rome, having no doubt heard so much of all its splendours.

They travelled to Assisi as promised and celebrated the Holy Week and Easter ceremonies there. Leaving Ireland, Oliver would have had money with him, gifts certainly from the different branches of his family and some friends. Continuing on their journey, their pockets and purses empty after their abduction and except for what little help Fr. Scarampi might have arranged for them on the way, they had become totally dependent on the charity of strangers for food or shelter. As they entered Assisi, the home of St. Francis, the symbolism of their poverty must then have seemed rather appropriate to them. This journey under the guidance of Fr. Scarampi taught Oliver valuable lessons and would have helped him on many of his own difficult journeys later on.

[1] Bennett Fr. Martin 'Blessed Oliver Plunkett' London 1973. p.7

[2] Moran Cardinal Patrick 'Memoir of Oliver Plunket' Dublin 1895. p.5

3. Seminarian in Rome

They finally reached Rome in May 1647 after a journey lasting about three months. Their first sighting and experience of Rome would have been a most dramatic one, with the magnificence of Rome's fine churches, gardens and fountains contrasting greatly with what they had been used to back home. The Irish College could not take Oliver immediately so it was the good Fr. Scarampi who again came to the rescue by organising his studies and accommodation and arranging payment for the pauper student. A shortage of money would be something which Oliver would suffer from on an almost continuous basis when he would return to Ireland many years later.

Eventually enrolling in the Irish College, the group of seminarians undertook an oath to return to Ireland after their ordinations. Oliver proved to be an excellent student, the Rector of the college is later quoted as saying that Oliver was among the foremost in talent, diligence and progress. His small class in the Irish College must have been quite an extraordinary group, for of the five students who travelled out with Fr. Scarampi, three would be offered archbishoprics in Ireland. Oliver Plunkett went to Armagh, John Brenan was translated to Cashel from

Collegio Romano

Waterford, and Peter Walsh not the 'Peter Walsh' of Irish Remonstrance[1] notoriety, was forced to decline the option of the archbishopric of Cashel on health grounds. Peter Walsh must also have come under the strong influence of the Oratorians, as he entered[2] the Oratorian congregation of St. Philip Neri at Perugia and lived a devout life thereafter. During their time at the college which was situated on the Via Degli Ibernesi or the street of the Irish, they walked each day across the buried and yet undiscovered Roman Forum for lectures to Collegio Romano the renowned Jesuit institute.

Old Irish College

The year after his arrival in Rome, Nicholas Plunkett and Bishop Nicholas French of Wexford visited Rome as emissaries of the Confederation of Kilkenny. Sir Nicholas was knighted by Pope Innocent X during the visit. Oliver later wrote of Sir Nicholas: "who reared me as a boy." Oliver must have been delighted to again meet his mother's first cousin from Killeen Castle, a location where he must have had so many happy childhood memories and to hear news from Ireland of relatives, neighbours and friends. In the following year of 1649, Ireland was invaded by Cromwell and was rapidly overwhelmed by his superior forces and tactics. The country soon became a wasteland for Catholics. Drogheda was the location of Cromwell's first major engagement in Ireland, he finally broke through its defences on August the 11th and soon made the town an example for any other town which might dare not to submit to his forces. Within a month, Wexford so dared and probably paid an even higher price. Bishop Nicholas French a friend of Oliver had a narrow escape from the terrible onslaught of Cromwell's forces in his native County Wexford. In a letter written some years later, Bishop French recounts that at his house in Wexford town, a sacristan, a gardener and a sixteen-year old boy were killed. Bishop French then hid in the Irish countryside despite a determined search for him by those same forces, until his escape into exile some five months later. While hiding in the woods, his hideout was discovered and surrounded at one stage, but he broke through the ranks of the soldiers at speed, later thanking God and the swiftness of his steed. Indeed, the Cromwellian forces hanged three of Bishop French's fellow Irish bishops at this time and another bishop died as a prisoner from ill treatment. Cromwell's model army quickly conquered the country, ruthlessly teaching the Irish a lesson and overcoming all opposition in their path.

It certainly became one of the worst periods in all of Irish history, as the Cromwellian conquests were consolidated at pace. Arriving in Ireland with a bible in one hand and a sword in the other, his model army gave Catholic Ireland an unenviable choice. Either give up their Roman Catholic faith and convert to the new strands of religion or become dispossessed of land, property and positions. Almost unanimously, Catholics refused and were made to suffer severely for holding onto the beliefs of the ancient faith. Many were sent into exile, or given the choice, 'To Hell or to Connaught.' where it was not planned to replant with foreign settlers a portion of the land, which was of much poorer quality in any event. Thousands, upon thousands of Irish were transported into exile, many of whom were sent as slave labour to the sugar plantations of the Barbados. Many small-holdings were combined to give Cromwell's officers or English investors of his Irish campaign huge estates. Land and property was confiscated on a wholesale

Way of the Irish street,
where the old Irish College was situated

basis and the native Irish could count themselves lucky to become paying tenants on even a small portion of what was formally their own land. When further settlers arrived from England or Scotland these tenancies would then lapse and be given to the newcomers. It must have seemed as if Ireland had been selected to re-experience the

Roman Forum

persecutions of the early Church. If all of this was not enough suffering, the people then had to endure plague and famine in the years 1652-53. One account says that the effects of the famine were so bad that one could travel for many miles in the countryside and not meet a living creature. During this time, it is on record that Oliver spent many long periods in prayer in one or other of the many churches, shrines or in the catacomb, all located around the city of Rome. The pilgrimage of visiting Seven Churches in Rome was popularised by St. Philip Neri, founder of the Oratorians. The pilgrimage was mentioned by Archbishop Oliver in one of his letters and must have been undertaken by Oliver himself on a regular basis. Ireland was in trouble such as it never had been before, and all he could do was pray. It is safe to assume that his prayer during all those years, along with the prayers and sacrifices of the now strong contingent of Irish exiles in Rome, was a fervent one for peace and reconciliation back home in their troubled Ireland.

[1] Irish Remonstrance : See Chapter 8
[2] 'Collegio Hibernorum De Urbe' Rome 2003. p.133

4. FATHER OLIVER

Oliver was ordained on the 1st January 1654, a joyous occasion for him, but he would surely have missed the company of his family on this special day. His thoughts would certainly have turned to all his relations who continued to face an uncertain future. Back home in his native Ireland, the bishops and priests were hunted and persecuted. Some were killed, many were in hiding and others went into exile. Five pounds was the princely sum offered as a reward on the head of any priest. Everywhere, churches and monasteries were burnt and destroyed. A catchphrase used by the Cromwellian soldiers and supporters was "Priest, Tory or Wolf" and as the priest was mentioned first, perhaps his capture would evoke the greatest acclaim. About three years later an Irish MP while speaking in the Parliament about Priest, Tory or Wolf, said: "We have three beasts to destroy that lay a heavy burden on us." The Church in Ireland was forced underground with numerous martyrs, some of whom are still unknown to us.

Oliver and his colleagues in Rome must have continually worried for their families and friends and would have prayed intensely for an end to the turmoil in Ireland. Oliver wrote[1] of a Fr. George Plunkett: "He was imprisoned for a year... tied to horse's tails and dragged through the streets of Dublin... exiled to the Barbadoes, but by accident was taken to France." Oliver was well aware therefore, what priesthood could mean for him, but he went ahead nevertheless during this period, with his sub-diaconate in the John Lateran Cathedral,

Santo Spirito Hospital

his diaconate in the Chapel of Propaganda Fide and finally his ordination to the priesthood in the same chapel. After ordination, Fr. Oliver and his young colleague priests were naturally released from their promise to return to Ireland at that time, Bishop MacGeoghegan of Clonmacnoise who ordained Oliver, would no doubt have concurred with that decision. He could not go back to Ireland, that road was blockaded and the country thoroughly fortified. Oliver wrote to his superiors at the time and promised that he would return to Ireland whenever they would wish him to do so in the future.

[1] Hanly 'The Letters' no.13

5. DOCTORAL STUDIES 1654 - 1657

Along with his friend John Brenan from Waterford who had travelled with him from Ireland and who had studied with him for the priesthood in the Irish College, they undertook higher studies in the renowned La Sapienza University in Rome. During his studies he stayed with the Oratorians as chaplain at San Gerolamo della Carità, apparently still under the protective wing of Fr. Scarampi. While undertaking his higher studies, Fr. Oliver also ministered in the Santo Spirito hospital near the Vatican. It was noted at this time that he was, "everywhere and at all times a model of gentleness, integrity and piety." During his time in Rome, Fr. Oliver is also recorded as frequently visiting the poor in the hospital and helping to feed and cleanse the poor patients as best he could. During those times he must often have wished to be home in Ireland, assisting those who were poor either in spirit or in body.

Around this time a plague struck Italy and his friend Fr. Scarampi who had volunteered to assist the victims, died as a result on the Island of St. Bartholomew in 1656. Fr. Oliver had already written advising him not to do such a thing and received a strong rebuttal from the zealous Fr.

Scarampi in reply. Fr. Scarampi[1] admonished Oliver: "O ye of little faith, why do you fear…Would you have us withdraw from so laudable a work, which God wishes us to perform…I am now over sixty…I may die. What of it…Should I then, merely for the sake of living another ten or fifteen years, refuse to face death now. And for all that I may be snatched away prematurely. Besides if God does not will it, death cannot touch me." Within days of Oliver receiving the letter, Fr. Scarampi had died after contracting the plague. This letter must have become one of Fr. Oliver's prize possessions and one can imagine him often referring to it; the letter is now kept in the Vallicellian[2] archives, Rome. Fr. Scarampi's death was a terrible loss to Oliver who regarded his mentor and benefactor as a father figure. Indeed without his great example and help, Oliver would

Sapienza University, Rome

certainly not have achieved all that he did. He wrote that he was afflicted with an unspeakable sadness, some of his relatives had been put to death or sent into exile, he was deprived of his father and friends, the whole Irish people were living in extreme misery, and Fr. Scarampi has died. Fr. Scarampi was closer to him than an earthly father. Undoubtedly, Fr. Scarampi had promised to look after Oliver before they had left Ireland some nine years earlier. True to his word he had cared for him on the journey, paid for his studies and arranged

The Oratorian Church of San Gerolamo della Carità

accommodation for the pauper student in Rome. Oliver wrote that Fr. Scarampi had brought him to Rome at his own expense and that he had maintained him in the city for three years. He had put him up in the Oratorian house during his university studies, arranged his chaplaincy work and other work for the poor in the Santo Spirito hospital and he trained him in many other works of charity and mercy. Even in death, Fr. Scarampi's care of Oliver would continue, shortly before his death he wrote a letter in recommendation of Oliver, arranging that he would be placed under the protection of Cardinal Barberini. Oliver then continued his studies at the Sapienza University, confining himself to his books, he thus distinguished himself with a doctorate in Civil and Canon Law under Mariscotti, the celebrated professor of law.

[1] Moran Cardinal Patrick 'Memoir of Oliver Plunket' Dublin 1895. p.6
[2] Concannon 'Blessed Oliver Plunket' Dublin 1935. p.57

6. DOCTOR OLIVER 1657 – 1669

Oliver had obviously earned a very good reputation from his studies, as he then joined the staff of Propaganda College as Professor of Theology and later Professor of Apologetics or Controversies. Dr. George Crolly[1] the first biographer of Oliver, wrote in 1850: "He filled this important office for twelve years, in a manner which gained him the highest reputation and the esteem and admiration of the Sovereign Pontiff himself."

It is said that Oliver helped improve standards in the college a great deal, a foretaste perhaps of his great zeal for reform some years later as the Archbishop of Armagh. He also became a consultor at this time in the Congregation of the Index with a duty of reviewing books, which

Propaganda College, Rome

would have been another very responsible position. His friend John Brenan became a Professor of Philosophy in the same college.

Chapel of Propaganda College

Propaganda College was an impressive establishment located in the same building as the Sacred Congregation for the Propagation of the Faith and as such, the whole complex was a hub of activity. Oliver wrote "Propaganda in a word all Rome, is a great book. How many nations and their customs are observed, Poles, Germans, Spaniards, French, Turks, Ethiopians, Africans, Americans all rub shoulders and one learns with what prudence such widely divergent affairs referring to such opposing interests and countries are handled. One treats with cardinals and prelates of great wisdom, of consummate experience in the spiritual and temporal affairs of so many monarchs and princes. It is impossible that a person of even mediocre intelligence would not profit very much both in the fields of learning and experience, and indeed for the purpose of training a missionary, there is not another college in the world more suitable than the Propaganda." Oliver was well respected in the college and his knowledge of the religious affairs of Ireland was obviously valued as many letters to the College concerning Ireland had markings to indicate that they should be referred to him. In the year 1666, Oliver became aware that one of the young students from Ireland was badly in need of funds to attend the Irish College, so he organised a collection which funded a burse to provide for him. Oliver was no doubt mindful of many others who had helped him in his own time of need.

Over the previous two centuries, the Renaissance had transformed Rome, leaving its mark in the form of fine marbled churches, palaces, piazzas, fountains and gardens. Art and sculpture saw a great revitalisation and from his new home in Propaganda, Oliver would have experienced this ongoing revival at first hand. During his time in Rome he witnessed three popes; Innocent X, Alexander VII and Clement IX. He saw the genius of Bernini's work, with his spectacular Fountain of the Four Rivers in the Piazza Navona. He witnessed the excitement when Queen Christina of Sweden made her grand ceremonial entry into Rome in 1655 having shortly before-hand renounced her throne and become a Catholic. Oliver would also have witnessed the installation of the 'Chair of St. Peter' high up in the Apse of St. Peter's basilica in 1666. Exactly eight years later, on the feast of St. Peter's Chair, while on the run in South Armagh during a snowstorm, he was almost suffocated in snowdrifts. He later thanked God for being able to suffer for the Chair of Peter, praying: "I hope will in the long run, break the violence of the tempestuous waves." Oliver also saw the commencement and completion of the colonnades of St. Peter's square; like great outstretched arms, they welcome all who come to St. Peter's square. If these stones could talk, they would relate much history. Other work was still ongoing on St. Peter's Basilica, particularly much of the decorative work, as the dome had only been completed some fifty years earlier.

[1] Crolly Dr. George. 'The Life and Death of Oliver Plunkett' Dublin 1850. p.12

7. News of Ireland

The news from Ireland continued to be grim, indeed Oliver's brother Edward and family had been deprived of the estate in Loughcrew. Oliver rarely mentions his relations in correspondence, although he does mention a Robert Plunkett, son of the Lord of Loughcrew who may have been another brother but more likely an uncle. He described him as a priest in the Trim area who had amazing stories to tell as he constantly avoided capture in that locality. It is interesting to note that for some time there was only one active Catholic bishop in the country namely, Bishop Patrick Plunkett, Oliver's tutor of old. He too had been forced into exile for several years during the tyranny of Cromwell's commonwealth regime. In 1649, there were twenty-seven[1] bishops in Ireland, within five years the only one remaining in the country was Dr. Owen MacSweeny from the diocese of Kilmore. He was then an invalid and remained throughout the Cromwellian regime.

Oliver Cromwell

Shortly after Cromwell had died, Charles II was restored to the throne of England in 1660. Because the English Parliament and Council still exercised huge power there was no great reversal of the strict anti-Catholic policies which had been enforced previously, either spiritually or materially and many people soon became bitterly disappointed about this fact. There was often great hatred between the members of the different religions both in Ireland and in England, but this had more to do with power, land and the income from rents, than with religion. Indeed some of the old Gaelic chieftains could be every bit as harsh in enforcing their rights, as some of the new landlords had become. Bishop MacGeoghegan, the Bishop of Meath left Rome and slipped back into Ireland. In August 1660, he wrote[2] to Rome: I still live in the caverns of the earth and so do all the other members of the clergy. Because though the Stuart King, for whom the Irish had fought and endured so much, was back on the throne of his father, the Cromwellian's were still the rulers of Ireland." Ormond became the viceroy for the second time in 1662, but the situation did not improve a great deal thereafter; over the next seven years he actively promoted division within the Church in Ireland.

[1] Curtis, Fr. Emmanuel 'Blessed Oliver Plunkett' Dublin 1963. p.28
[2] Concannon Helena 'Blessed Oliver Plunkett' Dublin 1935. p.71

St. Oliver Relic, Parish Church, Oldcastle

8. IRISH REMONSTRANCE

In Ireland, the government had failed miserably in their efforts to impose the Protestant religion on the people, using bribery and the seemingly ever-increasing harshness of the rule of law. The Irish had been given a choice, they chose to give up their land, property and positions, rather than to relinquish the great treasure of their Catholic faith. Guile was then necessary, so the state, with the Duke of Ormond as viceroy tried the obvious tactic during the 1660's of divide and conquer. A 'Remonstrance' or declaration of loyalty to the King was proposed for the Irish Church, which was of course totally unacceptable in Rome, as it denied the Pope influence in the temporal power of monarchs. Some Catholics were in favour however, in the forlorn hope that the confiscated lands might be returned, since the monarchy had been restored only a short time previously.

A small number of priests under the leadership of a Franciscan friar, Fr. Peter Walsh were also in favour of this Remonstrance and they tried their best to encourage many of the leading Catholic families to follow their example. Only sixty-nine priests signed the Remonstrance out of a grand total of eighteen[1] hundred and eight clergy, a number calculated by Walsh at the time. In order to increase their influence amongst Catholics, they were even allowed by the viceroy to open chapels in some of the principal towns and cities, with priest sympathisers as chaplains. Priests refused to sign with the exception of a small number, although many of the Catholic gentry did so. Oliver wrote later: "I would rather lose an arm or even my head than sign a protestation of loyalty which would not be Catholic in tenor." Fr. Walsh and some others were actually receiving quite an amount of money from Ormond's payroll and as can be imagined, they were the cause of serious disharmony and disquiet within the Irish Church throughout the decade. Thankfully every cloud has a silver lining, because after the supporters of the Remonstrance were finally subjugated, these chapels remained open for another ten years or so, under the control of priests who were loyal to the Pope, which also facilitated the opening of some other chapels during this period. Within a few years, Oliver could remark: "In the wealthiest and most noble city of my diocese and of the whole province, there are three very fine, ornate chapels, one of the Capuchins, one of the Franciscans of the reform and one of the Jesuits. There is also one belonging to the Augustinians, but it is a poor one." Across the rest of the Northern Province, the mass-rock was the order of the day as no Catholic chapels were allowed and even if they were permitted, the Catholics did not own any land on which to build such chapels. Viceroy Ormond failed to split the Church in Ireland but as a result of the mayhem, Bishop Patrick became the only active bishop in the country. He was a relative through marriage of the viceroy and undoubtedly this fact helped him to remain on in the country. This became important for the Church as he gave vital leadership during the remaining and difficult years of the 1660's.

[1] A Sister of Notre Dame 'Blessed Oliver Plunket' London 1920. p.24

The Beatification Ceremony 1920

9. FR. JAMES TAAFFE

To add to the confusion of that decade, there arrived in Ireland in 1668 a Fr. James Taaffe, who forged a commission document from the Holy See to become vicar apostolic for the whole of Ireland. His original commission was one to try and win back Friar Walsh and the other supporters of the Remonstrance in allegiance to the Holy See. Changing sides, this forged document gave him the authority to visit, correct and assign as he saw fit, vicar generals throughout the country. It also gave him full command over all clergy, with the right to extract a levy from every priest to pay for his extensive commission. The forgery appeared perfect in every respect, Bishop Patrick Plunkett at that time the Bishop of Ardagh was initially fooled by it and told others that they should also accept it. Friar Taaffe then delegated his huge powers to other priests who deposed, censured and excommunicated around the country, particularly those who opposed Walsh and company. As a result of their outrageous conduct, Bishop Patrick soon realised that this brief could not be genuine and denounced it, even before Oliver had written back to him informing him that it was a forgery. Oliver as agent of Irish bishops was kept well informed of Irish affairs and he helped to uncover the truth behind the bizarre events unfolding in Ireland. Bishop Patrick wrote back stating that he was most gratified to obtain confirmation of his suspicions. Friar Taaffe was then challenged by Bishop Patrick and he initially put up a strong resistance, however he must have thought better of it and submitted to the commands of the Holy See.

As a consequence of the great obedience the Irish Church had for the Holy See, many people at least initially, dared not question his brief. Although he was but a simple Franciscan friar, he had good family connections since he was the brother of the Earl of Carlingford and so it was not long before even greater disharmony erupted amongst Catholics. Dr. Edmund O'Reilly, Archbishop of Armagh who lived in exile for ten out of the twelve years of his Primacy, wrote[1] from the continent: "The villainy of James Taaffe has done more harm to the faithful priests of

Ireland than the combined tyranny of Cromwell, Henry VIII, Edward VI and Elizabeth." Friar Taaffe and his associates had already excommunicated the vicar general of Armagh and many of the priests living in County Louth were threatened with a similar sanction. It was only towards the end of the 1660's, before Rome felt it safe to appoint a small number of bishops who could be sent to Ireland. In January 1669, bishops were appointed to Dublin, Cashel, Tuam and Ossory. Oliver was also confirmed by these new Irish bishops to act as their agent in Rome and as a result he would have been only too well aware of the tragic circumstances back in Ireland. In the same year and at Oliver's request, Bishop Patrick Plunkett was translated from Ardagh to Meath; for the three preceding years he was the only active bishop in the country, having ordained an estimated two-hundred and fifty priests in his time. The lessons of the ongoing debacle of the Irish Remonstrance and the fiasco of Friar Taaffe were not lost on Rome. Something needed to be done about Ireland and quickly, it was an opportune time to appoint bishops to the Irish mission.

[1] Curtis, Fr. Emmanuel 'Blessed Oliver Plunkett' Dublin 1963. p.41

St. John Paul II at Killineer - 1979

10. ARCHBISHOPRIC OF ARMAGH

In March 1669, the Archbishopric of Armagh became vacant upon the death in Saumur, France, of Dr. O'Reilly, who had spent his last few years there in exile. There were great political and cultural divisions in the Archdiocese of Armagh, between the Gaelic clergy of the northern end of the diocese and of the Anglo Irish clergy of the Pale, based more or less in County Louth. Since the beginning of the century, Armagh had rarely had a resident archbishop, Peter Lombard primate for twenty five years never set foot in the diocese, Hugh MacCaughwell was archbishop for only a few months. Primate Hugh O'Reilly was completely taken up with political events for most of his twenty-five years, pre, post or throughout the time of the Confederation of Kilkenny. The see was then vacant for five years in the 1650's and Edmund O'Reilly spent only two years out of the following twelve in the diocese. Order, peace and a sense of hope were urgently required; otherwise the Church would completely fall apart in the archdiocese and throughout the Armagh province generally.

Due to the fragility of the situation in the province, Rome was exhorted from many quarters to make an appointment without delay. With the clergy and laity split into factions, strong leadership and a calming influence were qualities which were needed more than ever in the Irish Church. As agent of the Irish bishops in Rome, Oliver was only too well aware of this. Order can emanate from disorder. As a consequence of the uproar in the Irish Church after the supporters of the Remonstrance and of Friar Taaffe, Rome moved quickly by appointing archbishops to the three vacant metropolitan sees. The newly appointed Archbishop of Dublin, Peter Talbot, wrote to Rome three times in the space of a fortnight, expressing urgency because of: "The tumults of the clergy of Armagh." The lack of strong leadership during the enforced exile of Archbishop O'Reilly was just another factor, which exacerbated the mistrust and the ill will between those groups in the archdiocese. In the meantime, Dr. Talbot had suggested three names to Rome and

Oliver's name was not among them. In private his name must have been mooted for the position however, since the agent of the Armagh clergy in Rome wrote to the Holy Father and requested that no person from the Pale and especially no Meath-man should be appointed to Armagh, adding: "If not, nothing is more certain than that an uproar will be to be feared in the Church, and without doubt the Apostolic See will have to support the primate, intruded from elsewhere, abandoned by Armagh." There had been tensions for centuries between Gael and Pale and the Archbishops of Armagh who were usually of Anglo Irish stock and therefore more acceptable to the government, lived in Drogheda or Termonfechin, while the vicar general who was invariably of Gaelic stock would reside in the northern end of the archdiocese.

Oliver loved Rome, his work in Propaganda College and the company of his many friends, however, he must also have realised that the time had come for him to offer his humble services to the Church back home. Although Oliver was impressed with the grandeur of Rome, from his writings it can be seen that he was much more captivated with the Church martyrs, the lives of the saints, the one known catacomb in Rome at the time and what all of these represented in God's overall design for the salvation of souls. The Church in Ireland was in turmoil and at the precipice, so perhaps Oliver felt somewhat obliged to offer his services and to honour the oath he had made some twenty-two years earlier upon entering the Irish College; to return to Ireland after his ordination. He must also have had in mind his second promise which he made after his ordination, that he would return to Ireland whenever asked to do so in the future. This alone would be a compelling reason for him to accede to any such prompting. Perhaps he believed he could offer some little help at that crucial time in a defence of the Church in Ireland. His time had now come to stand up and be counted, whatever faults Oliver may have had, a lack of courage was certainly not one of them.

Petitioning for a benefice was counted as normal procedure in those days, quite often with the support of royalty or the leaders of governments. Indeed in Oliver's case his petition seems to have been no more than a formal acknowledgement of his readiness to accept this important position if requested. Even though he worked in the Propaganda College and mixed regularly with cardinals and others of great influence, rather it was from the president of his beloved Irish College that a reference was forwarded on his behalf, so it is clear that he did not canvass for the position. Some years later, in September 1674, he wrote that his superiors had appointed him to Armagh and this may well have been another way of saying that he was prompted to put his name forward at that time. But for whatever reason and however it came about, in early June 1669, Oliver wrote a short and a rather matter of fact

First ever Procession in Honour of Blessed Oliver - Lamspringe, Germany - 1920

petition, neither signed nor dated, to the Holy See for the important position of Archbishop of Armagh and then obviously left all in God's hands.

"Oliver Plunkett, most devoted petitioner of Your Eminences having taught two courses of speculative theology and moral theology for one year, and Christian controversies for three years in Propaganda College, and having served for many years as a consultor of the sacred Index, desiring to return to his country for the service of souls, begs Your Eminence to honour him with the archbishopric of Armagh, the petitioner being a native of the province of Armagh; and he will pray God for your Eminences."

11. ARCHBISHOP ELECT OLIVER

On 9th of July 1669, at a meeting which took place in Rome to discuss the merits of the various candidates for the position of Archbishop of Armagh, Pope[1] Clement IX intervened: "But why delay in discussing the merits of others, whilst we have here in Rome, a native of that island, whose merits are known to us all, and whose labours in this city have already added so many wreaths to the peerless glory of the 'Island of Saints.' Let Doctor Oliver Plunkett become the Archbishop of Armagh."

While many of the clergy of Armagh were no doubt greatly disappointed at his appointment, numerous letters of thanks for Oliver's nomination were written to the Holy See. Bishop Nicholas French of Ferns, then living in exile in Ghent, wrote: "To your influence we owe it, that such a prelate, of noble birth, and adorned with exalted talents, benevolence and virtue and yet of no proud conceit should be raised to the government of the Primatial Church...to which office he will be a light to all who hope in the Lord." John O'Maloney working in Paris at that time and soon destined to become the Bishop of Killaloe, also wrote to Rome giving thanks: "You had already laid the foundations of our edifice, erected the pillars, and given shepherds to feed the sheep and the lambs: but now that the work should not remain imperfect, you have crowned the edifice, and provided a pastor for the pastors themselves, appointing the Archbishop of Armagh... One therefore in a thousand had to be chosen, suited to bear so great a burden, that one you have found, one whom none better or more pleasing could be discovered."

Relic of St. Oliver - St. Patrick's Chapel, Rosario, Argentina. 'Cabra Relic'
See p.264 & p.275

Much to Oliver's disappointment, it was decided that his episcopal ordination should take place quietly in Flanders on his journey back to Ireland, lest a well-publicised ceremony in Rome might antagonise the government back home. He had obviously hoped that his many friends could pray with him at such a ceremony in Rome and so speed him on his way before setting out to labour in the vineyard of the Lord in the far-flung outpost of Ireland. Or that he could be like so many apostles and martyrs before him, who down through the centuries were appointed in Rome just as St. Patrick was, and who then set out from the eternal city fully armed for the challenges of spreading God's Word. He appealed the decision, which was turned down and he humbly accepted the outcome, Flanders it was to be. On reflection, the Roman authorities must have later questioned the wisdom and indeed the reasoning behind that judgement because within two years, his friend John Brenan would be consecrated Bishop of Waterford at such a ceremony, performed in the centre of Christendom. The difficulties and the delays about to beset Oliver on his journey might indeed have been a catalyst for that Roman change of heart. Oliver clearly understood that the task he was about to undertake was a daunting one, fraught with danger. Nonetheless, he was willing to give up a relatively comfortable lifestyle in Rome, all in the service of the Church back home. Like St. Patrick before him, he was willing to leave a secure and regular way of life, to answer the call of Ireland, so as to work amongst an impoverished Church and people, knowing of course that countless hardships awaited him as Primate of Ireland.

[1] Stokes Mgr. John 'Life of Blessed Oliver Plunkett' Dublin 1965 p.11 & Moran 1895 p.36

[1] Pope Clement IX, who as Cardinal **Rospigliosi was** Cardinal Secretary of State 1657-1667. In earlier years he served as a diplomat and would therefore have been quite familiar with **Propaganda Fide College and its staff. Mgr. John Hanly wrote that** Cardinal Rospigliosi had been attached to the College.

12. Oliver's Vineyard at Castel Gandolfo

As a student in the Irish College many years earlier, Oliver's annual two weeks summer holidays were spent in the college vineyard on the slopes of Castel Gandolfo, about twenty-five kilometres south east of Rome. He must have had very happy memories of those working holidays, because when working as a professor in Propaganda College, he acquired a small garden vineyard close to the one owned by the Irish college, overlooking the beautiful lake Albano. This, he now left to the Irish College along with some books and pictures, in appreciation for the education he had received there. The pictures must not have been used by the college at that time, as twelve years later and barely a week before his martyrdom, St. Oliver wrote a long and poignant letter to his former secretary and relative, Fr. Michael Plunkett in Rome, leaving the pictures to the Irish College and expressing his sorrow that they had not been framed. Many of the books, which he presented to the college library were scattered by the French during their invasion of Rome in 1798, however at least one of those books is still easily identified by his[1] signature: 'Oliver Plunkette, Collegio Hibern. Dedit.'

The garden vineyard, which he gave to the Irish College, was probably attached to their existing vineyard as a small extension. The time he spent in his vineyard must have been a joyful and a prayerful time for him and he would certainly have reflected on the scores upon scores of references to vines and vineyards in the Holy Bible. Doubtless Dr. Oliver was familiar with them all. Having the freedom of the house and library which was on the property of the Irish College vineyard nearby, meant that this whole experience must have been a most edifying one for him, so that when he wrote some years later about the delights of Rome, the vineyard must surely have been on his mind as one of those delights. One can well imagine the care and love with which he must have tended on those vines at Albano, and no doubt a little of the fruit of those vines was made into wine, for the sacred mysteries of some of his Masses. Indeed the crushing of those grapes was perhaps a foretaste of his-own willing sacrifice as a martyr at Tyburn.

[1] Moran, Cardinal Patrick 'Memoir of Oliver Plunket' Dublin 1895. p.43

13. PLANNING HIS RETURN TO IRELAND

Thinking ahead of his future apostolate while still in Rome and obviously hoping to waste no time or opportunity to reform the Church in Ireland, he made seven requests[1] on his own behalf and on behalf of the Irish bishops. The first request would allow existing bishops to appoint vicar generals in those dioceses that lay vacant, until further bishops or vicars apostolic were appointed by Rome. This would provide constant leadership in those dioceses, forestalling possible divisions, which often surfaced after elections by the clergy. Oliver's request was granted and over the following years he appointed several vicars to various dioceses.

He was probably also thinking ahead about the infamous Fr. Terrence O'Kelly, one of the first students of the Irish College in Rome, then the vicar general of Derry, who was living an openly scandalous life for over twenty years. Each time an attempt was made to remove him from office he remained defiant and reported it under the law of Premunire, which forbade any instance of foreign jurisdiction, especially from Rome. One vicar general had already been jailed when a previous attempt to remove

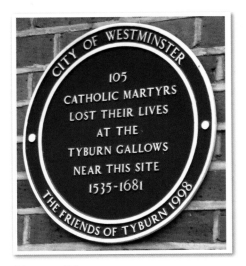
Plaque at Tyburn

him from office was reported to the civil authorities.

The other six requests made by Oliver before he left Rome, had to do with the blessing of the Holy Oils, indulgences granted to cathedrals and parish churches, the blessing of crucifixes with an indulgence for the dying, the control by a metropolitan bishop over other dioceses and their vicars and the problems concerning the performance of clandestine marriages by religious, sometimes against the will of the parish priest or bishop. Concerned also about Irish Catholics who were forced into slavery in the sugar plantations of the West Indies in the preceding twenty years, he also requested: "That the bishops should be enabled to communicate their faculties to Irish priests who, moved by God, feel called to the difficult missions of the American islands to succour the thousands and thousands of Irish Catholics sent into exile by the tyrant Cromwell, and now in grave danger as regards their eternal salvation because of the lack of priests."

Oliver was forever aware of the dangers to the Church if it should meddle in politics and before leaving Rome he had recommended: "Do not promote those who have been involved in intrigues and factions during these wars, and have become positively hateful to the King. And I also believe that it is not a good thing either to promote those who seek to advance themselves by means of the English Court because such men always subscribe to the doctrines of the Sorbonnists and their followers, doctrines which are favourable to the King but not to the Holy See."

[1] Hanly 'The Letters' No.20

14. SCANAROLO CROSS

Before leaving Rome, Oliver petitioned the Holy Father, for the return of a relic of the True Cross, which was given to the Church of Armagh by Archbishop Scanarolo[1] around 1654. It was given on the stipulation that it would be publicly venerated in Armagh. One report states that the cross was entrusted to Bishop Nicholas French of Ferns Diocese on his visit to Rome in 1648 and that the gift was renewed formally in the year 1654, when it was deposited for safe keeping with Fr. Luke Wadding and the community of St. Isidore's in Rome, awaiting an opportune time to send it to Armagh. The Scanarolo Cross was described in detail in an inventory of St. Isidore's in 1664, containing wood of the Cross of Calvary and relics of the Blessed Virgin, St, Joseph and other saints. Made of pure gold, it was an impressive reliquary and Oliver evidently felt that the time was right to take it with him to the Archdiocese of Armagh. In response to his request, the Sacred Congregation made enquiries as to whether the relic could be safely venerated in Ireland. The outcome of those enquiries remains unidentified and there is no known reference to the cross after that. As there is no record of any further petitions from Armagh for its return, it is possible that Oliver did take the treasured relic with him on his journey home. This is perhaps unlikely considering the risks involved, yet he did make a request for it, so obviously he had some plan in mind. If left in Rome it may have been stolen by the French one hundred and thirty years later just as some treasures from the Irish College were,

Relic of True Cross, St. Peter's Church, Drogheda

Unveiling of plaque in St. Bavo's Cathedral, Ghent. Bishop Gerard Clifford, Bishop Van Looy, Ghent, Mgr. James Carroll.

although one would imagine that some reference would have been made to the cross in St. Isidore's in the meantime.

It is surely more than a coincidence that on a pilgrimage which travelled to Ghent in 2008 to commemorate St. Oliver's episcopal ordination and journey home to Ireland, the Irish group led by Bishop Gerard Clifford were presented with a relic of the True Cross. The Relic was presented by Bishop Van Looy of Ghent to Bishop Clifford, thereby completing St. Oliver's seemingly unfulfilled desire on his own journey home to Ireland all those years earlier. The silver reliquary was mounted the following year in a beautiful triptych reliquary in St. Peter's Church, Drogheda, opposite the National Shrine of St. Oliver.

1 Moran Cardinal Patrick 'Memoir of Oliver Plunket' Dublin 1895. p.42

15. LEAVING ROME

After twenty-two years in Rome, Oliver had seven weeks' in which to prepare for his departure and say all his farewells. He was only too well aware that he would never return to his beloved Rome. Before leaving, Oliver paid farewell to all his friends not forgetting a visit to the poor of Santo Spirito hospital adjacent to the Vatican. Fr. Mieskow, the superior wished him well, along with the prophetic[1] words: "My Lord, you are going to shed your blood for the Catholic Faith." Oliver replied: "I am unworthy of such a favour but help me with your prayers that this desire of mine may be fulfilled." He would certainly have made a last pilgrimage to the seven churches and the other shrines of the city of Rome, popularised a century before by St. Philip Neri, founder of the Oratorian order, a religious community which had been so caring to Oliver while he was under the patronage of the saintly Fr. Scarampi. Dr. Oliver set out on his journey from Rome in the first week of September 1669 and before setting out he would certainly have recalled his outward journey to Rome all those years earlier. All journeys were considered risky so whatever precious money Oliver carried, his own savings and many little gifts, would have been well secured upon his person and were certainly earmarked for his mission to an impoverished Church back home in Ireland. He must have trusted and prayed that he would not be abducted and robbed a second time, so before leaving Rome he would surely have asked the prayers of his many friends and acquaintances for a safe journey and the success of his future apostolate.

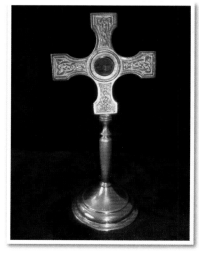

St. Oliver Relic which has travelled to parishes throughout Ireland

[1] Ó Fiaich & Forristal 'Oliver Plunkett' Indiana USA 1976. Ó Fiaich. p.20

16. JOURNEY TO FLANDERS

Oliver began his journey in the company of Fr. Edward Locke, a Jesuit who was president of the Irish College. The same rector had some months previously sent a reference in support of his appointment to Armagh. Fr. Locke had barely concluded two years of his term of office by that stage and he died in Dublin some two years later, so perhaps he was suffering from ill health at the time, which might explain his early return home. It is not known if they completed the journey to Ireland together or if they separated on the way, as no further reference is made to Fr. Locke on the journey. Perhaps their intention was to travel to Brussels together and to carry on individually from there, with Fr. Locke travelling directly to Ireland and Oliver passing through England.

The fifteen hundred kilometre journey to Flanders was completed in two months, almost certainly by horse drawn carriages, which plied between cities on the route, covering forty or fifty arduous kilometres per day. When he arrived in Bologna, he was advised that there was a plague and quarantine in Basel, so he decided to change his route by taking the longer road through Austria and Germany. He then travelled through the Brenner Pass to Innsbruck, through Munich, Augsburg, crossing the Danube at Neuberg, through Nuremberg, Würzburg and on to Mainz. From here he travelled by boat down the Rhine to Cologne, arriving in Cologne he found himself in yet another predicament. Should he risk the more direct overland route to Brussels, through an area infected with pestilence and which was also patrolled by Spanish soldiers who were roaming loose in the Belgium region. These soldiers were often unpaid and had a notorious reputation of not sparing anyone. Or should he travel further down the river Rhine and pass through Protestant controlled areas, which included parts of Germany and Holland.

Upon reflection, having been robbed before in the Ardennes region, he decided to risk travelling into the Protestant areas dressed in disguise, so he continued by boat further on down the river Rhine and on into Holland. Near Rotterdam the Dutch skipper who was drunk, allowed the boat to run aground on a sandbank. This was a serious incident apparently, as the twenty-five passengers were very much afraid for their own safety and were obliged to wait anxiously for the next tide to re-float the vessel. On the journey the skipper must have suspected that Oliver was a priest, for in a letter written to the College of Propaganda shortly afterwards, Oliver wrote: "And for four nights I slept on the bare boards exposed to the air and the winds because that devil of a Calvinist would not permit the door or the window to be closed in the cabin assigned to me in the ship. At last I reached Antwerp and then I went on to Brussels by the river." Oliver's description of the captain was obviously not intended as an unforgiving one but rather just another example of his dry humour, in a report that he knew would be circulated amongst his many friends, all eagerly awaiting news from him. It must also be remembered that Oliver had some way to go on his journey to sainthood.

Arriving in Brussels on the 3rd of November, Oliver sought out Monsignor Carlo Airoldi, the Internuncio who was based there and who also had the responsibility of looking after the Church in Ireland and England. Oliver's Bull of appointment from Rome had already been sent to him at an earlier date. Oliver's episcopal ordination was delayed

St. Oliver Procession, Drogheda

because Bishop d'Allamont of Ghent was away at the time and he became ill with fever upon his return. In a letter to Rome, Oliver explained his enforced delays: "I tell you all this so that your Lordship may see that my delay here is not voluntary, and Monsignor Internuncio can testify to this too, he is working hard for me in this great charity. I am well aware of the mind of His Holiness and the sacred congregation, and I shall obey not alone the commands of the Sacred Congregation, but even its hints and slightest indications. And with the help of God I shall conduct myself in the matter of obedience in a manner befitting one brought up and raised upon the milk of the Holy Roman See." The charisma of obedience was one which Oliver practised constantly and is quite evident in many of his later letters.

Not one to waste time, Oliver went to visit the famous St. Anthony's College at Louvain, a Franciscan friary of fifty friars where he met the fifteen friars who had recently arrived from Ireland. Writing from Brussels on his return from Louvain, he communicates his concern that the friars would later return to Ireland, young and inexperienced. He asked that a decision should be taken in Rome with regard to the novitiates in Ireland as he was apprehensive about the large number of novitiates and consequently the quality of their friars. In Louvain, he also spoke with disgraced friar, Fr. James Taaffe, who had recently arrived from Ireland. Friar Taaffe expressed great remorse for the actions he had taken and later went to Rome where he lived out the rest of his life quietly and in repentance. Oliver also met in Louvain the famous Jesuit theologian,

St. Oliver's Watch and Ring.

Richard Arsdekin. Cardinal Moran wrote[1] of Oliver: "Through his solicitations, the learned Jesuit, Arsdekin, a native of Kilkenny and at that time lecturing on divinity in the university of Louvain composed his learned work, Theologia Universa Tripartita which acquired for the author a universal fame." Some twenty years later, in the twelfth edition there is a section in which he writes glowingly about Oliver.

[1] Moran, Cardinal Patrick 'Memoir of Oliver Plunket' Dublin 1895. p.47

17. ARMAGH ALTAR-PLATE

While in Louvain, Oliver would undoubtedly have enquired about the remnants of the Armagh altar-plate, which was deposited there over sixty years earlier. The altar-plate, along with some church items and possibly some vestments, were brought out of Ireland for safe keeping by Hugh O'Neill, the Earl of Tyrone in the poignant Flight of the Earls, who had stayed with his party in Louvain over the winter of 1607/1608. The following items were listed in an earlier inventory[1] of 1644, a monstrance, ciborium, four chalices, two gilt crosses including a processional one, two thuribles, two silver spoons, incense boat, six patens, two statues, etc. They had been examined by Archbishop O'Reilly about eleven years before Oliver's visit and were generally found to be in poor enough condition at that time. Worried that these items would deteriorate and become almost worthless through use by the friars, Archbishop O'Reilly obtained the written agreement from the Dean and the Chapter of Armagh that they should be sold and the money used to provide a fund for the education of student priests from the archdiocese. He later changed his mind about this, so they remained in the safekeeping of the friars at Louvain until at least 1741 and may have been sold for such a purpose at a later date.

[1] Millet Fr. Benignus 'Ancient altar-plate and other furnishings of the church of Armagh' Seanchas Ard Mhacha 1958. p.87

18. CONSECRATION AS ARCHBISHOP OF ARMAGH

Oliver's consecration as Archbishop of Armagh took place on the 1st December 1669, the first Sunday of Advent, in a quiet ceremony in the bishop's private chapel[1] adjacent to St. Bavo's cathedral in Ghent. Bishop Eugene Albert d'Allamont, Count of Brandeville and Everghen performed the ceremony assisted by the Provost of the Cathedral, Rt. Rev. James Roose and the Dean of the Chapter of Ghent, Rt. Rev. John le Monier. Interestingly, Bishop Nicholas French was present at the ceremony and it can be assumed according to protocol, that if a third bishop was available, Bishop French would have taken part. This was the third time since May of that year that Bishop d'Allamont was involved in the consecration of an Irish Archbishop, namely, James

St. Bavo's Cathedral, Ghent

Lynch of Tuam in Ghent and Peter Talbot of Dublin, in Antwerp. Bishop French assisted at both of those ceremonies, when three bishops were available in each case. Oliver then made plans for the next stage of his journey to Ireland via London. Before leaving he gave Bishop French his personal items of devotion until such time as a ship would sail directly to Ireland.

Leaving Ghent, Oliver decided to change his route for at least the third time on his journey from Rome by sailing from Ostend instead of using the Calais-Dover crossing. Arriving in Ostend, Oliver was forced to wait twelve days for favourable wind before setting sail for England. During this time, he must surely have recalled his landing at that port all those years earlier, having survived the chase and the terrible storm at sea. He wrote: "I am thinking of passing myself off as an Italian tourist who is going out of curiosity to see the sights of London" and he added that he had given his papers and letters to an English gentleman to be brought to London. He eventually set sail from Ostend on board an English ship on Saturday 21st December (Gregorian calendar) and he arrived in London two days later on Monday the 13th December (Julian calendar). England and Ireland refused to adjust to the Gregorian calendar until 1752 and were ten days behind the continental calendar at the time.

[1] Curtis, Fr. Emmanuel 'Blessed Oliver Plunkett' Dublin 1963. p.50

19. LONDON

Travelling on through England he actually stayed for several weeks incognito in the Royal Palace, under the protection of Fr. Philip Howard, Grand Almoner to Queen Catherine who was a Catholic. Staying in the palace had a certain irony as there were already agents on the look-out for him, so perhaps the palace was the very place where he could best remain unnoticed.

Fr. Howard brought Oliver in his carriage to see the sights of London. Undoubtedly they witnessed the after-effects of the great fire of London,

Cardinal of Norfolk, Philip Thomas Howard

which had occurred only three years earlier in 1666 and of the rebuilding work which was ongoing at the time. During the hysteria of the Popish Plot yet to come, the Catholics would again be accused of starting the fire. Indeed a monument was erected to commemorate the event and a plaque blaming the Catholics for the fire placed on it in 1681, where it remained for almost two hundred years. The 1660's were momentous times in England, 1660 saw the restoration of King Charles II to the throne. Five years later saw England at war with the Dutch and also a year of plague with a large number of deaths. Called the great plague, it claimed the lives of an estimated one-hundred thousand inhabitants of London. The great fire of London took place the following year, destroying the medieval centre of the city and jumping over the river Thames over the course of the conflagration. King Charles II showed remarkable courage and leadership to the fire-fighters as they arrested the fire, perhaps it was his finest hour. The following year, saw the Dutch warships sail up the Thames estuary and destroy numerous English war ships and tow away a couple more, including a flag-ship; perhaps one of King Charles' lowest hours. It is no wonder then that the English were looking over their shoulders and the Catholics could always be relied upon to be an easy target.

Before travelling to England he had written: "I shall not delay long there, but shall go to my diocese where until my last breath I shall live in obedience to the Holy See and the service of souls, even if it should cost me my life." He had obviously made up his mind even before his ministry in Ireland had begun that he would never go into exile irrespective of the circumstances that might confront him.

He would have had many letters with him, including the one he carried from the superior of the Dominican order in Rome and addressed to the Irish provincial of the order. The personal letters he carried, including one addressed to the wife of King Charles II, Queen Catherine of Braganza, who was a Catholic and written1 by Cardinal Barberini, may even have been useful to help smooth his passage through customs or checkpoints.

1 Concannon Helena 'Blessed Oliver Plunket' Dublin 1935. p.109

St. James' Palace, London

20. ALWAYS ON DUTY

One suspects that during his stay in London he would have outlined his thoughts and feelings on the possibility of setting up of schools in his diocese. The day after his arrival in London, Archbishop Oliver was presented to the Queen by Fr. Howard. Writing to Rome on 17th December, Oliver announced his arrival in London and obviously having heard fresh news from Ireland, no doubt from his cousin Bishop Patrick, he recommended that Fr. Thady Keogh should become the Bishop of the diocese of Clonfert. A year later he was so appointed, in fact it was Archbishop Oliver who officiated at his episcopal ordination in Dublin in November 1671. In the same letter to Rome, he made a strong case that Fr. Howard should also become a bishop. Indeed two years later he was so nominated and within five years became Cardinal and moved to Rome, where in 1680 he became the Cardinal Protector of England. Some five years later, Cardinal Howard was destined to become the Custodian of the Relic of the Head of the martyred Archbishop of Armagh. Fr. Howard a brother of the Duke of Norfolk was the great grandson and namesake of the Elizabethan martyr, St. Philip Howard and an uncle of Blessed William Howard or Lord Stafford who was also martyred as a result of the Titus Oates plot. Oliver, who was martyred just six months later, wrote from Newgate prison that he was much obliged to the family of the same Lord Stafford for their kindness to him while in prison.

It is interesting to note that the Dominican Convent, which was founded by Cardinal Howard in Flanders a few years later, was the community to which Sr. Catherine Plunkett, believed to be a grand-niece[1] of Oliver, was sent to for further training some thirty years later. Upon returning to Ireland after her formation, she soon became the first superior of the new Dominican community of sisters at Siena Convent, founded in Drogheda in 1722. Fr. Howard had been ordained in Rome two years before Oliver and although they attended different seminaries, it is possible that they were already acquainted. They became good friends and wrote to each other subsequently. Oliver stayed with him in St. James' Palace, London, incognito for ten days, indeed there was a certain sense of irony in his staying in the royal palace as only a few weeks earlier, King Charles had written to viceroy Robartes in Dublin, stating that Oliver was lurking in Ireland to do mischief and that if he could be apprehended it would be an acceptable service. Charles had empathy for Catholics and it was just typical of his duplicity that he should continuously act in this way.

Perhaps staying in St. James' Palace was the very place where Oliver could best remain unnoticed. Friar Peter Walsh who had caused so much division and strife within the Church in Ireland as ring leader of those promoting the Remonstrance, was also in London, having refused an order from his superior to travel to the continent and was causing trouble

St. John Paul II venerating St. Oliver Relic at Killineer

as usual. His stories however were so fantastic that even when partially true they were not believed. Oliver wrote that the followers of Walsh, or Walsh himself had sent anonymous letters to the royal ministers concerning his activities. One report to the authorities stated that Fr. Howard had three hundred priests in hiding in the palace, who went out each night to convert the populace. Oliver wrote that Walsh had been ordered to go to Flanders under pain of excommunication. "He appealed to[2] the General and should the General send him such an order, he will appeal to the Pope and from the Pope he will appeal to the Council and from the Council to the Tribunal of God."

[1] See Chapter 94
[2] Moran, Cardinal Patrick 'Memoir of Oliver Plunket' Dublin 1895. p.48

Fr. Paddy Rushe & Tony Breen at the Spanish steps in Rome, during the making of a DVD on St. Oliver 2006.

21. CATHOLICISM IN ENGLAND

Without resident bishops, the church in England relied on a governing chapter of priests. Oliver met with Fr. Humphrey Ellis, dean of the chapter along with several other members and he found them all devoted to the Holy See. He also met many other resident priests and members of the leading Catholic families in the London area. Due to the harshness of the laws towards Catholics, England had a resident bishop for only eight[1] out of the previous one hundred years and it was exactly one hundred years since London last had a bishop, who died in prison. As there was no resident bishop in England for the previous thirty-eight years, it would be extremely surprising if Archbishop Oliver did not first exercise his role as a bishop over the three month period which he spent in England. It is unlikely that he ordained any priests, but it would be probable that he confirmed during his visit. Cosmo de Medici, Grand Duke of Tuscany who spent time[2] in England around the time of Oliver's stay, wrote: "The Irish bishops perform the episcopal functions for the benefit of the Catholics, and come over occasionally to exercise their charge in the best manner in their power."

While staying at the palace, Oliver was not to know of the secret negotiations in progress, between King Charles II and King Louis XIV of France, culminating in the secret Treaty of Dover a few months later. As part of that agreement, Charles agreed to publicly announce his conversion to Catholicism and eventually converted on his deathbed. Charles was a weak monarch however, continually bowing to the pressures of politics; Oliver would time and time again, find this out to his cost, right up to his failed appeal to the King for clemency in 1681.

Because of the impossibility of travelling with snow and ice, Oliver was obliged to stay in London much longer than he had intended. He was forced to stay most of the winter and he recalled that it was so cold while in London that the wine in his chalice had frozen, indicating an indoor temperature of minus four or five degrees celsius. The winters were very much colder than in modern times, the seventeenth century being among the coldest of what has been termed a mini ice age. Dr. Plunkett was to suffer from the effects of this harsh weather on many occasions subsequently, either on his long journeys, at mass-rocks, or in unheated hiding places or prison cells.

Knowing the lie of the land politically was always an important consideration and Oliver wrote: "I do not intend however, to remain in London since I know the designs of court." Under the patronage of Fr. Pulton a prominent member of the old English chapter of priests, Oliver went to stay with a Mr. and Mrs Slaughter at a country retreat outside London, where he cheerfully reported that the walks were good and solitary. Fr. Pulton had been an army officer previously and probably for reasons of disguise was still known as Captain Pulton. On the day that Oliver had left Ghent to travel to Ostend, Pope Clement IX who had appointed him to Armagh passed away. Writing now from his country retreat, Oliver asked Fr. Pulton to keep him informed about any news from London or Rome, but especially anything with regard to the next Pope. Obviously Rome was still very much in Oliver's thoughts and prayers at the time.

Reliquary of St. Oliver in Irish College, Rome

During his stay in England, he acquired two pairs of glasses, one pair of 'first vision,' the other pair suitable for a person of fifty years of age; he later expressed his satisfaction with them. Although he was forty-four years old, he needed glasses for a person of fifty years, a first inkling perhaps of the weakness of Oliver's eyes, from which he would suffer greatly thereafter. No doubt, reading and attending to his correspondence for long hours under candlelight, would not have improved the weakness of his eyes. A man who intended to maintain a voluminous correspondence, he ordered a quire of paper, which amounted to twenty-four quite large sheets of paper; this would undoubtedly be largely used up before his return to Ireland. He also bought books and placed orders for extra books at this time. Oliver's Bull of appointment from Rome, his seal of office and his other private papers were left with a Mr. Warren. Another very helpful gentleman to him at this time was an Irishman, Mr. Daniel Arthur. He was a trusted Catholic businessman living in London, whom he could safely use as a conduit for his ample correspondence and who is mentioned time and time again in his letters over the following couple of years.

[1] Bennett Fr. Martin 'The Way of a Martyr' London 1974. p. 17
[2] Concannon Helena 'Blessed Oliver Plunket' Dublin 1935. p. 116 From the Rawdon Papers.

22. MAN OF CHARITY

Having already distinguished himself in Rome for his works of charity, Archbishop Oliver when writing to Fr. Pulton, asked him if a position could be found for a local servant girl, Christian Coles, who was a Catholic. He described her as suitable for dressmaking, sewing, etc., a devout, able and obedient girl of twenty years of age and not with red hair. Due to the fact that she had a Presbyterian aunt who was not pleased with her; Oliver was concerned for her faith and was hopeful that a placement could be provided for her as he mentions her a second time in another letter to Captain Pulton. A few years later, in spite of his poverty, Oliver would again show his charitable side by pawning some of his valuables so as to give bread to the poor during a season of famine.

23. Captain William Browne

In the series of letters[1] addressed to Captain Pulton, Oliver signs himself as William Browne, the first use in his letters of the nom-de-plume; within weeks he himself would adopt the costume and accoutrements of an army captain. Using such a disguise had many advantages; as army officers were a common sight on the roads, had the freedom to travel and would usually not draw any suspicion. No doubt, Fr. Pulton sowed this idea with Archbishop Oliver and perhaps even supplied the uniform with all its trappings.

About the third week in February, despite the rigours of the weather, he set off again on his journey for Ireland so as to fulfil his desire to reach his province during Lent. The English leg of his journey proved to be the most traumatic part of his overall passage from Rome, and he wrote: "I suffered more between London and Holyhead, where I boarded ship, than during the whole journey from Rome to London; severe cold and strong winds and then heavy snow and finally as the snow melted, the rivers were so high that three times I was up to my knees in water in the carriage."

[1] Westminster Archives

24. Arrival in Dublin

Another delay awaited him in Holyhead, while he waited twelve days for a favourable sailing wind. At 9am on[1] Monday 7th March 1670, he finally landed at Ringsend, Dublin, after a ten hour sailing time. This date was coincidentally celebrated on the continent as St. Patrick's Day, feast of the National Apostle of Ireland and founder of the See of Armagh. Surely it is more than coincidence that his many friends in Rome would around that very hour be remembering him in a special way in their prayers at masses on that feast-day morning. Archbishop Oliver's first sighting of the landscape and of the green hills of Ireland, early on that spring day, would undoubtedly have stirred his emotions after an exile of over twenty-three years. He must have wondered about his future and what trials lay ahead for him; his homeland had changed completely since he saw it last. When leaving, he had experienced the joys of Irish freedom, with the exception of some of the major walled towns and cities. During those few short years of the Confederation of Kilkenny, the Church was glorious once more and many churches and monasteries were being used once again in giving glory to God.

When Oliver left Ireland as the young and insignificant Don Oliverio, he was under the protection of the Papal Envoy, Fr. Scarampi and was waved off by thousands of people at the quayside at Waterford. Now, as the Primate of Ireland, Archbishop Oliver disembarked in secret

Penal Times Vestments in Armagh - reputedly worn by St. Oliver

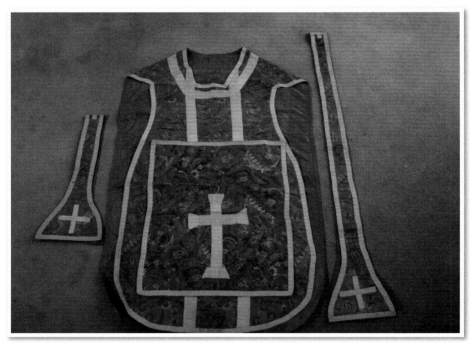

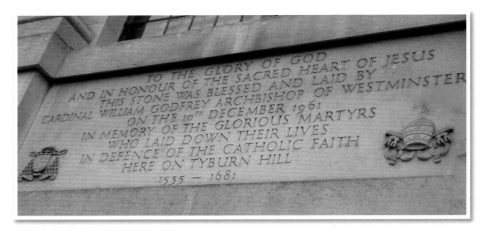

Plaque at Tyburn Convent, London

at the tiny little promontory of Ringsend. Almost certainly dressed as the military officer Captain Browne, he went directly to the 'Inns' in Dublin city centre, where Sir Nicholas Plunkett had his home. He wrote letters of thanks to Fr. Pulton both on his arrival at Chester and again upon his safe landing at Dublin. He requested from him some further spiritual books of specific authors of the day, with money, which Oliver had shortly beforehand left with the afore-mentioned Mr. Warren. He stayed for only three days in Dublin, in the house of Sir Nicholas, who gave him his carriage. Oliver was delighted to see Bishop Patrick looking so well. The Earl of Fingall offered him a home and three other knights all married to cousins of his, also offered their hospitality to him at this time.

For the greater part of the previous two hundred years, the archbishops of Armagh had resided in the southern end of the archdiocese, at or near Drogheda, leaving the day-to-day running of the northern end of the diocese in the hands of a Gaelic vicar general, who lived there. Oliver was resolute not to be an absentee archbishop and was determined to mend bridges between the clergy and peoples of the 'Gael' and the 'Pale,' so he decided to accept the offer of the Baron of Louth a distant relative, writing: "I have decided to attach myself to this gentleman because he lives in the heart of my area." Based at Louth Hall, the Baron also had other properties in mid-Louth. Writing to Rome to report his arrival in Dublin, Archbishop Oliver asked permission to consecrate the holy oils with just two priests, instead of the stipulated five, because of the difficulty of assembling that number of priests during holy week, as all would be busy hearing confessions.

During those three days in Dublin he also met many more of his relatives and he wrote: "I find such a heart-warming welcome and companionship among my relations that the pain of departure from Rome is eased." Soon after Oliver's return to Ireland, James McKenna became his servant; this was undoubtedly arranged for him by his relations upon his arrival in Dublin and James was subsequently maintained by Oliver's relatives. James would be his loyal servant until the very end, some eleven years later. During that time he was destined to experience many good and bad times with Oliver, including many months spent in prison.

[1] Ó Fiaich & Forristal 'Oliver Plunkett' Indiana, USA 1976. Ó Fiaich. p.25

25. Political & Religious Situation in Ireland

The political situation in Ireland was extraordinary in many ways. The laws on the statute books were strongly anti-Catholic and it depended on the viceroy or any one of the many hundreds of local officials, dignitaries or Protestant ministers as to how strictly these laws were enforced. This often depended on how much outside influence or pressure was exerted on them. If Catholics showed any form of resilience or if an individual Catholic appeared to be feisty in any way, then a complaint could be made to a Protestant minister or to a magistrate. In a cabal of self-interest and self-preservation, it was ever the concern of Protestants that the status quo of property possession be maintained at all costs. Any Protestant who overly showed softness or leniency towards

Catholics would be seen as turncoat, called a 'Papist' and might be ostracised within their own community. Going 'native' was one of the greatest insults and hurts which could be inflicted. Whenever a complaint was made, whether it was right or wrong, the authorities felt pressurised and obliged by a sense of group-think to uphold the status quo. 'Croppy lie down' became a common cry over a hundred years later but it was already much in vogue as a tried and tested strategy throughout the second half of the seventeenth century to keep the Catholics subjugated.

Throughout the countryside, Catholics formed the large majority of the overall population while the Protestants were generally in the majority in the larger towns and cities. It seemed to be more expedient to supress and kill Catholicism off by a thousand small cuts, including an odd severe wound administered every so often, rather than a complete and total ban on their activities. If a total prohibition was enforced on the religious practices of Catholics they would rise up and rebel, just as they had done almost thirty years earlier. Catholics had already proven more than willing to give up their property so as to preserve the ancient truths of their faith, and had also proven that under no circumstances were they willing to give up those self-same truths. Catholics greatly valued their land and many a feud began over the ownership of a sliver of land along a ditch. However, as much as they prized their bit of land, they had proven that they valued their faith even more. In any event, there were not enough working class Protestants to keep the wheels of the economy moving and so Catholic artisans and labourers would always be required to keep profits flowing back to the investors and adventurers. A minimum number of Catholic parish priests were therefore tolerated and allowed to minister, provided they operated strictly within the confines of their own area. Provided also that they kept an extra low profile and did not have any public displays or show any inkling that Catholics might rise above their station. In any event, those receiving Catholic sacraments such as baptism or marriage were penalised by being forced to pay a fine to the local Protestant church and so support the Protestant clergy and the established church structure throughout the country. Until such time as the government would have more control, it became the pragmatic policy in Ireland to allow Catholics a limited practice of their religion provided such practise remained invisible. To profess openly any religion other than the established one would immediately bring down the full rigours of the law. Bishop John Brenan in[1] 1672 wrote: "The Protestant ministers with their large income have never built a single church, and have not even repaired the old ones that were built and endowed by our Catholic forefathers; nay, more, when there is a question of repairing bells, organ, and similar things in the cathedral, they compel our Catholics to contribute."

Arriving incognito in Ireland, this then was the scenario in which Archbishop Oliver found himself. Word soon got out that he was back

Reliquary in Westminster Cathedral

in Ireland, not just as plain Mr. Oliver Plunkett returning from the continent, but as the Archbishop and Primate returning from Rome. Therefore, it was not long before a complaint to that effect was made to the Irish Privy Council, probably by the supporters of Walsh and company; Walsh having already been dismissed from the order, was on the payroll of the government. Luckily, Archbishop Oliver escaped arrest or possible exile at the time, because the influential Earl of Roscommon, a Protestant relative of his and a member of the Council, happened to be in Dublin and pledged good behaviour on his behalf. Oliver had been very good to him during his stay in Rome some years earlier. This sufficed for the time being, Archbishop's Oliver's card was marked, he was being warned not to rock the boat, either by straying into politics or by daring to ever become a visible presence in the community. This was just fine with Oliver as he intended to work along these lines in any event.

[1] Power Canon P. 'A Bishop of Penal Times' Cork 1932. p.28

Portarait of St. Oliver in Siena Convent

26. CATHOLICISM IN IRELAND

Catholicism in Ireland at the time could briefly be described as chaotic. The Church was teetering on the very verge of collapse for several decades before Oliver's return to Ireland. There were very few Catholic churches; many in the south of the country were small mass-houses with thatched straw roofs which were not suitable to reserve the Blessed Sacrament. Without the possibility of sanctuary lamps, these were not churches or chapels in the proper sense of the word, but proved their importance nonetheless. In the north of the country, the landless Catholics were invariably forced to rely on the mossy mass-rock for an altar. For thirty years before his return, there had been disorder and upheaval throughout the land. The 1640's had brought the Confederate wars; the 1650's saw the completion of the Cromwellian conquests; it also brought martyrs, a new breed of priest hunters, the iconoclastic and cynical smashing of statues and monuments, with the unruly damage and complete destruction of all churches which were surplus to Protestant requirements. It also saw transportation and an active slave trade to the Barbados, the cruel policy of 'To Hell or to Connaught' when a large percentage of the land mass of Ireland literally changed hands, as well as much other suffering caused by the tyrant adventurers. The 1660's brought the Restoration of King Charles II to the throne, but there was little respite for Catholicism or for the return of much of the confiscated lands to Catholics. The decade saw much talk, promise and negotiations on the issue, but hopes were soon dashed for a return of the confiscated lands. Only the lucky few would acquire some land. The Plunkett clan as loyal supporters of King Charles during his exile, retrieved the greater portion of their former estates, however, Oliver's family estate at Loughcrew was not returned. The 1660's also saw the policy of divide and conquer by viceroy Ormond. Ultimately this policy was unsuccessful against the Church in Ireland, primarily because of the resolute leadership given by those few bishops still in residence. In England which had been without Catholic bishops for several generations, the Church collapsed completely as a result of detachment, a lack of leadership and the consequential divisions which arose within it. In Ireland, as a consequence of the Remonstrance, the duplicity of Friar Taaffe and the almost total lack of Church leadership throughout the previous two decades, the Church was deeply divided and disorganised in the 1660's. A large number of the priests throughout the country were uneducated; the religious orders often had quite serious arguments amongst themselves, almost coming to blows on occasions. Some members of the religious orders would not accept their leaders. In Munster, Friar Martin French, an Augustinian friar, beat up a Franciscan friar. Archbishop James Lynch of Tuam having dealt with the case was then brought before the courts and accused of Premunire or foreign jurisdiction; he was jailed for a time in 1670, as was the Augustinian friars superior. The same Augustinian friar ultimately succeeded in having Archbishop Lynch sent into permanent exile some four years later. Many of the religious orders argued with the diocesan clergy and all wished to continue to do things

Old Siena Convent, Dyer Street
1725 - 1796

in their own way, without any outside interference.

The provincial of the Franciscans was not accepted by factions of his own order and one of their provincial synods had all of its acts subsequently quashed.

The Irish Church had reached a crossroads and was then in grave danger of taking a wrong turn. But into the 1670's and not a moment too soon, by the grace of God, steps Archbishop Oliver, who wrote of these dissensions: "altar has been erected against altar." With the strong cultural differences of Catholics of the 'Gael' and of the 'Pale'

St. Oliver - Bronze Image

adding to the mix, the potential fault line in the Irish Church was much more pronounced in the Northern Province than in any other province. Providentially, it was here that Archbishop Oliver firmly took the tiller, writing later: "I imitated the Patriarch who without appearing on the stage, directs the whole show." Without his strong leadership, the Church dissensions could only have gotten worse and one can only wonder how things might otherwise have turned out. Without that calming and guiding presence, there was a real possibility that the Irish Church could have become 'a house divided against itself'. Having already gone through more than a generation of serious strife, the Catholic Church in Ireland badly needed reform, order, regularity and hope. Otherwise, it would have been completely annihilated and gone the way of the Church in England; this was a lesson too often repeated elsewhere, a dreadful consequences of church discord. Reform was badly needed in the Church in Ireland and while nobody knew it at the time, Rome had sent a reforming Primate who would more than fit the bill and literally save the day.

27. ARCHBISHOP OLIVER ARRIVES IN HIS DIOCESE

Oliver was anxious to travel to his diocese and he arrived in time for the Holy Week and Easter ceremonies of 1670, where he received a tumultuous welcome from the populace. He reported: "It was as if St. Patrick himself had come in person." He said at the time that what pleased him most was the loyalty and faith of the people, for which they had suffered so much. He was impressed with Fr. Patrick Daly, the vicar general of Armagh and he confirmed him in his office. He had been vicar general of Armagh for almost thirty years and had 'borne the heat of the day' during that time. During the previous decade, Dr. Daly had helped to organise widespread opposition in the province against those in favour of the Remonstrance and had been excommunicated by the pretender Fr. James Taaffe for his considerable successes in this regard. A year later

St. Oliver's Shrine, St. Peter's Church, Drogheda

in 1671, he resigned as vicar general and became a Franciscan, by that time he would have been well into his seventies.

Lord Oliver Plunkett the Baron of Louth lived at Louth Hall which he had regained after the Restoration. It was on some of his land that Oliver's brother, Ned and family later[1] occupied at Ardpatrick. Oliver also lived and spent much of his time at Ballybarrack just outside Dundalk where he had a small house and garden. Shortly afterwards in about 1672, Oliver took up residence at Ardpatrick, in Louth village and lived there with his brother Ned and family.

As any local magistrate, Protestant minister or regional governor throughout the country could cause trouble for him at any time, he thought it expedient to remain invisible and to continue on his travels in disguise. Viceroy Robartes had spies actively trying to apprehend him, so for the first few months of his apostolate he was a daring figure travelling in disguise as Captain William Browne, wearing a wig and complete with sword and pistols as befitted an officer. He admitted in a letter, that he found it necessary on occasions to sing in the taverns in order to protect his identity, perhaps he was within earshot of some soldiers at the time and no doubt he could tell them he was on a special mission, a very special mission at that. He wrote later that viceroy Robartes had been his enemy and had harassed him at this time.

[1] Ó Fiaich & Forristal - Oliver Plunkett Indiana, USA 1976. Ó Fiaich. p.122

28. Setting To Work

The Duke of Ormond was another powerful figure in Ireland at the time, a previous viceroy and a man of huge wealth and extensive land holdings. Many would say that Ormond was the power behind the viceroy and his policy was a consistent one of divide and conquer. He would support and encourage any group who had ideas which would sow dissension, or cause trouble between the Irish, doing so primarily to defend his own very large properties. About two months after Oliver returned to Ireland, Viceroy John Berkeley replaced the more hard line John Robartes and this appointment greatly eased the tension. Berkeley was married to a Catholic, had a Catholic secretary and was much more tolerant than his predecessor. The climate of tolerance having changed for the better, Oliver soon discarded the disguise and proceeded with his work more openly, but invariably with some caution. Unhindered by wig, sword or pistols, Archbishop Oliver swung immediately into a high gear. This was the beginning of the period of his greatest freedom and of a very high work rate, which lasted for almost three and a half years. It also corresponded to the time when the King might have conceded freedom of conscience to Catholics, but was thwarted in this by an increasingly truculent Parliament. Setting up his headquarters in Ballybarrack and Ardpatrick suited Oliver as these areas were fairly central in the diocese and were also in rural areas where locals could warn him of any approaching search parties. His brother Edward and family were now also living in the area and Edwards's wife was expecting another child to add to their other children, Jemmy, Joe, Mick and Catty. Undoubtedly Archbishop Oliver would have performed the christening ceremony of Thomasina the new-born baby girl. Later from his condemned cell in Newgate he would also refer to the education of Nicky, who was probably another nephew and perhaps an offspring of one of his sisters, Katherine, Anne or Mary.

Coming from the eternal city of Rome with all its ceremony and splendour; witnessing the Holy Year ceremonies, the erection of the Four Rivers Fountain, the decoration of St. Peter's Basilica and having experienced a renaissance of art and culture in Rome, Oliver now willingly answered the call to come back to the impoverished Church and people of Ireland, knowing that countless hardships awaited him. The native Irish were poor and largely uneducated and they were often looked down upon, but here was Oliver, a Plunkett, highly educated and a teaching professor from Propaganda College, coming back from a very cosmopolitan and cultured Rome as the Archbishop of Armagh and their

Primate. A man who was very well versed in theology or controversies and who could certainly hold his own in any company, such a man deserved and therefore received the highest respect from all quarters.

At the time of his return, he had spent over half of his lifetime away from Ireland and he had no doubt dreamed, planned and prayed about his return to his native land for many years. Priests out of necessity and to their great credit, had operated on their own initiative for many years previously. However, this also meant that the Church organisation was just non-existent in most places. The task he now faced was huge and it is understandable why he should feel the need to spring into action immediately.

Loughcrew - St. Oliver Celebration

29. SADDLED HIS HORSE

With the new viceroy in place, Oliver understood that he had to move with all haste during this period of relative calm, if one could call it calm. Within three months he had held two diocesan synods of priests, confirmed ten thousand persons, performed two ordination ceremonies and completed a diocesan visitation of parishes. Many of his diocesan meetings took place[1] in Blykes Inn, Dorsey, Co. Armagh for priests of the northern end of the diocese and in Pierces Inn, Dunleer for the priests of Co. Louth. This had another advantage, as generally speaking the priests in these areas were of two different cultural backgrounds, predominately Gaelic in the north and Anglo Irish in the Pale. He sent a report of his diocese to Rome and before the year's end he had undertaken a thorough visitation of six of the northern dioceses. After his visitation of these dioceses he travelled extensively in subsequent years across the broad expanse of the eleven dioceses in his province, an enterprise which was a real act of stamina for him. Even today with good roads and every modern means of transport and comfortable accommodation, this would still be quite an exhausting exercise. While most priests stayed with relatives or moved from house to house amongst friends, the accommodation of a few priests left much to be desired. Some were described as glorified hovels located in the unclaimed wastelands of woodland or along ditches, one was sometimes required to go down on hands[2] and knees before entering through a rather low doorway.

In June 1670, a meeting of bishops and Church leaders was held in Dublin to assist in Church reorganisation throughout the country. This small assembly marked the beginnings of tension between Archbishop Talbot of Dublin and himself. Oliver called a synod of Church leaders in Clones and held various meetings of priests in his own diocese. He often wrote to Rome to recommend those who were suitable to become bishops or vicars of the various dioceses. His work rate was prodigious and over the next six months, he held Church synods, conducted many meetings with priests, confirmed thousands, celebrated ordination ceremonies, built schools, brought peace to the Church, brought peace to the province and made a thorough visitation of the province. It was to be the first of several extraordinarily busy and successful years of his apostolate. In truth the twenty-two years he had been in Rome were well spent; prayer, penance, pilgrimages of the seven churches and regular works of mercy, all left him spiritually well prepared for the many challenges which now lay ahead. To many, it also must have seemed like a whirlwind for good was sweeping across the land. He wrote: "The harvest is great but the workers are few." Few workers there may have been, but Oliver was doing his utmost to make up for that. He thanked God for the successes of his ventures, indeed during those early years, all of his enterprises had successful outcomes.

This was a man who behind a desk, was a manager and also an academic par excellence and here he was out in the field, a man in a hurry right across the province, proving himself as the people's pastor par excellence. An odd priest may shine in one or another but it must be rare indeed, for a man to excel in all three. He wrote: "But I, to avoid talk among the Protestants, go from village to village with the parish priests to confirm them." But having a confirmation ceremony in

each of the smaller villages during those first few months after his return, must have been very time consuming and tiring for the new Archbishop. Of Anglo Irish stock and a Meath man, there would always have been some doubt if he would ever be accepted by the native Ulster people, but they soon came to admire his boundless energy and untiring work rate. Starting off with this double disadvantage, it was to his credit that he soon won people over and was indeed accepted by the clergy right across the province, whom he then inspired to even greater ardour. He achieved this largely by his own example as a good pastor and administrator, through his exceedingly hard work and also by his living of a simple and frugal lifestyle. Through his reforming zeal, improvement was effected little by little. This was not always welcomed by some of those priests whom he had occasion to correct for drunkenness and banditry, a few of whom would later wreak their revenge.

He appointed a new vicar to the diocese of Raphoe and it was he who accompanied him on the long journey to Donegal to show him the passes and to introduce him around the diocese. The vicar wrote to Rome shortly afterwards: "It is for spiritual motives alone that I have undertaken on the responsibility for so barren, rough and rugged a place. I admit too that I was moved by the words and even more by the example of the illustrious Primate; for he has on many occasions administered confirmation to the children in these very mountains and woods. On many occasions too he has had nothing to eat but oaten bread, salty butter and stirabout, and nothing to drink but milk. We are all amazed that a man of such a delicate constitution, who accustomed (as I know myself know) to so many amenities in Rome, should be able to undergo so many labours, so many journeys, so much hardships and adversities. It is quite certain that if he does not change his way of living and acting, he will lose his health and become useless to himself and to others." A first reference to the Archbishops health, but all this was of no consequence to Oliver, the wind was at his back. This was his window of opportunity to do good and so nothing less than full sail was called for.

A trip from Co. Louth to Co. Donegal or to Clonmacnoise would have been a major undertaking; people rarely left their own small area at the time. Even up to the mid 1950's, many people in rural Ireland had never been to Dublin. Today, one could now travel to Australia and back a couple of times in the time taken for Archbishop Oliver to make a trip to Donegal. While there was a mail carriage to Dublin the roads were atrocious and it really was the rocky road to Dublin. Endless hours spent in the saddle would not have been any more comfortable, but just another one of the many hardships to be endured, all of which he offered up for the success of his ministry. Writing about his travels in his own diocese and around Donegal, he wrote in a letter to Rome: "What Alps and Apennines I have crossed the Lord knows." His mode of transport on all of his journeys was by horse and by foot.

Oliver was a meticulous planner and one can just imagine him, brushing up on his native Irish language even before he had left Rome,

Pilgrims from Lamspringe, singing hymns on steps of St. Peter's, Drogheda

probably with the help of one of the many native Irish speakers living there. Now was the time to put his undoubted language skills to good use. He led the faithful in prayer, administered the sacraments and preached the good news to them, all in their native tongue. His congregation, although impoverished materially, he recognised them spiritually as being very rich. Their faith was strong and they sometimes travelled for miles to these ceremonies. A few months after his arrival, the six vicars of the northern dioceses could write the following in a letter of thanks to Rome: "For sending such an illustrious Primate to Ireland, he is so untiring in good works and so exemplary in his life and conduct that he has won for himself and the clergy the love and reverence even of the enemies of our faith." Everything he touched seemed to be fruitful, saddling his horse it is difficult to comprehend how one man could

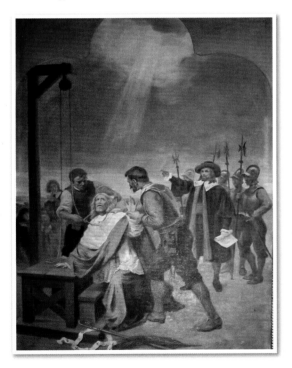

achieve so much in such a short span of time, effectively achieving a lifetime's work in a few short years. Despite this, he was humble in his many successes by always thanking God. He was keenly aware of his many faults and failings and knew only too well that he was certainly not a saint. Not yet at any rate, but he seemed to be working hard on this aspect of his life.

[1] Ó Fiaich & Forristal - Oliver Plunkett (Both books in same edition) Indiana USA 1976. Ó Fiaich. p.31
[2] Power Canon P. 'A Bishop of Penal Times' Cork 1932. p.30

30. PREMUNIRE

Under the law of Premunire it was illegal to exercise any authority from an outside jurisdiction and especially from the Pope. Oliver wrote of the earlier Premunire laws enacted in England, which had become law in Ireland following the passing of Poynings law and its plethora of statutes, passed at a parliament in Drogheda over the winter of 1494: "An Irish Parliament held in the time of Poynings, the Viceroy accepted all these laws." Referring to a more recent law he wrote: "An act passed in the second year of Elizabeth was the most severe[1] of all...passed in the Irish parliament on a Catholic feast day, the Protestants taking advantage of the absence of Catholics, otherwise the law would never have passed...Whenever some rascal charges a cleric before the courts, it is only with the greatest of difficulty that the infliction of some penalty can be avoided."

This law was an all-encompassing one and meant that anyone who wrote, spoke or acted in favour of papal jurisdiction even in spiritual matters would be liable to exile along with the confiscation of all fixed and movable property. Oliver had to be always careful in case a complaint would be made against him to the authorities. The advice of Oliver's second cousin, Sir Nicholas Plunkett, a prominent lawyer and brother of Bishop Patrick Plunkett was to prove invaluable to him on many occasions. He advised him what not to do under the law of Premunire, as many had fallen foul of this law and Oliver would later see its effects enforced by the imprisonment of a bishop and some priests during his tenure as Primate. Sir Nicholas strongly advised Oliver never to excommunicate any priest of bad life but to suspend him from saying Holy Mass and hearing confession and in this way he should not incur the law of Premunire. Later during his trial in London, Oliver stated that he was innocent of all the charges levelled against him, but if he had been charged with Premunire he would gladly have pleaded guilty to it.

1 Hanly 'The Letters' no.105

31. CHURCH SYNODS

A critical element for the success of reform of the Church in Ireland was the holding of synods. Shortly after returning to Ireland, Oliver organised a national synod in Dublin which was attended by the four archbishops along with the Bishop of Ossory and Bishop Patrick Plunkett of Meath. It was held in the house of a Mr. Reynolds in Bridge Street. It would have been the first national synod organised in over two decades. Before the synod, Archbishop Talbot let it be known that the viceroy wished to have a remonstrance from the bishops. But what type of remonstrance, alarm bells must have gone off in their minds as the last one was completely unacceptable to Rome and to the Irish bishops. If insisted upon again, it would certainly cause untold confusion, division and possible persecution for the Church in Ireland. Oliver met the viceroy, entering Dublin castle through the secret door and he must have been greatly relieved to hear that a general declaration of loyalty would suffice. This was duly passed at the synod with all present signing an innocuous document declaring loyalty to the king in civil affairs, a simple case of rendering to Caesar the things that are Caesar's. However it was a warning to those present that the Church was never far away from walking a tightrope and always needed to be careful in its approach. Oliver was determined to steer clear of all political matters and always urged others to adopt the same policy.

The synod was called to help renewal by regularising and bringing uniformity to the Church across the country. Order needed to be brought into the question[1] of who had faculties for the dispensation of marriages; some religious insisted that they had such rights, giving themselves more privileges in this regard than even the bishops could lawfully exercise. The Tories were not to be supported. Diocesan chapters needed to be regularised; this was a cause for concern as irregular chapters were often the cause of disharmony in those dioceses without serving bishops. Dioceses had different regulations regarding abstinence from meat on Wednesdays and it was suggested that it could be eliminated altogether;

it was also customary to refrain from eating eggs on Fridays. The synod agreed that a few new bishops should be appointed in each province and forwarded the names to Rome of a few candidates from each province. This was an important consideration as each province would require at least a few bishops in each. It was also at this meeting that the first inklings emerged of the differences between Archbishop Peter Talbot and Oliver on the Primacy.

A Provincial Synod was held in Clones in August 1670 at which the resolutions of the National Synod in Dublin were[2] adopted. Drinking at wakes was banned as was the practice of all night wakes. The decrees of the Council of Trent were adopted; this had relevance as it affected the legitimacy of clandestine marriages. Vicar Terence O'Kelly of Derry agreed to abide by the decision of the Synod to depose him, but later went back on his word. Priests were expected to have a fixed place of abode and a fixed place for saying Mass. Other regulations concerned

St. Oliver Procession, Lamspringe, 2013 - Bishop Norbert Trelle and Cardinal Seán Brady

stipends for Holy Mass and the contributions that parish priests should make to their bishop. Following the synods of 1670, his plan of action was becoming clearer and falling into place. His strategies brought hope, regularity and normality to the dioceses, eliminating many of the abuses which had crept in. Crucially, his exploits also cared for the education and reform of the clergy. The wind was at his back, the sails fully unfurled, the four horses that he owned were saddled and ready to go. For a man of quite delicate constitution, he undertook remarkable feats of physical endurance and achieved quite remarkable successes in his work over the following three years or so.

His last Provincial Synod was held in[3] August 1678, in the tiny little church at Ardpatrick, the location of so many of Oliver's ordination ceremonies. Three bishops were present; Archbishop Oliver, Bishop Patrick Plunkett of Meath and Bishop Patrick Tyrrell of Clogher, along

First ever Procession in honour of Blessed Oliver in Drogheda 30-5-1920, seven days after the Beatification Ceremony

with representatives of all the dioceses of the province. It must have been quite cramped for space in the tiny church as there were twelve delegates in total.

During the synod, the Tories were again condemned, as was drinking by priests in taverns or the drinking of whiskey by priests. Priests should possess a silver chalice and good vestments. Another decree stipulated that no marriage between Roman Catholics shall be valid without the presence of the parish priest and two witnesses. Oliver explained it as follows: "The decrees of the Council of Trent were accepted here in the time of Monsignor Rinuccini and in the province they had been accepted in the time of Elizabeth. However, since there were doubts about this in some places, particularly regarding marriages, etc. here we do not dare to speak formally about the Council of Trent, since it is illegal to do so, we decided to draw up this decree. Similarly we do not dare to excommunicate here or to issue censures in formal and express terms, but only in equivalent terms, because it amounts to premunire."

Many modern day committee members might well agree that the second part of decree number ten from the synod would be a great idea and should be universally accepted: "We decree and lay down that there be held each month, during the three winter months, conferences for the discussion of cases of conscience in the areas subject to each vicar forane and whoever is absent shall pay five solidi to those who are present." This sum was significant in itself as it amounted to one crown or five shillings, at a time when the standard Holy Mass contribution was one shilling. The last of the twenty eight decrees was one instructing all the clergy: "To pray for the King, Queen, Royal Family, Viceroy, and to pray for peace in our country, and for peace among the princes of Christendom, and to recommend these intentions to the prayers of their respective flocks." Oliver signalled his intention to undertake another visitation of all the dioceses in the province.

The provision of meals and overnight accommodation for the participants of the Ardpatrick synod and their companions/servants must have posed quite a headache for Oliver, as the tiny church was only one field distant away his home. His relatives and friends would have stepped into the breach and uncle Oliver, would no doubt have relied on his young nephews and nieces to help out as well. Undoubtedly, his servant James would have had the care and foddering of more than a score of horses well under control. The delegates were already proscribed men and this meeting proved to be Oliver's last big assembly. By 1678, dark clouds had already gathered on the horizon and Oliver would find himself under arrest within a period of sixteen months. It proved to be an important synod, as it left the Church much better prepared as an organisation, to face the impending storm.

[1] Curtis, Fr. Emmanuel 'Blessed Oliver Plunkett' Dublin 1963. p.58
[2] Ó Fiaich & Forristal 'Oliver Plunkett' USA 1976. Ó Fiaich. p.50
[3] Concannon Helena 'Blessed Oliver Plunket' Dublin 1935. p.191

St. John Paul II at Killineer 1979

32. DIOCESE OF DERRY

The diocese of Derry was destined to be without a bishop for a hundred years, indeed most other dioceses had not had a bishop for almost a generation and some dioceses had not even seen the sight of a bishop for forty years. Oliver had countless disputes to adjudicate upon and settle, because the Church had been effectively leaderless for so long. Many of these disputes were between the religious orders and the parish clergy, or between the religious orders themselves. Some were over questing rights and others concerned the ownership of abandoned religious houses, disused for so long that their title was in doubt. Some may think that scandal in the Church is a comparatively new phenomena, well Oliver had more than his fair share of Church scandals to contend with, he removed the vicar of the Derry diocese who had been living a dissolute life for many years and later on he removed the vicar of Kilmore.

Terrence O'Kelly was the long-time vicar of Derry. He was among the first batch of students of the Irish College in Rome, as vicar he was living an openly scandalous life for over twenty years as a consequence of his lady friend and numerous children. He was also considered guilty of simony or the charging of money for spiritual benefits. Each time an attempt was made to remove him from office, he remained defiant and reported it under the law of Premunire. One vicar general had already been jailed, when a previous attempt to remove him was reported to the civil authorities. Within months of his return, Oliver who obviously had everything well prepared having received much advice from his cousin lawyer Sir Nicholas Plunkett, did indeed replace him in the following manner. Typical of Archbishop Oliver, he approached Fr. Terrence O'Kelly in[1] kindly fashion, who agreed to abide by whatever decisions the Synod of Clones might come to. The synod held in August agreed there should be a replacement vicar appointed to the diocese of Derry but shortly afterwards, Kelly went back on his word. Oliver went in person to Derry, convoked the clergy, deposed him and appointed Dr.

Conwell instead. O'Kelly as vicar apostolic of the diocese, thought that he could only be replaced by Rome, but Oliver already had all this taken care of. By having the council oust the vicar, it meant that Oliver was not leaving himself open to the probable charge of doing it himself as a representative of the Pope in Ireland. The respect that the President of Ulster, the Earl of Charlemont had for Oliver was also another important factor that stood in his favour, as when the anticipated appeal was made to the civil court, the case was summarily dismissed. After his failure at the court to retain his position, Terrence O'Kelly shouted out: "The Italian Primate, The Roman Primate has unhorsed me." The success of his action had a positive outcome throughout the whole province. The message was sent out loud and clear, that Oliver Plunkett the new broom in Armagh meant business, and more importantly, that he had the capacity and determination to put his reforms into full effect. Dr. Conwell the new vicar later gave a report to Rome which included a reference of the good work of the new Archbishop of Armagh: "Nothing more useful ever happened to this province than the deposition of Terence O'Kelly, since it struck terror into all those who imitated his depraved example."

[1] Dease O. 'With Blessed Oliver in Ireland' Dublin 1939. p.43.2

Canonisation Ceremony:
Pope Paul VI,
Giovanna Martiriggiano and
Mgr. John Hanly

33. Ballybarrack and Ardpatrick
Oliver's Pro-Cathedrals

Upon his return to Ireland as the Archbishop of Armagh in 1670, St Oliver based himself in north Louth and for several months, the locals would have become accustomed to seeing him dressed in disguise as a Captain William Browne. Living in north Louth held several advantages for him, as it was nearer the centre of his archdiocese and within easier reach of many other dioceses of the Northern Province. Living on the border of 'Gael' and 'Pale' enabled Oliver to reach out to these groups and he was able be to reconcile many of their differences. Ballybarrack is located on the outskirts of Dundalk, while Ardpatrick church is conveniently out of view, in a saucer like dip on top of the hill, which overlooks Louth village. Ardpatrick must have seemed like the perfect location for Oliver. It had a small church, which was central in the diocese but was also off the beaten track; it even had a great view of the sea and of the surrounding countryside. Without pillars or spires, these tiny churches have been described as St. Oliver's pro-cathedrals. In rural areas, they were obviously considered of little value to those who had commandeered almost everything else. Throughout the 1670's, these tiny churches were destined to serve St. Oliver's humble mission to his flock in fine manner. He lived in both locations, ordained many priests in both small churches and held an important Provincial Church Synod at Ardpatrick in 1678.

He conducted most of his ordination ceremonies in the north Louth area; the vast majority of these were held in Ardpatrick and Ballybarrack, with Ardpatrick hosting the greater recorded number. In his earlier years as Archbishop, Ballybarrack figured largely as[1] his preferred location for ordinations. However, Ardpatrick soon took over the mantle and became by far the most popular location overall for his ordinations ceremonies. At the time of Ballybarrack's excavation in the early twentieth century, the top of a sixteenth century thurible[2] was found with a Celtic motif. It may be viewed in the Museum of Maynooth

College. Ballybarrack church now measures fifteen metres by five metres, but could well have been shorter than this as it is believed that St. Oliver's home may have been situated towards the front of the church, alongside the road. We know that his homes were not lofty palaces but simple, humble abodes. At his trial he attested: "The house I lived in was a little thatched house, wherein was only a little room for a library, which was not seven feet high." That did not confine him however in his hospitality to friends, strangers and visiting priests, as he wrote occasionally of his many visitors. Located in rural areas, safe from prying eyes, there must have been a lot of coming and going at these locations in north Co. Louth. The Earl of Charlemont presented Oliver for use during his lifetime, a house with garden along with an orchard and two fields; the location is unknown but was possibly Ballybarrack. This must

Ballybarrack Church

St. Oliver Oak Tree, Ardpatrick

have been like a gift from heaven, a place to live and rest after his many long journeys, particularly during his hectic early years, as archbishop. It was also a place to keep and feed his horses, before his next expedition, in the service of the Lord.

Ardpatrick church was only uncovered in 1935 and the remaining walls stand at a little over a meter high. The church is even smaller than Ballybarrack, measuring only eight and a half meters by five and a half metres. It must have proved quite a squeeze for many of Archbishop Oliver's church ceremonies. St. Oliver is renowned for his letter writing and his faithful servant James McKenna, must have been a regular traveller on the roads around north Louth, as he looked after the mail. He discretely delivered or collected mail from the other dioceses in Ireland and would have connected regularly with the mail service for London, the Internuncio in Brussels or with Rome. The four horses, which St. Oliver owned for a time, must have been kept well exercised

Ardpatrick Church

by Oliver as he continued with his visitation to all of the dioceses of the Northern Province. From north Louth, he frequently travelled to Drogheda and his schools there. He journeyed to meetings with his diocesan priests at Dorsey, Dunleer or further a-field and he frequently visited Dublin. Archbishop Oliver must have come to know most of the mass-rocks dotted across the province, but in north Louth, particularly in the Ardpatrick, Ballybarrack or Castletown areas, it would be no exaggeration to say that he must have known every hedge-row and tree. Local tradition points to the location of the Archbishops house at Ardpatrick, close to the garden wall of the now demolished Ardpatrick House. Local tradition also points to an ancient oak tree still standing, in which Oliver is believed to have hidden and slept. This tree is known locally as 'St. Oliver's Oak' or 'St. Oliver's Bed'.

[1] Matthews Deirdre 'Oliver of Armagh' Dublin 1961. p.46
[2] Ó Fiaich & Forristal 'Oliver Plunkett' Indiana USA 1976. Ó Fiaich p.122

34. FRANCISCANS VERSUS DOMINICANS

Oliver advised Rome of the volatile and serious situation that existed between the Franciscans and the Dominicans, as they hotly disputed the ownership of abandoned religious houses in three dioceses. Also at stake, were the consequential rights of the owners, to remain on and to collect money in the three dioceses concerned, Armagh, Clogher, Down along with the diocese of Dromore. After the Restoration of King Charles II to the throne, the Franciscans were among the first to re-establish themselves in any numbers. The Dominican convents at Gaula in the Diocese of Clogher, Newtownards in the Diocese of Down and at Carlingford in that of Armagh were abandoned and largely destroyed. When the Dominicans tried to return, the Franciscans refused to give them up and without a Dominican presence in the areas, they disputed the Dominicans right to seek alms in those areas. Invited to a conference of arbitration, Oliver was given two hours' notice by the procurators of both orders, of a meeting which was to be held near Dundalk, at which it was hoped to settle the matter. Told that the numbers would not exceed three or four from each side, Oliver was shocked to find over twenty from each, including lay brothers, stable boys and even the novices. Nothing was or could be achieved in such a setting and Oliver wrote: "Tempers grew hotter and after my departure they all but came to blows...The meeting created such a stir that the local officer would have thrown them all into prison but for the respect he has for me."

Writing to Rome, he offered his services to adjudicate on the matter and his proposal was accepted. The Holy Father, Blessed Pope Innocent XI upon hearing of the problem, ordered that the dispute had to be sorted out. Oliver indicated that he was happy to settle the argument, writing: "This decision will be a difficult and thorny one, after all my efforts I shall not harvest other fruits than the thorns of calumny and lies, as your Lordship shall see." Continuing in the same letter he writes: "I shall hear their allegations and the evidence in support of them, and then I shall give sentence in conformity with these. Even if the world should cease to be, let justice be done…if the whole globe should disintegrate and come crashing down, the ruins will strike an undaunted man." Oliver could prophesise the huge trouble that lay ahead for him after such a decision, but he could not have realised that his decision on these and other matters, particularly the one of questing or the collecting of money, would ultimately lead to his death.

Oliver went to each disputed convent and after careful investigation at each location he decided in favour of the Dominicans on all counts. He wrote that the Dominicans had many positive arguments for ownership including witnesses and documents, while the arguments of the Franciscans was mostly of a negative kind, such as the following; even if it was true that the Dominicans once owned them, they had given up on them and so reneged on any possible rights they may have to them. Locals had not seen the Dominicans in these convents. The Dominicans would not fit in with the secular clergy. The people would not be able to provide for both orders in these dioceses.

While it may have been the correct decision, it proved extremely unpopular with the Franciscans, exemplified by the story written by Oliver in one of his letters. Two of the young Franciscan students purposely broke a bust of Oliver which was in St. Isidore's College in Rome; both students were expelled but allegedly regained admission to the Franciscan order in Spain where they completed their studies. Both characters[1] resurface in our story by having a disgraceful career and some ten years later they would reappear as some of the principal prosecution witnesses against Oliver at his trial.

In his writings to Rome, Oliver predicted that many calumnies would be written against him following his decision. But he could not have expected the quantity or the vicious nature of the complaints that followed. That he was corrupt in favouring the Dominicans, he was a tyrant, he was a secret Protestant, he was too friendly with the Protestants and the ruling classes, he was a drunkard, he was guilty of simony or gaining financially in spiritual matters, he was a womaniser and while

Carlingford Priory

the name Mary Kelly was even mentioned in this regard there were no times, dates or witnesses quoted and this allegation quickly died off. One allegation which was destined not to die off however, was his agreement with the Tories the previous year which had brought peace to the province. His peace agreement was supposedly in favour of the government and the landed classes and not in the best interests of the dispossessed Catholics. In a letter to Rome, Oliver answered each allegation in turn. When somewhat similar allegations re-emerged some years later with regard to being too friendly with Protestants or over conciliatory towards the government; Oliver could pose the question, how is it then that I am in prison while my accusers are free.

Some of the religious orders had in times of persecution the wide ranging powers of missionaries apostolic and it was inevitable that there would be tensions later when these powers were being reined in or withdrawn. Oliver was also concerned about the large number of novitiates the religious orders maintained, over fifteen in his own province, and he recommended on many occasions that this number should be reduced to a more manageable number so as to improve standards in these novitiates. He often suggested that greater use should be made of the novitiates on the continent, stating that they would provide a better training and the young students would also benefit from seeing the magnificence of the Church in other lands. He added that in Ireland, there was only the shadow of a Church, writing: "Indeed it is a first class miracle that in the midst of so many persecutions suffered since the Reformation it has been preserved in the state in which it is." The Franciscans must also have been aware of the need to improve standards, as in a letter to Oliver; the Provincial of the order expressed the need for a brief to be able to expel incorrigible friars after a threefold warning had been given to them.

Another thorny issue which very much concerned him at the time was the practice by the various religious orders to take up collections before the parish Mass. This was an abuse which he often wrote to Rome about. Some Masses were delayed for up to two hours while the collection of grain, sheep, goats, hens or money was taken up, or such pledges given for collection later. He was concerned that some people might stop going to Mass altogether because of the delays and the embarrassment caused by this practice. In March 1672, Oliver wrote: "In the parish near where I live they fought at the altar about a fortnight ago and gave great scandal, and in another parish in Co. Tyrone there were similar scenes." Because of Oliver's involvement in the curtailment by any of the orders to quest at the parish masses; his decision in favour of the Dominicans and the decision to allow the Dominicans to collect in four dioceses; it is hard to believe the outcry and the hostility which soon arose against him.

For those who were unwilling to implement any type of reform in the Church in Ireland, so badly needed at the time, Archbishop Oliver was becoming public enemy number one. Exaggerated reports, complaints which included many lies and calumnies were soon flying in all directions against Oliver. The Franciscans appealed the decisions and Oliver's judgement in these great controversies was confirmed by Rome a few years later. The arguing between the religious soon became irrelevant as during the next round of persecution, all the convents were closed and the religious banished. This soon put an end to the petty rows over the ownership of the convents or of questing. A small number of the Franciscans firmly believed that Archbishop Oliver was out to harm their interests and that he wished to reduce their influence within the province. There are several examples to show that this was patently not true. Lord Berkeley the viceroy had decided to refuse permission to the newly appointed Bishop of Clogher, Franciscan, Dr. Patrick Duffy to enter the country. Oliver went to meet the viceroy and after quite a long conversation, he ably persuaded him to change his mind on the matter. Dr. Duffy led the Diocese until his death in 1675. Over a long period of time, Archbishop Oliver devoted a lot of his energy to successfully encourage Franciscan Friars, Harold and Coppinger to submit to their provincial. As Primate, Oliver often commended the Franciscans on their work. Even from the scaffold at Tyburn, martyr Oliver acknowledged the Franciscan order, stating that the action of a few members of that order: "…ought not to reflect upon the order of St. Francis, or upon the Roman Catholic clergy. It being well known that there was a Judas among the twelve Apostles."

[1] Chapter 87

35. TROUBLESOME PRIESTS

Priests, out of necessity and to their great credit, had for many years lived on their wits. For sheer survival, they had found it necessary to operate largely on their own program of initiatives. While there were a few wicked priests causing untold harm, it was a marvel that there were not considerably more of them at the time. Living a life of poverty, they might easily be tempted with bribes of money from the organs of the state, as a handful had already done. While it is easy to focus on a few bad priests, they were in fact only a tiny minority. However, despite their very small numbers they were the cause of untold damage within the Church in Ireland. On the other hand, it must be remembered that it was really quite miraculous, how the Church had withstood all that was thrown at it. This was due in no small part to the vast majority of the priests, who were loyal and quite heroic in the practice of their duties.

However, as a direct outcome of the troubles of the previous thirty years, the education of many of those priests was seriously lacking in many respects. Oliver, who was essentially a reforming bishop, met many obstacles in his way; it was only to be expected that not all would welcome a tightening of discipline and an improvement of standards. A few priests were always troublesome and some refused to repent of their ways and many lies were written about him. He answered these calumnies, point for point, adding: "Lies have short legs, and time will tell who has written what is true." On another occasion he wrote: "However by their lies I shall not suffer in the least, while they will lose credit."

He also had to manage a couple of uncontrollable priests in his own diocese, including one who was associated with bandits and who along with a small number of religious clergy remained disobedient. All were later suspended. These then formed the nucleus of a group, who a decade or so later, would be persuaded to take the stand and give false evidence against him. Oliver also had to cope with many questions of theology and some religious houses even had two factions within them and as a consequence two superiors. This was an extraordinary situation in which he found himself and he quickly rose to the challenge of it all. Recognising that reforms were badly needed in the Church in Ireland, Oliver was not prepared to shy away from taking whatever action was necessary to bring about change for the better. Unconcerned about his own popularity, he carried on regardless, despite the many dangers to himself.

Writing of those priests who promoted the Remonstrance: "I was able to send away all the followers of Walsh and thank God have not a single one; but I used craft, I won over certain pious and good gentlemen who proceeded to discredit them everywhere, so that nobody received them into his home." Standards were steadily improving and within a year a and a half of his return to Ireland he could write: "Thanks be to God the deposition and deprivation of Terence O'Kelly, of McColyn, of Maginn and of two or three others decreed by me in the course of visitation has led to a great reformation of the clergy in the whole province, and I have never deprived anybody unless after four or five warnings, even though the law requires only three." Fr. Bernard Murphy was a thirty year old parish priest in his diocese, who went astray because of women and the taverns; Oliver issued a sentence against him and deposed him of his parish. Murphy undertook to travel abroad for further study so Oliver did not publish his edict out of respect for the good name of the Murphy family and the shame which they would have incurred; such was Archbishop Oliver. Oliver always insisted on the highest standards from priests and was willing to live up to those high values himself. Inflexible with the scandal giver, but if they repented he was always quick to praise them. Religious orders on the continent regularly sent their undisciplined and restless friars back to Ireland where they would be cause of even more disorder; writing to Rome he suggested that the good friars should be sent to Ireland as well. Many priests amended their ways and he was ever willing to accept their assurances of good behaviour in the future as in the cases of Friars French,

Coppinger and Harold. Oliver reported to Rome the story of a young man named Michael from the diocese of Down, who after falling out with a young Catholic student from the same diocese, then reported him to the authorities for the murder of an English merchant and of burying the body. The student spent eighteen months clapped in irons in prison, when lo and behold the English merchant unexpectedly returned from England and stated that he never seen the young man in his life. An order for Michaels arrest was issued with the intention of cutting off his ears as a perjurer and for the paying of the accused's expenses. Michael quickly went into hiding by joining the Franciscans in Armagh where he made his profession. Shortly after his profession, he fled to the Franciscan friary in Drogheda having heard that the police were onto him in Armagh. When Oliver was informed, he went to the community in Drogheda and met the Guardian, Friar John Brady. Oliver interviewed Michael who admitted his guilt and expressed remorse for what he had done. The Guardian promised he would send him out of the country, but fourteen months later Oliver was flabbergasted to see Michael hearing confessions in Drogheda. Oliver also discovered that two other young friars without instruction were also hearing confessions. Oliver said he wished to examine them, but was refused permission by Friar Brady who added that Oliver's vicar general had already approved them. Oliver inquired from the vicar, who denied giving any such permission. When challenged on this he got nothing but abuse from Fr. John Brady the then Definitor and Guardian of the community on Oliver's previous visit. In the same letter, Oliver informed Rome that he had a second perjurer operating in his diocese, Friar George Codden of the Armagh Friary, who had sworn in court against Dr. Daly the previous vicar general of Armagh, after he had tried to restrict the friars from questing at the parish masses.

A year after publishing his controversial decree on the ownership of the three abandoned friaries, Oliver wrote in October 1672, to the provincial chapter of the Franciscan order, meeting at Elphin. Wishing to encourage reforms and seek better training of the friars, he suggested that they should greatly reduce the number of novitiates. He also wished to motivate a greater observance by the friars to their charism of living out their vocation, through a life of poverty.

In a letter[1] dated 30th October 1672: "On my arrival as the unworthy successor of St. Patrick, I regarded nothing as important as that I should set about the reformation of the clergy in the province of Armagh...There are as many novitiates almost as thee convents...It would be more than enough to assign one single convent in the province...in this way, far from the noise of the crowd and free from all worldly attractions, they might give themselves to God alone and lay the foundation of solid virtue...There is a second point...the constitutions of the order command that journeys be made on foot, all should observe this. It is not more difficult to observe here than in Germany, Belgium and other countries...in your convents here hardly a priest is found who does not himself use a horse and have a servant on horseback too, whenever he has to go anywhere. And this multiplicity of servants and horses cannot but be a heavy burden on convents...A third point, many fathers both young and old, buy themselves, at considerable expense, rich clothing of French material with collars, adorned with woven goffered fringes and such like. They ought to refrain from buying such things and use the money for better purposes, e.g. the support of novices, the purchase of sacred vessels and books...which many of you say suffer from a serious lack of almost all things."

In August 1673, Oliver informs Rome that the Franciscans had not fulfilled their promise to him, to correct their ways: "They promised amendment, but so far there is no sign of this amendment in my province." He acknowledges receipt of a letter from the General of the Franciscans and promises its safe delivery, writing: "I do not think the friars will obey the general, nor do I think that there will ever be a remedy for the multiplicity of novitiates unless the Holy See takes the matter in hand." It wasn't in the interests of any of the Franciscan convents to be downgraded so naturally enough, they were not in favour of any such proposals. Oliver was later proven correct as to the lack of any lasting reforms. However, the question would soon become an academic one, when all the convents were closed and the friars dispersed.

In another letter, Oliver recounted that the friars were well dressed, many in Dutch cloth, wore good shoes and travelled on horse along with a servant on horse. He reported that there are many in Ireland who went without horse and wore plain shoes and simple Irish cloth. The cheaper Irish cloth was called frieze; Oliver wore the cheaper cloth himself, to save money for his work and to give good example. In his letter to Rome, Oliver requests that Rome should arrange for a visitator to inspect the Irish convents, either Italian or Flemish: "A visitator from a different nation who would have strong convictions about proper observance and the spirit of God and St. Francis." Later he would recommend Bishop Tyrrell of Clogher diocese to complete such a visitation. In order to improve standards of the Irish Franciscan province, he often suggested that the smaller Franciscan communities should be amalgamated, the number of novitiates should be greatly reduced and the Irish province should be split into two. Adding that because of the size of the country, the ten convents of the Northern Province were rarely visited by the Provincial.

Oliver was resolute and unyielding in his pursuit of reforms which were so badly needed in the Church in Ireland. It is easy to see why as a reforming bishop he was becoming hated by those who resisted change and he wrote: "The zeal of God has eaten me up and I would like to see my province holy and good, and reformed both as to secular and regular clergy." Archbishop Oliver sided neither with the 'Gael' nor the 'Pale'; he did not concern himself by being pro-Irish or pro-English and he urged others to do likewise. Archbishop Oliver steered consistently clear of politics, he was straight down the line, pro-Catholic, writing: "God knows that I think of nothing else, day and night than the service of souls." Many failed to appreciate this fact and unbeknownst to himself,

Oliver was beginning to sign his own death warrant; Friar George Codden was one of those who would travel to England some eight years later as a prosecution witness against him, although in his case his testimony was not used at the trial. If Oliver had compromised on his principles and meddled in politics, he would certainly have lived a longer life, but such a policy would have been disastrous for the Church in Ireland and would almost certainly have signalled its demise. Having focussed so much on a few bad apples, it should not be forgotten that the vast majority of priests in Ireland at the time, performed an outstanding job in the most difficult of circumstances.

[1] Hanly 'The Letters' No.125

36. PEACE TO THE CHURCH

Oliver undertook extensive visitation of all the dioceses in the Northern Province, sorting out numerous problems in each, thereby bringing peace to all of these dioceses. He was obviously very successful in this work as he would soon write in a letter to Rome: "I found serious divisions in them, but by the grace of God, all is now quiet in the dioceses which I have visited."

He was patient yet firm in his correction of abuses, always insisting on high standards and there are also numerous examples when he was ever ready to forgive those who were mending their ways. In each diocese that he visited, he soon settled the numerous disputes, which had festered for so long because of a lack of Church leadership. Quickly rising to the challenge of it all, he brought much needed peace to the Church in each diocese. Franciscan friars, Thomas Harold and Francis Coppinger were a case in point. As a result of complaints to Rome after a new provincial was elected for the order; the election was set aside and all acts of the council of 1666 were nullified. Friar Peter Geanor was appointed in place of Friar Coppinger, who[1] along with Friar Harold

St. Oliver's Vestment, Mullingar

organised opposition to the new provincial. Archbishop Oliver was asked to try and resolve matters and have both defer to the new provincial and to the wishes of the Holy See in this affair. Oliver succeeded in bringing back Friar Harold, writing: "without any fuss and with gentle treatment." He spent several weeks in Dublin, as he waited until Friar Harold was safely on board ship for the continent. At a later date, he helped Friar Coppinger to make peace as well.

[1] Concannon Helena 'Blessed Oliver Plunket' Dublin 1935. p.161

37. CONFIRMATIONS

Another example of his commitment to the service of others was his administering of the sacrament of confirmation to tens of thousands of people, many of whom were adults who had not previously had the opportunity. Archbishop Oliver was aware that it made sense for the Church in Ireland to maintain a rather low profile, so as not to provoke a possible backlash from the politicians, writing: "But I, to avoid talk among the Protestants, go from village to village with the parish priests to confirm them." This meant having a much greater number of such ceremonies, rather than just a few in the larger centres of population. He was obviously happy to increase his workload for this reason and it was common practice at the time for him to perform two confirmation ceremonies on the same day. All of his work in this regard explains why St. Oliver is now renowned for the numerous confirmation ceremonies he performed. Within a month of arriving in his diocese he wrote: "The people are so devout that they will go three miles to hear Mass, very often in the rain, and they will go twelve miles to receive confirmation...sometimes men and women of thirty and forty years of age present themselves to me to be confirmed."

St. Oliver administering confirmation – stained glass window – St. Peter's Church, Drogheda

He was also conscious that most districts would not have seen a bishop for at least a generation and he wrote: "There are bearded men of sixty who have not yet received the sacrament of confirmation." It was also not uncommon for the old and the infirm to be carried by the strong and healthy, some distance to a mass-rock for confirmation. There were hardly any churches allowed around the Northern Province, so the ceremonies were usually[1] at mass-rocks located outdoors in the valleys or in the woods. While it might be nice to contemplate that they were all under the canopy of heaven, they were also at the mercy of wind, rain and occasionally a priest hunter, leading a band of militia. Keeping meticulous records and accounts, Oliver wrote that he had confirmed forty-eight thousand, six hundred and fifty-five souls in his first three years and that he had kept a list of them all. No doubt, counted and recorded by his gallant servant James. Often on a diet of oaten bread and milk and exposed to all weathers, it was reported that Archbishop Oliver was sometimes barely able to stand with weakness after his long journeys and the prolonged open air ceremonies.

[1] Bennett Fr. Martin 'Blessed Oliver Plunkett' London 1973. p.22

Mass Rock Carnally, Co. Armagh

38. HEBRIDES

Before he left Rome, he was given a special mission with regard to the Hebrides, a large group of islands off Scotland where Gaelic was spoken. He planned to send some priests to the islands and he wrote: "Three have written asking to be sent, but I wish first to examine their standard of learning and I shall go to where they live in order to have exact knowledge of their[1] way of life. Your Lordship can rest assured that the persons who will be sent will be men of sufficient learning and integrity." He stayed at Dunluce, Co. Antrim but was unable to get agreement from the Marquis of Antrim to allow them to travel at that time and the mission was postponed. With a sense of humour, Oliver typecasts the Marquis as similar to a certain Monsignor Alberici who was unable to find a suitable servant in the whole of Italy. Oliver had proposed the names of twenty priests to minister on the islands, but the Marquis found fault with each one of them. The Marquis who was a Catholic had control of a number of the islands, but was ever so cautious and very much afraid of rocking the boat. Oliver on the other hand felt there was still a window of opportunity to establish a mission on the islands and wished to use that time favourably. He urged Rome to write to the Marquis and request his assistance in facilitating a mission to the islands. He also wished to go there himself, saying that it will be necessary to dress according to the custom of the place which is very different from the rest of the world.

Such a visit would have been a major undertaking because of the large number of islands and the long distances involved, the islands being spread over several hundred miles in total. Somehow he sensed the urgency of a mission on the islands as he wrote: "Let us gather the grapes before the hailstorm and tempest strike." His fears were proven correct and the trip never became possible because the political situation soon worsened as a result of the proposed amalgamation of the English and Scottish parliaments. Sometime later he wrote: "We are in greater fear and trembling here, now that our neighbour is on fire."

1 Curtis, Fr. Emmanuel 'Blessed Oliver Plunkett' Dublin 1963. p.75

39. Primacy Controversy

Ireland was a most complex society at the time and there were many divisions within it. The relationships and attitudes between those divisions and the extent of their loyalty towards the viceroy and officialdom in Dublin, the king or to Rome, all varied between groupings and over time. Only a good diplomat or historian could understand the nuances of all of those interdependencies. These groups included the new settlers who were mainly English or Scotch and were Anglican, Presbyterian or Puritan. The native Irish who were Catholic and the old Anglo Irish, who were also Catholic, the latter group were often divided with regard to tactics in civil and religious matters. The old Anglo Irish were having similar debates to those going on throughout Europe among many Roman Catholics; some wished to have dialogue and co-operation with the temporal powers, while others favoured that faith and obedience should have precedence over political influence.

Both Oliver and Archbishop Peter Talbot of Dublin belonged to this latter grouping and their[1] differences surfaced at the meeting of Church leaders in Dublin. They would have had distant family ties, as would nearly all of the prominent Anglo Irish families of the time. Archbishop Talbot shocked those present at the meeting when he claimed that the King had given him visitation rights, or jurisdiction over the Church in Ireland. When asked to show this commission from the king, he would not or could not. He also stated that the See of Dublin should have precedence over the See of Armagh, or should at least be equal to it and he should sign the meetings proclamation. Oliver's appointment as the Primate of Ireland was already well documented in his papers of appointment from Rome, whereas Archbishops Talbot's papers did not specify this. The Primacy of Armagh over the other dioceses in Ireland had also been very well established since the time of St. Patrick, although it had been questioned previously by a Dublin which was growing ever more powerful.

Uttered almost in the same breath, these two statements by the Archbishop of Dublin if taken together could even be interpreted as part of the argument for the power of the Monarchy over civil and religious matters. That is the right of the Monarch or Government to appoint or even influence the appointment of Bishops or the Primate. The Archbishop of Dublin was certainly not saying anything of the sort, but on the other hand by using his commission from the King as a possible support for the argument of his Primacy it could be interpreted as such.

Archbishop Talbot would have been familiar with court diplomacy and intrigue having been involved in his earlier years, as a strong supporter of Charles II, who at the time was trying to regain the Monarchy during the years of Cromwell's Commonwealth. His brother, Richard Talbot, was then in London as the agent of the dispossessed Catholic landowners of Ireland and was actively canvassing on their behalf, which as it happened was very much against the interests of the viceroy. Archbishop Talbot was drawn into some of those controversies and was loathed by the viceroy as a result.

Archbishop Peter Talbot of Dublin

Oliver was always insistent that there should be no involvement or meddling in politics of any kind, he understood it as a sure recipe for grief and was obviously determined that it would never happen during his Primacy. A year and a half later, Archbishop Talbot wrote to him saying that he had: "procured a new authority from the King, to superintend and correct all the clergy of the whole country and if they did not obey, to imprison them by means of the secular arm." The Archbishop of Dublin had no doubt felt, as he had been given some jurisdiction by the King over the Irish Church, that he could therefore act within the law for the betterment of the Church. But the idea of the civil authorities or monarchy having influence over religious affairs or appointments, had already caused countless problems elsewhere and if anything it was a growing problem throughout Europe. Oliver would have been ever watchful for any sign of straying away from Rome even in small things and would always have been alert to detect even the

Jus Primitiale Book

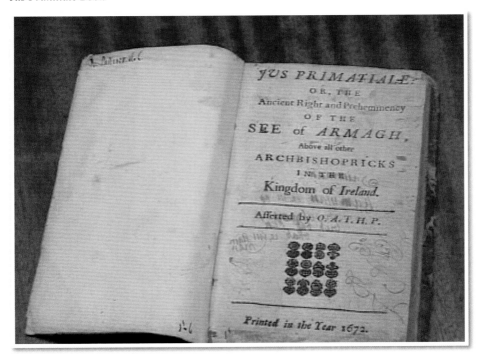

slightest sign of a nationalist church developing. There were many examples of this in other countries such as in France where some of the Church leaders had acquiesced, to the great detriment of the faith there. Shortly before leaving Rome, Oliver had recommended: "Do not promote those who have been involved in intrigues and factions during these wars, and have become positively hateful to the King. And I also believe that it is not a good thing either to promote those who seek to advance themselves by means of the English Court because such men always subscribe to the doctrines of the Sorbonnists and their followers, doctrines which are favourable to the King but not to the Holy See."

Armed with his invaluable experience from Rome, Oliver believed as a first principle in the importance of being ever faithful to the See of Peter in all things. Otherwise, he knew it could spell disaster for the Church, would certainly lead to local disagreements and the Church could even collapse completely, as happened in several countries as a result of such divisions. Archbishop Talbot was sincere and well-meaning and he was also very loyal to Rome, as exemplified by his trenchant and continued opposition to the group promoting the Remonstrance. These advocated a declaration of loyalty to the King to the detriment of Rome. This declaration had already caused great confusion in the Irish Church throughout the previous decade. Oliver strongly believed that the Archbishop of Dublin was treading on dangerous ground on both counts. He as the Archbishop of Armagh and a successor of St. Patrick could never back down therefore from his principles and he was quite determined in his arguments. Oliver has been criticised for the non-compromising attitude he adopted on these matters, being described as bad tempered and touchy, but for him they were crystal clear and this was his way of showing them to be non-debatable.

Oliver published a book in 1672, entitled 'Jus Primatiale' which outlined the ancient rights and precedence of the Archdiocese of Armagh since the time of St. Patrick. Stating Armagh's case calmly but resolutely, he quoted many sources of Irish history and indicated his willingness for the whole question to be judged in Rome. In his[2] book, he wrote: "Prelates of the Church in giving honour, ought one to go before the other, not in seeking honour. Archbishops and bishops should increase their reputation by modesty and not by ambition."

Used to spending much of his time on horseback, he used a horse-riding metaphor: "He of Armagh is in the saddle." As far as he was concerned, neither the King nor anybody else for that matter could appoint the Primate, or a co-Primate as this was solely the prerogative of Rome. One can certainly understand why it became an unwelcome topic for him, particularly coming from those whom he probably felt, should really have known better. Oliver wrote: "He would have no superior and I would have no equal." Archbishop Talbot did not help matters when he overturned Oliver's dismissal from their posts of a couple of priests in the Armagh province; criticised his handling of the Tories, ordered Oliver not to ordain so many priests, disagreed with Oliver's right to declare that the clan with the slang name of Magouna or Chaoich should revert to their original name of O'Reilly. In a letter to Rome, Oliver totally exasperated wrote: "It were better for us if that man had never been born." Archbishop Talbot was a good man but he had the unhappy knack of making even a saint swear. Many of the Franciscans naturally favoured Archbishop Talbot. A few Dominicans in turn reported Talbot for Premunire and he was exiled a few years later. Many prominent families took sides in the dispute and a directive was soon issued from Rome to cool matters. Oliver wrote: "I shall be prepared to swallow many bitter pills for the sake of peace and to avoid scandalizing the little ones." Oliver still showed determination and in a letter to Rome, wrote: "I suppose however, that this order or desire only commands silence as to writing for or against in this matter, and the avoiding of disputes about precedence, all of which I will most strictly obey. The Sacred Congregation and your Excellency cannot mean that I should omit to exercise my jurisdiction in matter of appeals from the courts of other metropolitans…to interdict this to me would be to suspend the rights of the see of Armagh, even before the sentence of decision is made."

Obedience was a virtue which Oliver cherished and there are many instances of his complete obedience to the instructions coming to him from Rome or even to the hint of such instructions. Rome had already appointed him as Primate and it would have been disobedient of him were he to accept the argument of the Archbishop of Dublin even if he had wished to and there was also the question of obedience and respect due towards the Primate. The Irish bishops and people already had a fine history in their loyalty to Rome, his stance and example on this and other occasions ensured that this would continue in the future. The question of the primacy was referred at the time to Rome for a decision, which eventually went in favour of Oliver and the Archdiocese of Armagh and so ended another defining episode of Irish Church history. The argument about the primacy strained relations between them for some time, although the two Archbishops were reconciled afterwards and Oliver wrote appreciatively of the efforts of John O'Maloney the Bishop of Killaloe who helped to bring this about. Shortly after Archbishop Talbot returned from his five year exile, although quite ill, he was arrested and jailed in Dublin. In June 1680 when both archbishops were imprisoned in Dublin Castle, Oliver brushed past his guards at one stage and he was able to minister spiritually to the then dying Archbishop of Dublin. Archbishop Hugh MacMahon, the second successor of Oliver as Archbishop of Armagh wrote a full treatise on the question of the primacy in 1728, but as there were much more pressing matters during penal times, the question effectively became a non-issue. The whole episode of the primacy was not one of Oliver's finest hours, but then he still had a little way to go on his journey to sainthood.

[1] Curtis, Fr. Emmanuel 'Blessed Oliver Plunkett' Dublin 1963. p.94
[2] O.A.T.H.P. (Oliver Plunkett) 'Jus Primitiale' Dublin 1672. p.2

40. PEACE TO THE PROVINCE

One major problem was the Tories or Raparees, a group who were fighting a hit and run type campaign of robbery from the hill regions of Tyrone and Armagh. At national and provincial synods, priests were asked to instruct the laity not to support the Tories, but yet Oliver had sympathy for them nonetheless, writing: "It would break your heart to see the great families…who were princes in the time of Elizabeth… deprived of their property…and yet with joy they accepted their spoliation for the sake of the faith." They had been dispossessed of their lands a generation or so previously and Oliver could sympathise somewhat with their loss, just as his brother Edward had been dispossessed of the family properties at Loughcrew. Huge swathes of land in Co. Armagh were owned by the Church of Ireland, Trinity College and by old and new Protestant settlers. A portion of poorer and hilly land of the Fews and of the huge parish of Killeavy was largely left to the Catholics. Much of it was of rough and woody terrain where the rule of law might not easily prevail, thus lending itself to lawlessness and to the rise of the Tories in the area. Hanging around their areas in the hope that the fortunes of war might somehow change, the Tories were causing great distress and hardship in the whole province. Many of the local families, who had been forced by the Tories to help them, were then fined for having done so. These fines were often unpayable by families who were landless poor and had barely enough to live on.

Oliver recounts: "To remedy this state of affairs the Bishop of Meath and all the vicar generals, knowing that I enjoyed some favour with the viceroy and the governor of Ulster, besought me to find some way to free the country of these problems. Oliver undertook the role of mediator; he met with the governor of Ulster and must have negotiated an offer of terms with him. Bringing a priest and a servant, he went to the Tories hideout and spoke for one hour in Irish to them, he asked them to give up a life which was full of spiritual risk and personal danger to themselves and reminded them about the widespread hardships they were causing throughout the province. He persuaded them to give up fighting. The authorities granted to Oliver, the lives of three men tried and condemned to death in the city of Enniskillen. They also conceded a general pardon for all, along with the release of prisoners. The authorities guaranteed safe conduct to the continent and the viceroy gave a commitment to assist with such passage financially. Oliver wrote: "This action was applauded by all the Catholics who raised their hands to heaven." Always willing to go more than half way, Oliver met the Tories and saw them safely on board ship in Dublin. He must have had total and absolute trust in Viceroy Berkeley, because if Berkeley had gone back on his word and arrested the Tories, Oliver would have had a serious credibility problem on his hands.

Oliver wrote: "Hundreds and hundreds of families benefited from the general pardon," this would be as expected, when one considers the

Stained Glass Window, St. Patricks, Dundalk

number of Tories involved and also the number of families who had been fined. Oliver added: "I obtained pardon for them, for all their previous misdeeds and for all those Catholic families who had been put on trial because of them." There is no commentary available on his meeting with the authorities, perhaps he would have been loath to commit such details to paper, but it might be fair to assume that all his diplomatic skills were invoked, to extract concessions such as these. In going to the Tory hideout, Archbishop Oliver proved yet again that he was eager to go out in search of the lost sheep and ever willing to go much more than half way in his efforts.

Probably no one other than Oliver would have had the respect from both sides to carry out a diplomatic coup such as this. It was a remarkable achievement when one considers the type of shuttle diplomacy which is required nowadays to effect modern day peace agreements even with the aid of all the latest communication equipment and gadgetry. Oliver had only one chance to get an agreement and his pre-planning and diplomacy again proved flawless, just as in the case of his removal of the vicar of Derry. In another of his letters he states that he undertook this affair with the consent of all the clergy of the province. As so many people from the different dioceses were involved with this initiative with the Tories and the outcome being so successful, there can be no doubt that there was a concerted campaign of prayer for its success, and for peace and reconciliation in the province at the time. Later in that year Oliver could write: "The province has not had greater peace in thirty years," and in the following year he wrote: "By Divine favour my province enjoys deep peace, God grant that it may continue."

While Oliver's peace agreement brought peace to the province, it only took a few years before other Tories gained in notoriety. Not all of these were willing to accept Oliver's first offer. Patrick Fleming was a prominent Tory who was ambushed by soldiers from Ardee at an inn near Iniskeen in February 1678. On his person was found a letter from Oliver Plunkett to a local parish priest, which entreated Fleming to leave the country and requesting him to fulfil this promise which he had already made to Oliver. Always willing to go more than half way, Oliver promises in the letter, to provide Fleming's wife with a sum of ten pounds[1] per annum for the duration of his absence, which he expected to be a short one. While Oliver was consistent in denouncing the Tories, he continued in his efforts to bring their remnants into an agreed settlement. The most famous Tory was undoubtedly Redmond Count O'Hanlon who was shot dead by his foster brother, who then received a pardon for his crimes and a one-hundred pounds reward. Redmond was a Robin Hood type figure, who was popular, well educated, had perfect English and was able to mix with soldiers who were on his trail; he was killed only two months before Oliver's martyrdom in 1681. Local tradition states, and there is evidence[2] to suggest that O'Hanlon refused an offer of pardon, in exchange for giving evidence against Oliver, thereby paying the ultimate price.

There were many other instances when Oliver settled other types of disputes throughout the province, such as his declaration that the clan with the slang name of Magouna[3] or Chaoich should revert to their original name of O'Reilly. A branch of the O'Reilly clan had turned Protestant a few generations earlier and even after returning to the Catholic faith, the slang name stayed with them. The O'Reilly clan would not recognise them as members of their clan and this in turn had led to many fractious disputes. Oliver's pronouncement was accepted and so yet another dispute in the province was settled once and for all. At the time when the Primacy controversy was at its height, Archbishop Talbot perhaps seeing an opportunity to take Oliver down a peg or two, reported Oliver's action to the authorities in London, as he felt that it was solely the king's prerogative to make any such decree for a change of name. Nothing seems to have come from his action.

1 Murray P.G. 'A Previously Unnoticed Letter of Oliver Plunkett's' Seanchas Ard Mhacha 1975. p.33
2 Gibney John 'Ireland and the Popish Plot' Palgrave MacMillan. p. 126/127
3 Ó Fiaich & Forristal 'Oliver Plunkett' Indiana USA 1976. Ó Fiaich. p.56

41. DROGHEDA SCHOOLS

Within weeks of his return to Ireland, he wrote to Rome: "In my diocese there are some young priests poorly instructed in Catholic doctrine. They are poor, and their relatives are poor. What can I do with these? Could the sacred congregation give them some extraordinary burses in the college of Louvain, to enable them to learn some moral theology for a couple of years? There are also some boys here, sons of noble families, who are inclined towards the clerical state. What shall we do with these? The nobility is impoverished having been without their incomes in the time of Cromwell for sixteen years, and after the king's restoration the greater part of their possessions was divided up among the soldiers of Cromwell. Oh what a sad situation."

Before he undertook any new ventures, Archbishop Oliver first prepared the ground, so that by diplomacy he could smooth out a path towards success, as when he negotiated a peace agreement with the Tories/Raparees or the delicate task of removing the corrupt vicar of Derry. The schools were another good example; despite the fact that Catholic schools were outlawed and notwithstanding the strong opposition to them, he diplomatically obtained permission to open a school in Drogheda. He had already explained his intentions and allayed the fears of the viceroy in Dublin. Writing: "I could not

St. Oliver's Tomb, Downside Abbey

divulge what I had in the bag; the secret word of the viceroy that they would not be molested during his time." Oliver wrote that Archbishop Margetson, the Protestant Archbishop of Armagh knowing that Oliver enjoyed favour with the viceroy gave his permission for schools with Catholic masters in the diocese. This would have been necessary, as without their toleration, he could not have gone ahead with the project. When established the viceroy hindered or remained neutral towards the many complaints, which were put forward against them. As forty Protestant boys were educated at the school, it no doubt helped to overcome some of the local opposition to them, although others must have been aghast, that good Protestant boys were attending a school run by the Jesuits.

The school formed a crucial part of Archbishop Oliver's plan of reform for the province and must have been on his mind even before his return to Ireland. Catholic schools were outlawed and Dr. Plunkett, a former professor in Propaganda College, recognised a great need for schools to educate both young boys and priests in Ireland. Young Catholic boys had no opportunity for any type of formal schooling and the scholarship of those priests who had been solely educated in Ireland, left a lot to be desired. Over the previous three decades, good men were ordained in their hundreds; the lucky few went to seminaries on the continent, but the vast majority, often got little chance of a proper spiritual formation. Remarkably, the school and college, which he paid for and built from the ground up, was in operation within months of his return as the Archbishop of Armagh. He also built a large 'comfortable house' called St. Ignatius for the three Jesuits priests, Fr's Rice, Murphy and Browne along with a Brother Nicholas who ran the school. Oliver wrote that Fr. Browne preaches at every festival in the principal chapel with great acclaim. Soon afterwards the staff of the school was augmented by a Fr. Cronin S.J. In 1672, Fr. Edward Drumgoole of the diocese of Armagh joined the staff. Oliver described Fr. Drumgoole as: "The ablest and best priest I have."

The school in Drogheda, could accommodate one hundred and fifty boys, including forty who were Protestant; it thus became the first integrated-school in Ireland. It was his hope that the school for boys might encourage some to go on for the priesthood and he wrote that he would like to pick six of the best for further studies; thoughts of a junior seminary were obviously already on his mind. A section of the school was reserved for the education of priests and this college would later cater for up to fifty-six at a time. All the clergy of Armagh must have attended the college and no doubt priests from Meath or the other dioceses of the province were also given the opportunity to attend. The expense of all this was considerable and Archbishop Oliver mentions in one of his letters that in order to help financially with the schools upkeep, he dressed himself in clothing made of inexpensive or rough material and he kept a most sparing table.

In a letter from Drogheda, dated 26th April 1671, he wrote[1] of the school for boys: "Apart from three, the nobles and gentry of the whole province of Ulster were deprived of their possessions, and from being landlords and proprietors have become leaseholders. They are unable to educate their children. The young priests ordained over the past seven years to fill the parishes vacated by the death of the older priests are very deficient in learning: they do not have schoolmasters fit to teach them, nor were Catholic masters tolerated, and thus even the sons of gentlemen deprived of learning and skill grew up to become rogues and highwaymen, and many of them were hanged. Seeing this state of affairs I undertook a risky project: I called in the Jesuits into my diocese, I built for them from the foundations quite a comfortable house and two schools where they train up to one hundred and fifty boys and twenty five priests... I have supported for the past nine months two very learned and hardworking fathers, a brother and a servant; one instructs the priests for an hour in the morning and an hour in the afternoon in cases of conscience, and the manner of preaching and catechising, and he also teaches rhetoric for two hours in the morning and two in the afternoon, and on feast days and free days he gives instruction in ceremonies and the administration of the sacraments, the other father teaches syntax and concordances. Besides, both of them often preach. I have kept them these nine months at my own expense, and have bought for them even the frying pan."

Even though Drogheda Grammar School, an Erasmus school had opened a year earlier in 1669, there continued to be much opposition to the Catholic school in Drogheda and undoubtedly to the fact that Protestants boys were attending a school run by the much maligned Jesuits. Within eight months of his schools start up; Archbishop Oliver was summoned on no less than nine occasions to the viceroy's court in Dublin because of the school's existence and for his exercise of foreign or papal jurisdiction. In one of his principal arguments in favour of the schools, he claimed that if the Catholic youth were educated they would become virtuous and less inclined towards any form of criminality but would instead become upright citizens and be of some good use to the state. His diplomacy and his experience as professor of controversies in Rome obviously stood to him, as he won the argument before the council on each occasion, thus enabling the schools continuance for a little while longer. Oliver wrote of Berkeley: "He kept his word despite all the efforts of Protestant ministers and governors of Drogheda and even of the Protestant primate."

One wonders if his plan for schools was crystallised before he had left Rome and that he may have progressed the matter further when in London on his journey back to Ireland, as it is known that he met the Queen during his stop-over. Within months of his visit to London, a new and more benign viceroy was on the way to Dublin. Perhaps his visit to court had initiated a new form of thinking for the kingdom of Ireland. At any rate, within weeks of his return to Ireland Oliver was writing to Rome requesting help for the schools: "Help me in this matter of the young uninstructed priests and the sons of gentlemen so that they may be educated and if it is necessary, to inform the Holy Father."

He also wrote requesting a salary for the three Jesuits who were teaching in the schools. All told it was a remarkable accomplishment when one considers that the schools were functioning with Jesuit teachers, a brand new building and also great hopes of a grant, all within months of his arrival back in Ireland. A short time later he was assigned a yearly pension of two-hundred pounds from the King upon the recommendation of the viceroy Berkeley; this was in gratitude for his work in bringing peace to the province with the Tories. The conferring of this grant was also a remarkable achievement in itself and would have solved most of his financial worries for the future. To his great sorrow however it was revoked in the first year after the initial moiety had been paid. Lord Ranelagh had objected to the payment from the treasury as a result of numerous complaints, including loose talk by Archbishop Talbot and his friends. Archbishop Talbot appeared peeved that Oliver had regular dealings with the viceroy, was in receipt of a substantial grant and that he had a school up and running in Drogheda, only hours from Dublin.

The winds of toleration soon changed for the worse shortly after the Test Act was introduced and the schools in Drogheda were levelled to the ground by the authorities in November 1673, after only three years and five months in operation. This was a terrible blow to Archbishop Oliver, having expended so much effort and resources on the school and college, he witnessed their great potential stamped out. Nevertheless their influence for good, even after such a short time in operation, would have been felt in the Irish Church and in society generally, for many years afterwards. Later he wrote: "There is nothing which gives me greater interior pain however, than to see the schools established by me thrown down after such expense. O what will the Catholic youth do now, so numerous and so talented." Rome promised financial help with regard to the schools but this was often slow in coming and after the demise of the schools, he was left much in debt. The Catholics who greatly outnumbered the Protestants were not allowed even one school in the country, not even if they allowed Protestants to attend them.

The exact location of St. Oliver's schools in Drogheda remains a mystery; some evidence suggests they were in Trinity Street, in the area of the Star and Crescent, although this location would have left them outside the town walls. Others believe that they were in the Shop Street or Dyer Street area. Canon Francis Carolan PP Mellifont, wrote in 1943 that all agree the schools were located in Shop Street. He surmised that they may[2] have been on the grounds of the Augustinian Church or Friary in Shop Street. He recounted a story that the Augustinians while building their Church or Friary in Shop Street had to have the ownership and title deeds of a certain property transferred from the Jesuits to the Augustinians before building work commenced.

Oliver also set up a school near Dundalk almost certainly before the large Drogheda schools; he mentions it in a letter but no more is known about it, it was probably located at Ballybarrack. A Jesuit was his secretary for a time and he probably had a cottage school established in the area. Oliver always saw education as an important priority and undoubtedly he oversaw the education of his young nieces and nephews at Ardpatrick; writing from his condemned cell in Newgate barely a week before martyrdom: "Jemmy and Joseph begun their philosophy and Nicky ended his prosedy."

Peace and Reconciliation Banner

ST. OLIVER PLUNKETT

PEACE AND RECONCILIATION

[1] Hanly 'The Letters' No.79
[2] Carolan Canon Francis 'Blessed Oliver Plunkett and Louth' Drogheda 1943. p3

42. A DIPLOMAT

St. Oliver was a diplomat, who astutely steered clear of politics, kept on good terms with many leading citizens, including the Earl of Charlemont, President of Ulster, who allowed him the use of his courtyard in Armagh for confirmation ceremonies and Henry Moore the Earl of Drogheda who allowed him a public church with bells on his estates, which were exempt from the jurisdiction of the royal ministers. Only a diplomat could have engineered the deposition of the vicar of Derry, or the bringing of peace to the dioceses of the Province and the brokering of a peace agreement between the Government and the Tories. He also proved his diplomatic skills and powers of persuasion by overcoming the strong and determined opposition to the setting up of his schools at Drogheda. Later when arrested, Archbishop Oliver had no objection to an all Protestant jury at Dundalk. He was then brought to London to face trial there because of the common belief that no Protestant jury in Ireland would ever believe the trumped up charges of treason which had been levelled against him.

43. CONTROVERSIES AND DIFFICULTIES

Dr. Thomas Fitzsimons was vicar general of Kilmore diocese; but after 1675 his health deteriorated, particularly his mind. He then became involved in numerous disputes and deposed several good priests in Kilmore. These priests appealed to Oliver as Metropolitan of the province and because Fitzsimons refused repeatedly[1] to appear before Oliver to explain his decisions, Oliver deposed him in May 1676. Fitzsimons garnered support for himself in the province and many of the dissidents who resented Oliver as their archbishop, now rallied strongly behind him. It only takes a few to cause a lot of trouble and shortly afterwards, another round of complaints was made to Rome, very similar in nature to those made a few years previously. Oliver was too friendly with the Protestants, he was not a Gael, he was a Meath man of Anglo Irish stock, he was unfair in his dealings, he was determined to diminish the influence of the Franciscans, he wished to do likewise with the other orders and he preached against the Tories. Many of those who had been censured or who did not favour reform or high standards of conduct in the Church also came on board behind Fitzsimons. The round of complaints was widespread and so intense, that Bishop John Brenan of Waterford was asked for his opinion and he vindicated Oliver on all counts. Rome decided that the deposition of Fitzsimons would stand and ordered that all calumnies against Oliver must cease, but there was little chance of that happening.

Friar Felim O'Neill a son of the great Sir Phelim O'Neill hoped to be appointed to lead an Irish diocese and when fellow Franciscan, Dr. Patrick Tyrrell of St. Isidore's College in Rome, was appointed Bishop of Clogher it was not a very popular decision with him. Dr. Tyrrell found much opposition to his appointment in Clogher, indeed the opposition to him was extremely interesting; he being a Franciscan did not appear to make up for the fact that he was a Meath man. The cultural differences of 'Gael' and 'Pale' seemed more important; he was also a friend of Oliver's from his time in Rome and indeed the prosecution witnesses against Oliver at his trial also tried hard to weave Bishop Tyrrell into the plot. After the Fitzsimons debacle, Bishop Tyrrell was appointed by Rome to take charge of the diocese of Kilmore as administrator, as well as looking after his own diocese of Clogher. Any opposition to him previously soon paled into insignificance, as he then found a huge amount of opposition taking charge of the second diocese. Fitzsimons and company argued that no bishop could be appointed unless such a request was made by the clergy. Oliver replied that the Holy See had already established this right centuries before. Oliver was also well aware of the dangers brought about by Jansenism and Gallicanism, menaces which were already quite active in some of the Catholic countries of Europe. To settle the problem in Kilmore, Oliver accompanied Bishop Tyrrell on a tour of the diocese and persuaded the vast majority to accept him.

Friar Anthony Daly was another Franciscan who maintained a strong hatred for Oliver, he became guardian of Armagh Convent in 1675. He was notorious and having been suspended by Oliver in the presence of Bishop Tyrrell the following year, he continued to operate in disobedience within the province. He later went to the continent, where the calumnies against Oliver continued unabated. Oliver wrote defending himself later from prison: "This Friar Anthony…sought to take away my life here, instigating the bandits to kill me; about six years ago (1674) they came to the house of my vicar general, where I was staying, and broke in the door about midnight and took away all the money which both my vicar general and my secretary – Michael Plunkett who is now in Rome had with them, and they stood with a sword to my throat. The leader of the band was later captured and before his death in prison he told the parish priest of Armagh and his curate that it was Anthony Daly who told them to kill me, and that he would give me absolution." It can be deduced from the above account that Oliver, poor as always, did not have any money with him, as it seems that no money was taken from him but only from his secretary and from his vicar general.

Reliquery Of St. Oliver, Lamspringe, Germany

The principal witness against Oliver, Friar John Moyer (MacMoyer) was vicar in the Armagh convent to guardian Anthony Daly. Anthony Daly was replaced as guardian by Friar Anthony O'Neill, son of the great Owen

Roe O'Neill. Friar Felim O'Neill was guardian of Armagh for the three years from 1672; Oliver had originally held him in high esteem but that was to change and he wrote disapprovingly of him in several of his later letters. Seemingly ambitious, Friar Felim had caused enough trouble for his time, particularly in his opposition to Patrick Tyrrell's appointments. Although he was never in the same league as Moyer or Daly, as son of the great Sir Phelim O'Neill, he still had a following and held quite a lot of influence in the province. He became guardian of Drogheda in August 1678 and Oliver wrote disparagingly of the great celebratory banquet he put on in the convent at Drogheda on the feast of St. Francis, October 4th of that year, calling it a scandal at the time. Soon afterwards with the religious houses closed, Friar Felim went abroad and he served a couple of terms of office, as guardian of Louvain from 1681.

[1] Curtis, Fr. Emmanuel 'Blessed Oliver Plunkett' Dublin 1963. p.120

44. THREAT OF HERESIES

The Catholic Church in Ireland was renowned over the centuries for its loyalty to the See of Peter. While opinions supporting Jansenism or Gallicanism were rare in seventeenth century Ireland, nevertheless a cohort of Irish priests who had spent time on the continent would have had some exposure to many new ways of thinking, some of them good, others not quite so good, while some other ideas were quite heretical. Oliver often referred to the dangers of Jansenism, writing: "The relics of Jansenism and other novelties which are widespread in France and Belgium…which have been published in print and are spread abroad concerning the fallibility of the pontiff, the authority of St. Augustine as prevailing over the pontiff's decisions, the invalidity of absolution if the penitent does not have the love of God above all things, the need to reform in many ways the cult of the Mother of God and the saints." He was concerned about this threat which had a following on the continent of Europe and which had exerted some influence in Ireland. He suggested that the Holy Father be informed and he recommended that Cardinal Howard's secretary in Rome should be asked to translate a book written as commentary and explanation of the Council of Trent as an antidote to some literature which was already in circulation in Ireland.

The dissidents in Ireland had already used Gallican arguments during their opposition to the appointment of Bishop Tyrrell as bishop of Clogher and even more so when he was appointed to take on the responsibility of the neighbouring Kilmore diocese, as already discussed in the previous chapter. Decrees two, three and four of the twenty-eight decrees of Oliver's provincial synod of Ardpatrick in 1678, were obviously drawn[1] up to overcome many such ideas. 'We decree that appointments to dioceses by the supreme pontiff are not dependent on their acceptance by the clergy and people. We decree it to be false that the supreme pontiff would be bound by the clergy, people or lay nobility if they recommend a candidate for appointment to a diocese. We decree it false that it rests with the people to choose for themselves whom they wish as their pastors.' Less than four years later in France, thirty-six Catholic bishops would codify such beliefs, thus conceding considerable powers to monarchs over the Church. England had lost the true faith because bishops had become extinct, were replaced by a chapter of priests who did not give proper leadership, were often divisive in strategy and the Church soon became like the house divided. In France, a Catholic country, the interference of politicians and the monarchy in the life of the Church soon led to all sort of shenanigans and division within the Church, which ultimately led to its ruin in that country also. Monarchs and governments of other countries, such as the low-countries were quick to seize similar opportunities. Contrast that to Ireland, the synod at Ardpatrick along with Archbishop Oliver's consistent and strong leadership in this regard, ensured that any such new or fancy ideas were quickly nipped in the bud. Assuredly, one of the greatest legacies Archbishop Oliver left to the Church in Ireland.

Archbishop Oliver's refusal to go into exile and his encouragement to the other bishops to follow his example meant that while the Church leaders were few in numbers and very often on the run, nevertheless they were still available to give the leadership necessary for Church survival. We must not forget the prayers and sacrifices of countless other holy people of the ages, who chose to endure great hardships rather than give 'up the pearl of great price,' which was their faith and those others who suffered martyrdom, including the Drogheda martyrs. All of these by their loyalty have contributed in a major way to the preservation of the faith in Ireland. Over the centuries Ireland became renowned as the 'Island of saints and scholars' and had many of each, but the martyrs were few and far between, until after the reformation. Indeed many of those who gave their lives across the country are still unknown to us.

Oliver always insisted that the Church in Ireland would not look for succour to any political masters in Dublin, Paris, Madrid or London, but always to the Holy See. St. Oliver was ever conscious that Jesus did not establish a democratic Church but a hierarchical one, built upon the See of Peter and sanctified till the end of time by the Holy Spirit of God. Despite the huge, huge problems of the Church in Ireland, Oliver left the Church unwavering in its beliefs, undivided for the future and it remained largely intact until well into the twentieth century. We pray that we may soon see a revival of faith in our country throughout the rest of this, the twenty-first century.

[1] Moran, Cardinal Patrick 'Memoir of Oliver Plunket' Dublin 1895. p.146

45. Embarrassments

Early in 1673, Archbishop Peter Talbot of Dublin decided to validate a marriage although he knew of a possible prior impediment to the legality of the marriage. An appeal was made to Archbishop Oliver as Primate, who having been led to believe at the appeal that the impediment was only then coming to light, overruled the previous decision. Archbishop Talbot had already received a dispensation of the said impediment and when Oliver found this out, he corrected his mistake and apologised profusely to Archbishop Talbot.

Some months later a public enquiry was held into Archbishop Talbot on the orders of the London parliament. Oliver was summoned to give evidence before the tribunal and he would much rather if he had not been required to do so. While he was criticised by some, his evidence did not bring anything new to light that had not already been brought out in evidence by others at the tribunal, including that of Bishop Patrick Plunkett. This was the beginning of Archbishop Talbot's five year exile.

The following year Oliver was involved in another incident, this time in the Province of Tuam. A Fr. John de Burgo was appointed vicar apostolic for the diocese of Killala with the usual proviso that he should go to the diocese within four months. Not having fulfilled this condition he sought a new brief which was issued the following May; this one coming without a time stipulation. Meanwhile the Metropolitan, Archbishop James Lynch of Tuam had reappointed Fr. John Duley as vicar general of the vacant diocese. De Burgo showed his new brief to Oliver who proclaimed it as legal and official. The Archbishop of Tuam appealed to Rome, who upheld his appointment of Duley and upgraded the appointment to vicar apostolic of the diocese.

46. ECUMENISM

Still in the long shadow of the Reformation and indeed of the Council of Trent, ecumenism was far from anyone thoughts. Yet Oliver was a man of reconciliation, and an ecumenist way ahead of his time. He was respected by the viceroy, the governor of Ulster, also the Protestant Archbishop of Armagh and his vicar. Oliver had a long meeting with the Protestant Bishop of Derry and he so cleared his doubts on many points of controversy that he forever spoke about Oliver in the most glowing of terms. The respect he had for Oliver proved to be an advantage for the treatment of Catholics in the region. Oliver was scrupulous not to get embroiled in politics or to have any correspondence of a political nature, consequently he was not seen as a threat to anybody and this fact stood to his advantage on many occasions. Oliver wrote: "As for temporal affairs, I do not wish to know anything of them, and to this effect I exhort the others also and if I am exiled or if I must suffer, it will be for the administration of the sacraments."

He recounts: "The Protestant Primate asked to speak to me and he gave me precedence in his own house and he promised that he would never interfere with me in the smallest matter." Indeed the Earl of Charlemont could offer him the use of his courtyard in Armagh for confirmation and the Earl of Drogheda allowed him a public church with bells on property under his control. Remarkably, he had been allowed build the schools in Drogheda, it being the second city of the kingdom and only four hours journey time from Dublin. Oliver was on good terms with Dr. Dudley Loftus the Protestant vicar of Armagh, he shared his beliefs with him and could write of Loftus to Rome: "If he was not afraid of losing his income he would become a Catholic, he is already one in his beliefs. He is writing to Cardinal Barberini; please get his Eminence to write him a kindly reply." As with the Protestant Bishop of Derry, Oliver shared his beliefs in a

Tyburn Scene, Synod Hall, Armagh

respectful and open way with the Protestant vicar of Armagh, which is yet another mark of a true ecumenist.

In June 1671 the Protestants of Dromore Diocese were[1] suspicious of a Catholic plot against them. When Oliver heard of the rumours he immediately went to Hillsborough fort and gave assurances that there was no basis to the rumours and offered to remain prisoner if his assurances should prove false. Yet again, it appears that merely going half way was not an option for Archbishop Oliver.

[1] Edwards R. Dudley 'Historical Studies - Blessed Oliver Plunket' League of Prayer Dublin 1937. p.18

47. DISCRIMINATION

Discrimination or the persecution of Catholics was never far below the surface. On one occasion when Oliver was in Dungannon for a confirmation ceremony, he was impeded by the governor of that location. The Earl of Charlemont however then gave a vigorous rebuke to this governor. It was common practice that Catholics were ordered to remain off the streets while the Protestants went to or from church on Sundays. There are several examples where Oliver courageously defended the victims of injustice, such as the occasion when the magistrate of Armagh gave orders that all Catholics of the town should accompany him to the Protestant church on Sunday's under pain of being fined each time they missed. Oliver appealed to the President against the decree and it was revoked. Oliver reported that he went on four occasions to the Protestant vicar of Armagh to defend his own clergy, adding that before his own coming to the diocese, they were often brought to court for the administration of the sacraments and imprisoned or fined. On another occasion, when the Protestant chancellor of Clogher diocese began to persecute the small farmers for sending their children to Catholic clergy for baptism, Oliver drew up a letter for the viceroy and the supreme council. He showed it to the Protestant Bishop and the Primate, and they both pleaded with him not to send it, promising that this practice of the chancellor would end. Oliver noted that more than three hundred families had already been impoverished because of this persecution.

48. ORDINATIONS

Oliver performed many ordinations and he wrote: "The fruit of fifty priests give me more spiritual consolation than the temporal consolation of a chest full of gold." Priests always had to be careful, as there was a danger that the law of Premunire would be used against them; many priests and bishops suffered imprisonment or banishment after being cited under this draconian decree. Oliver only ordained those who were worthy and who had passed a strict examination and in the 1704 registration of Catholic clergy, over one hundred and twenty priests were still alive who had been ordained by the Primate. Of those who registered, over half were ordained in north Co. Louth and the figure of forty-seven[1] for Ardpatrick easily outnumbers any other location. Besides Ardpatrick and Ballybarrack, he also ordained at Rosmakea in the parish of Knockbridge and at Castletown-Bellew outside Dundalk. He ordained in each year of his active ministry and by 1704, priests whom he had ordained were living in a total of twenty-five counties.

Archbishop Oliver must have ordained several hundred priests in total, as some priests would have died before 1704 and many others would have gone into exile. This large group of dedicated priests fired with the same ardour as he had, was surely one of his most important legacies, as it left the Irish Church and people well prepared to face the worst excesses of the penal laws which were yet to come in the first half of the eighteenth century. These young men were admired throughout Europe, as they were undertaking a most dangerous apostolate at great cost and sacrifice to themselves, proving yet again that youth will not run away from a challenge and the bigger the challenge the better. Oliver's witness and martyrdom is characteristic of so many others of the period. These women or men should not be forgotten as they all helped to pass the baton of faith on through the succeeding generations, right down to the present day.

Concerned that priests must be well educated, he provided schools and training for them and it was his policy on his visitations to forever encourage priests by word and by action. He asked that a greater number of students from the Northern Province should be taken in the Irish College in Rome, as the other provinces already had greater access to the Irish colleges in other countries. This was something which greatly concerned him and he drew attention to the difficulties which would result in the province in providing Church leaders for the future. The Irish College in Rome agreed to his request to accept two students from the Northern Province and they increased it to three students[2] from the year 1672. Thinking 'outside the box' he made a bold suggestion to Rome, requesting that if his scheme is accepted it should be kept highly secret until all could be accomplished. He proposed that the Irish College would be sold along with the vineyard and the house thereon; he estimated that a sale value of eight thousand scudi could be realised in total. If this money was deposited at four percent interest it would yield two hundred and forty scudi per annum, which when added to the one thousand scudi annual grant for the college, should

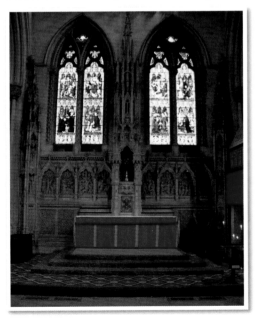

128: St. Oliver's Altar, Downside Abbey – Consecrated in 1935 by Cardinal MacRory

suffice to double the number of students from eight to sixteen, if these were accommodated in Propaganda Fide College. He reckoned that the students could be catered for much more economically in Propaganda College as the expenses of the Jesuits and of servants in a stand-alone college would thereby be eliminated. Obviously thinking about this a great deal he suggested in quite some detail how the objections and legalities might be overcome, writing: "For the greater service of the missions." This suggestion of his was never implemented, and although the Irish College experienced many difficult periods in the intervening centuries, thankfully it has since grown and grown into the fine institution it is today.

[1] Concannon Helena 'Blessed Oliver Plunket' Dublin 1935. p.285
[2] Ó Fiaich & Forristal 'Oliver Plunkett' Indiana USA 1976. p.39

49. A RAP ON THE KNUCKLES

Everybody needs a supervisor, we may much prefer to do things in our way at times, but a manager will help to keep us on our toes and they are also good for our humility. Archbishop Oliver reported to Rome, in the person of the secretary of Propaganda, short for the Sacred Congregation for the Propagation of the Faith and which is known since 1982, as the 'Sacred Congregation for the Evangelization of Peoples.' The trouble with Oliver was that his work rate was so hectic and his reforms so many and so uncompromising that when the reports, lies, calumnies and boundless complaints started flowing to Rome about him, they seemed to be just never ending. So much mud was thrown by so many people that some of it was bound to stick and after all, there can be no smoke without fire. They must have thought in Rome: 'perhaps he is going over the top.' Enough was enough, eyes must have been raised to heaven on almost a weekly basis in Rome as the wild reports about him just kept on coming.

Rome had had enough and soon chastised him for consorting with the Tories. Archbishop Talbot hadn't helped when he wrote to Rome complaining about Oliver who was in the company of a party of Tories as they awaited a ship in Dublin with a hundred pounds travelling money from the viceroy: "Here he is now with his fifteen bandits in tow, all arrived in the capital city of my archdiocese." Oliver replied to Rome and gave a detailed account of his activities, stating that at the request of the Bishop of Meath and all the vicar generals, he had reached out spiritually to the Tories who were the cause of untold suffering in the region. Bringing a priest and a servant he went to the Tories hideout and spoke for one hour in Irish to them, he asked them to give up a life which was full of spiritual risk and personal danger to themselves and reminded them about the widespread hardships they were causing throughout the province. As a result he could report that the province was at peace and had not seen such peace in thirty years. The fines payable by many poor families as a result of the Tories activities were cancelled. Arms were decommissioned, the release of prisoners agreed and the lives of three men were spared who were due to be hanged in Enniskillen. Oliver asked that he should not be judged so quickly until they had at least heard his side of the story; Rome soon replied; reversed their rebuke and complimented him on his good work.

Something similar happened with the appointment of Gerard Farrell as vicar apostolic of the diocese of Ardagh. Rome admonished Oliver for his slowness in installing the new vicar. Oliver knew that it was going to be a difficult assignment as the existing vicar had given decades of service in that capacity. Oliver was a man of courage and determination, he was fully prepared to obey the will of Rome and replace the vicar despite the danger of being subjected to the law of Premunire, and he wrote: "When the brief arrives I shall go in person to put Fr. Gerard Farrell in possession of the jurisdiction and if necessary, I shall inflict censures upon the said vicar Cornelius Gaffney if he does not obey. Although this course of action is a dangerous one, yet to carry out the commands of my superiors I shall not spare myself fatigue and I shall not fear danger…I shall put it into operation, even if it should cost me my life." Oliver wrote that he had been waiting for a decree for the appointment to arrive from Rome which would strengthen his hand, adding that it was a good journey to Ardagh and that he had been occupied with visitation when the winter had intervened, which in turn had prevented him from travelling. The new vicar was not accepted by many within the diocese, including the existing vicar as word had got out that Farrell was not well educated, was illegitimate and had spent a year in prison in Rome. To ease the new man into the diocese, Archbishop Oliver asked that they divide the diocese between them, but upon reflection by Farrell, this was not acceptable to him. The argument soon became academic upon the death of the existing vicar a little over a year later. In this instance, Rome may well have been correct in suggesting that Oliver had procrastinated ever so slightly in this matter, but if this is the case, he would have done so for the sake of peace in the diocese and Oliver after all was still travelling on that journey to sainthood.

The argument of the primacy also drew the ire of Rome as did the numerous complaints made following Bishop Tyrrell of Clogher's appointment by Rome to look after the diocese of Kilmore. After Oliver deposed Thomas Fitzsimons because of illness, many protesters rowed in behind the deposed vicar and the complaints were coming from a broad spectrum of people. Oliver wrote: "These are all calumnies, since I do nothing to deserve contempt I shall despise lies, insults will have no effect on me; if they should make me angry they would seem to be noticed, but if ignored they vanish." It seems that Oliver had just taken another small step on the ladder of sainthood. It was a sad reflection on the times, that Oliver's first letter from prison in Dublin castle was mainly one defending his actions. One very positive outcome of the myriad of complaints made against Oliver and of his having to defend himself point for point and in great detail, is that we are much more knowledgeable of his work and of the times in which he toiled. Unfortunately for

Archbishop Oliver, the lies and calumnies of some of those who were out to get him one way or another, would soon progress into deadly perjuries.

50. HIS LETTERS

St. Oliver is renowned for his letter writing and for the sheer volume of his correspondence, undoubtedly one of his strong charisms. This is exemplified by an addendum made by Bishop John Brenan to one of Oliver's letters, written while they were in hiding in an isolated location, he wrote of Oliver: "Even in this desert he has a most exact correspondence with all parts...From the desert 13 February 1674." Oliver's letter writing was so prolific either to Rome via the Internuncio in Brussels, or to his fellow bishops throughout the country, that the topic deserves to be dealt with in a little depth. His correspondence formed an important part of his apostolate; he was assiduous in reporting regularly to Rome as he had undoubtedly promised to do and was happy to receive letters with news, advice and instructions in return, often beginning his letter with: "I have received your most welcome letter of 'such and such' a date."

When sending an important letter he sometimes sent a duplicate through a different route in case it got lost or was intercepted. He wrote and received reports from various locations on the continent especially Antwerp and Brussels as it was important to know the lie of the land politically. It was even more important to know the designs of the Royal Court in London, as whatever happened in London would sooner or later have a direct bearing on Ireland. His letters with Fr. Howard and Irishman Mr. Daniel Arthur in London would have helped him greatly in his intelligence gathering in this regard. We have seen that his income from his diocese was never more than fifty pounds and often only amounting to about fifteen pounds per year. His letters on the other hand cost him four hundred scudi or one-hundred pounds in the first three and a half years of his ministry. His letters are so detailed that much of our knowledge of Irish Church history for the period and of his work comes from his pen. Several times he mentions that he is in weekly communication with his fellow bishops in Ireland and two hundred and thirty letters of his remain in existence. With the exception of Fr. Scarampi's poignant and instructive letter to him, which is now held in Roman archives, very little other material sent to him survives as he destroyed his correspondence and voluminous files on several occasions. Writing in June 1671, a period when there should have been relative calm in the country: "But I when a certain persecution was expected in Armagh had to burn all my letters from abroad, and all the briefs I had in my possession, and even the certificate of my consecration…how many letters there were in my files, how many decrees and ordinances and briefs to be published throughout the whole province."

Of the[1] two hundred and thirty letters of his which survive, one hundred and ninety are now kept in the building of Oliver's beloved Propaganda Fide College, where he lived and taught for twelve years; this building on the Piazza di Spagna now houses the Sacred Congregation for the Evangelization of Peoples. Six letters are kept in the archives of Westminster Cathedral; eight along with his final speech are kept in Downside Abbey and the remaining letters are to be found in the Vatican Archives, Vatican Library or in other Roman

Bishop James Lennon, leading out the Relic of the Head of St. Oliver from St. Peter's Church, enroute for Killineer, 1979

archives. Cardinal Ó Fiaich has written of the letters from Oliver's condemned cell and which are now housed in Downside Abbey: "Historical circumstances have made our country rich in prison literature but these Newgate letters have never been surpassed." This series of letters from the condemned cell in Newgate prison, probably gives us the best insight into the man, as they clearly reveal the depth of his spirituality and faith. In this last series of letters he did not have a lot of news to relate so while writing he let his mind wander, expressing many diverse thoughts as he went. His last few letters were short notes of practicalities, thanks and acknowledgements. In his last major letter which was written to Fr. Corker, he states; "An end of tears the happy rope." Not yet as saint, but taking the steps of sainthood two steps at a time during his nineteen months in prison, he was very nearly there at that point.

His letters are quite long, usually well over a thousand words, many between fifteen hundred and two-thousand words in total; they are written on good quality paper and even today are clearly legible. The handwriting is firm and steady with the formation of sentences and words extremely consistent. The spelling or punctuation is not always consistent however and seems to follow the general pattern of the time. His letters do show a clear, logical and precise structure; written in one go and covering numerous topics. They show that he had a clear mind, as many people today would have great difficulty writing a long letter or article in one go. He was not interested in flowery prose, but in the sincerity of the message, writing in the English of the time: "I never hunted after florishes in any language...many taverns have faire and majestical signes tho there be no good liquor in the cellar." In one such letter he apologises for the long-windedness of the enclosed, adding that he did not have time to make it shorter and in another he writes: "I have not time to look over the letter because the post is leaving this very minute, please excuse errors and slips."

He felt obliged to keep his superiors informed on a regular basis and in total he must have written thousands of letters throughout his lifetime. The expense of all this correspondence was considerable, as there was no postal service as such, but a series of couriers and trusted agents who collected and distributed the mail, each of whom had to be paid along the way. A letter cost seven and a half baiocchi to Dublin (a baiocchi was Italian currency and was valued at slightly more than the old halfpenny), a further ten baiocchi to London, thirteen to Brussels, Brussels to Mantua twenty and the final journey to Rome a further two and a half, making a cost of fifty three baiocchi or almost three old shillings for a delivery to Rome. Initially, Oliver's letters for Rome were sent via Antwerp and he paid the complete cost of the postage to Rome. He later sent his mail to the Internuncio in Brussels who would then forward them to Rome, thus saving Oliver almost half the postage. A few of his earlier letters from Ireland were sent to his old friend Dr. John Brenan in Rome. In order to reduce the number of letters and his costs, he usually requested that his letters would be seen by various people, the Internuncio in Brussels, the secretary of Propaganda in Rome and the agent of the Irish Bishops in Rome. He also requested that no envelopes be used when writing to him because upon delivery, his charges would be halved. A portion of the cost of the letter was borne by the recipient, which gave some guarantee at least of the delivery of each letter. Each letter from Rome cost him thirty baiocchi to receive or one and a half old shillings; when one pound was equal to twenty shillings.

He often wrote on one side of a large sheet of paper and so as not to be wasteful he would complete the page with writing, sometimes writing sideways on the margin so as to fill the whole page. To save on postage he also stopped using envelopes, filling one side of the paper completely with writing along with most of the second side and folding the paper in such a way that the address and no other writing would appear on the outside. In one such letter, seeing that more space was available on the page, he continued the letter with another topic, beginning: "In order not to burden the post with blank paper." He often concluded a letter by writing "the paper is at an end" and then signing off. Some letters were in his-own secret code, using numbers to represent either letters of the alphabet, specific words or even named individuals; this was quite clever as it used over a hundred ciphers in total. Aware that many of his letters might be opened in 'The Castle' he was always careful what they contained and he painstakingly steered clear of all political topics. Oliver was safe enough in this regard as he scrupulously steered clear of all civil or political matters and he strongly advised others to do the same. He also requested Rome in some of his letters to advise others in the Church in Ireland to behave likewise. He was later proved correct in his suspicions that his letters were opened, as viceroy Berkeley later admitted to him that his letters were indeed scrutinised and he expressed satisfaction with their contents; promising him they would henceforth go unhindered.

Oliver signed some of his letters under the pseudonym of Thomas Cox or Edward Hamon, with a few of his earlier ones signed by William Browne during the time of his alias as Captain William Browne; that is with sword, pair of pistols and wig. Many letters are unsigned but there can be no mistaking the handwriting. Some have his initials or the abbreviation O A standing for Oliver of Armagh, only a few are signed Oliver Plunkett. He invariably spelled the name Plunkett with two t's although many biographers have spelt his name with one. He was also quick witted and sharp in his correspondence and he often included little sayings, such as: "When the cat is away the mice will play," "The blind man is no judge of colour," "The spirit indeed is willing but the purse is weak," "Happy the man who has one eye in the midst of blind men" and a common saying of his which reflected his valour: "If the whole world should come crashing down the ruins will strike an undaunted man." It is interesting to note that although he was fluent in four languages, he felt most comfortable when corresponding in Italian, obviously as a result of immersing himself completely in the language and culture of Italy for over twenty two years. Very few of his letters are in English, although

Treisé leat i measc na naomh,
Ionadaí ó chine gael,
Pléigh mo chúis i lathair Dé,
'S tú mo dhóchas, slánaigh mé.
    Curfá
'Oilibhéir ár bpátrún féin,
Cúntóir caoin is taca tréan,
Tabhair do chunamh duinn go léir,
Seas go buan linn, 'Oilibheir.

Buachaill seimh ó chlar na mí,
Sagart thall sa róimh ag guí,
Easpag ceilte ag oirniú cléir,
Cúrsa saoil dar nOilibhéir.
    Curfá
Hist, a Chríost, le glór a bhéil,
Fear a lean do shampla féin,
Tabhair dar dtir sa bhearna baoil,
Sagairt óir mar Oilibhéar.

Cardinal Tomás Ó Fiaich

Poem by Cardinal Tomás O Fiaich

one example was the extraordinary letter he wrote a few days before his martyrdom to his former secretary, Fr. Michael Plunkett a relative who was then in Rome.

An untiring letter writer, the cost of his voluminous correspondence added to the cost of the schools, meant that Archbishop Oliver was forever short of money because his income was so small. He often sought help in this regard in his letters. Some of his letters are detailed responses in defence of the many calumnies which were written about him: "If you ever find that I have written one word that is untrue… my whole case falls to the ground." In the words of Mgr. John Hanly: "The Archbishop's veracity emerges unblemished from this self-imposed test." For a time he wrote on half a sheet of paper, writing: "I do it in order to keep down the size of my letters and to save money; my correspondence is reducing me to penury." Half of his letters were written in his first three years as archbishop, while the other half were spread out over his remaining seven years, undoubtedly as a consequence of persecution and of his severe poverty.

[1] Hanly 'The Letters' p.xiv

51. St. Oliver's Personality

His letters are all fascinating; containing detailed reports of his work in Ireland or enthralling descriptions of the condition of the Irish Church and people. As reports go, it would be expected that his true personality would only occasionally break through. However over the whole series of his letters, his character, warmth and persona comes across strongly. He was intelligent and shrewd, while he steered completely clear of all politics, yet through his contacts and correspondence he had his finger on the pulse. We can say with certainty that he was a warm, compassionate man, he was a humble, forgiving man and he possessed great uprightness and integrity. He was a frugal man, not just out of necessity because of his poverty, or simply to help fund the schools or his regular correspondence but also because of the importance of giving good example. He was a teacher to his very core, and never lost an opportunity to encourage, to teach but most especially, to give good example to priests, laity or even his fellow bishops. He had strong courage, was never afraid to do the right thing and the following was a common refrain in his letters: "If the whole world should come crashing down, let justice be done." This was borne out by his life as he showed bravery and endurance irrespective of the difficulty, a true hero who never yielded any ground or showed any signs of fear in the face of adversity, not even the harsh cruelty that was Tyburn. Saint John XXIII, described[1] Oliver as: "The bravest of the brave" and no more needs to be added.

Knowing how crucial it was that his masters at Propaganda in Rome would make the right decisions for the benefit of the Church in Ireland, he kept them well informed on a continual basis of the dismal circumstances it found itself in, and of the dire poverty of its church leaders. After his umpteenth letter in a similar vein, the Primate still a teacher to his core and perhaps slightly exasperated or afraid that nobody might be listening, sent off a respectful missive, but then it must be remembered that Oliver was still on that journey to sainthood. The letter could be interpreted as 'please sit up straight there, and listen carefully,' writing in September 1677: "Please be good enough to note well what I am going to say, no bishop in Ireland has two servants; it is one and the same who acts as his valet and his stable-boy, and it is his stable-boy who serves his Mass, and if the bishop has a nose at all he won't fail to notice a trace of the odour of the stable at the altar. Besides no bishop has his own house, and to obtain his board he goes to-day to the house of this gentleman, tomorrow to the house of another, not without embarrassment and already the gentlemen are tired of these visits. I leave it to your Lordship to judge if this is not a belittling of the crozier." Having said all of the above, he was loyal and totally obedient to authority; Rome had asked him to do many things and he was fastidious in their execution. Whenever Rome made a decision he was happy to implement it, whatever the cost may have been to him personally.

He was a grateful man who never forgot to acknowledge any form of kindness bestowed upon; besides writing a letter of thanks he would invariable mention the kindness granted to him in a letter to Rome. When Captain John Hamilton a Catholic convert from Scotland, who lived in Cavan castle, accompanied him around the diocese of Raphoe, he wrote of him to Rome: "It would be a good thing to write him a nice letter, encouraging him to keep up the good work and thanking him for his good services on behalf of our religion." A man of many journeys himself, Oliver was generous and hospitable to his numerous visitors to his humble abode. Whenever a principle in which he believed was at stake, he would defend it robustly and courageously and his pen could be quite sharp in this regard. He was gentle in manner as when he brought back Friar Harold, writing: "without any fuss and with gentle treatment." He had a sense of humour, which also surfaces occasionally. He could poke fun at the sheer irony of the many new and harsh laws enacted in London, yet he knew only too well that they would have a severe impact and could even be a matter of life and death for him. While Oliver and his relations remained loyal subjects of the king, this was not a concern of his; he was first, second and last, loyal to Holy Mother Church. He was a man willing to go much more than half way; having gone and negotiated a peace agreement with the Tories in their hideout, he then went guarantor for their safe passage to the continent, by going with them himself to see them safely on board ship.

He was innocent of favouritism or nepotism, although he had been accused of these and numerous other offences in his time. Thus, he wrote of a priest who was considered for promotion: "Christopher Farrell, the Dominican is a relative of mine, but flesh and blood will not restrain me from what is for the good of our religion and the mission here. Neither for learning nor for personal qualities is he very remarkable." Through the evidence of his letters, he kept meticulous records and accounts, recalling that he had confirmed, forty-eight thousand, six hundred and fifty five souls and that he had kept a list of them all. A diplomat, he built bridges between the different traditions and he was soon respected in all quarters, until the power and influence of bigoted politicians took control. Despite the hardships he endured of persecution and harsh climate, his letters portray him continuing in his work across the province, revealing to us a man of extraordinary stamina, steely determination, devotion to duty and of personal self-discipline. A good teacher to the last, he wrote shortly before his death: "Being the first among the Irish, with the grace of God, I shall give good example to the others not to fear death." Yet during his squabble with Archbishop Talbot over the primacy, his impatience and exasperation with the topic clearly shows in his letters to Rome; his friend Bishop John Brenan then of Waterford described Oliver as bad tempered and touchy on this question. Having apparently to fight against his own disposition, which was somewhat hot and hasty; Oliver it seems was not yet a saint, he was however working on it.

[1] Faul, Mgr. Denis 'St. Oliver and Louth Village' 1962/1975. p.13

52. LOYALTY TO THE HOLY SEE

Archbishop Oliver was renowned for his love and loyalty to the Holy See; continuing the fine tradition of the Irish Church in this regard. He knew all the while that this loyalty would guarantee the faithfulness of the Irish people in the true faith. Even as far back as the early seventh century, St. Columbanus wrote the following to Pope Boniface: "For we Irish are disciples of St. Peter and St. Paul, and of all the divinely inspired canonical writers, adhering constantly to the evangelical and apostolical doctrine. Amongst us neither Jew, heretic, nor schismatic can be found; but the Catholic faith, entire and unshaken, precisely as we have received it from you, who are the successors of the holy Apostles. For, as I have already said, we are attached to the chair of St. Peter; and although Rome is great and renowned, yet with us it is great and distinguished only on account of that apostolic chair. Through the two Apostles of Christ you are almost celestial, and Rome is the head of the churches of the world." A Jesuit report of the Cromwellian era of the mid 1650's states: "So tenaciously and indomitable has the whole nation clung to the Catholic faith in its full integrity and purity, that in a thousand Irishmen, scarcely one can be found who is not thoroughly devoted to the Holy See." Indeed, not one member of the Irish hierarchy over the centuries has ever dared to show open opposition to any ruling or exhortation emanating from the Holy See and it certainly wasn't going to happen during Oliver's Primacy.

He was obedient to any instruction or even suggestion coming to him from Rome and he wrote: "The Holy See is the chief physician, I am the under-physician and to me is entrusted a great number of patients…The will to cure this illness is not enough for us under-physicians; the proto-physician must put his hands on it." This belief strongly permeated his thinking and he was always happy to seek and to receive advice or instructions from Rome, writing: "Teach what you command, command what you will, I shall carry out your command." It is interesting to note that some of Oliver's reforms were concerned with implementing the Council of Trent which had concluded some one-hundred and twenty years earlier. Yet we in the twenty-first century are often tempted to believe that the reforms of the Second Vatican Council of the 1960's should have been fully implemented within a short space of fifty years. Loyalty to the Holy Father had always been a characteristic of the Church in Ireland, but at a critical time when matters were potentially on a downhill slide, Oliver's strong and consistent loyalty to the See of Peter, helped in no small measure to reinforce in Ireland that essential charism of Christ's Church on earth.

53. ALCOHOL

Oliver maintained a high standard of conduct for himself, a professor for twelve years and as an Archbishop; he was a teacher to his core and ever mindful of the opportunities to teach the laity, the priests or even his fellow bishops by word and especially by example. One of the decrees from the synod in Clones forbade priests from drinking whiskey or frequenting taverns. He was patient yet firm in his correction of abuses, always insisting on high standards and there are also numerous examples where he is quick to forgive those who were mending their ways. Worried about drunkenness, Oliver, who had owned a small vineyard in Italy, cut out alcohol in order to give good example. Within months of his return to Ireland, he made a visitation[1] of the Northern Province after which he wrote: "I noted that the prevailing vice was the excessive drinking of beer and especially whiskey… I gave a great deal of attention to trying to eradicate this cursed vice, which is mother and nurse to all sorts of scandals and disputes…I ordered under pain of privation of benefices that priests refrain from frequenting taverns and from taking whiskey, and indeed the results were very gratifying, these past few months only two priests, and this on one occasion only, were drunk…Let us remove this defect from an Irish priest and he will be a saint." At the Provincial Synod in Clones, which was held less than six months after his return to Ireland, drinking at wakes was prohibited as was the practice of all night wakes. Concerned in this regard about the appointment of Daniel Mackay as the Bishop of Down and Connor, he asked Rome to send him a strong letter of warning so that he would not give bad example in the matter of excessive drinking.

It is interesting to note that the temperance movement which sprung out of sheer necessity in the nineteenth century had many branches dedicated to Oliver Plunkett. Cardinal Moran in his 1895, 'Memoir of Oliver Plunket,' states that many temperance societies had been formed under Oliver's patronage and that numerous successful outcomes had been realised where families had placed their prayers under his patronage, writing: "I may add that instances are known in which families that prayed to God to banish drunkenness from amongst them, and placed their prayers under the protection of the martyred Primate, have had the wished for blessing granted to them in a most wonderful manner."

Suggestion: One of Oliver's charisms was working for the eradication of alcohol abuse. Many families in the twenty-first century are driven apart by the curse of excessive alcohol usage or the misuse of drugs, perhaps there may be a remedy for groups, families or individuals to invoke St. Oliver's willing intercession in this regard.

[1] Bennett Fr. Martin 'Blessed Oliver Plunkett' London 1973. p.48

54. Reports on Archdiocese of Armagh

Oliver sent a report of his diocese to Rome: "The city I speak of, by the way is Drogheda, called Dreat in Irish or Pontana in Latin. It is about five hours journey time from Dublin and is the finest city in Ireland after Dublin." He reported that it had a population of six-thousand souls the majority being Protestant. The town had communities of Franciscans, Dominicans, Augustinians and he himself brought in the Jesuits for his new schools. Dundalk had a population of two thousand, a quarter of whom were Catholic and it had a Franciscan community. Ardee the seat of justice for the region with the county jail had a population of five hundred families but only a few of those were Catholic. Armagh had a population of three-thousand, almost all Scottish or English and although there were hardly any Catholics it had a community of Franciscans. Carlingford had a community of Dominicans. Of Oliver's diocese, Cardinal Tomás Ó Fiaich, estimated that there were between forty[1] and forty-two parishes; fifty-six priests along with forty to fifty religious. The archdiocese was seventy miles long and fifty miles broad.

[1] Ó Fiaich & Forristal 'Oliver Plunkett' Indiana, USA 1976. Ó Fiaich. p.34

55. POVERTY

His income from the diocese was tiny in comparison to his needs; it was the norm for the fifty-six priests in the archdiocese to give him a contribution of about a pound each year but this only amounted to a possible maximum of sixty pounds per year. Later he wrote that his income from his diocese never exceeded fifty pounds or two hundred scudi. Usually he received much less than this and during the years of persecution or famine he got almost nothing, as priests and people were so poor themselves. Bishop Brenan reported in a letter that the priests of Ireland were the poorest in the world and that the same dues given by people to the priests had also to be given to the Protestant ministers. In contrast to his own poverty at the time, Oliver estimated that the income of the Protestant Archbishop of Armagh was five thousand pounds per annum as a result of owning massive estates. Without the help of relative and friend benefactors, Oliver could not have survived nor could he have

Pawn shops were used by Archbishop Oliver

performed his ministry in any meaningful way. His relatives maintained his servant James McKenna which was a great help. However, Oliver was in really serious financial straits for almost all of his time as Archbishop. Colonel John Fitzpatrick and other Catholic benefactors kept him afloat at times, but even with those supporters he seemed to be constantly short of money. He had spent large sums of money on the schools, on his voluminous correspondence and he had incurred travel expenses on his numerous visitations or on the settling of all sorts of disputes in diverse parts of the country. Despite his shortage of money, Oliver was renowned for his generous hospitality to travellers and his frequent charity towards those in need.

Forever in debt, he wrote that if he had been in other employment: "The baker's bill would long since have been settled." Elsewhere, he wrote that the schools were indebted to the butcher, brewer and baker to the tune of forty pounds alone in the previous year. He often wrote to Rome to help him in his ministry as he had been promised that his expenses with regard to the schools would be reimbursed but the grants always followed any expenditure; seemed slow in coming and after the destruction of the schools, he was left in debt. He wrote of using pawn shops on at least two occasions, once during the famine of 1674 and again while he was imprisoned, some six years later. His outgoings for the time he was in prison left him greatly in debt and he wrote: "My expenses have been and will be intolerable." One can just imagine his servant James McKenna, bartering for a better price from the pawn-broker, and of course James's expenses in prison also had to be taken care of. As Oliver's servant, James was destined to spend numerous occasions in prison, which added to Oliver's financial burden.

Archbishop Oliver could have spared both himself and his wallet if he behaved as some others might, by taking it relatively easy and living the quiet life, but that was not his style. No, so much work needed to be accomplished and so many reforms needed to be implemented. As we have seen, Oliver was sparing on his clothing, housing, food, alcohol and was well used to hardship, yet even in the relatively good times and the peaceful atmosphere of 1672 he was still poor having spent all his resources on his ministry. He often wrote to Rome requesting money to help with his state of affairs and in the same year he wrote: "If I should die tomorrow who would pay my debts, I would not have a halfpenny to take care of my burial or have Masses said, nor would I have thought that after so many labours I should be reduced to living from hand to mouth, I commend myself to your kindness to help me in Rome, so that I may recover at least a part of what I spent and be able to pay my debts." Throughout his ministry as archbishop he was short of money, but during the bad times of famine or persecution and in the years when he endured both, he literally lived a hand to mouth existence, writing: "The Bishop of Waterford and I would greedily gobble down a piece of oaten bread."

56. STILL A MAN OF CHARITY

He showed his concern for the plight of the people on many occasions, the distress caused to the ordinary people by the actions of the Tories; the poverty of those left without land or a proper means of support, writing: "It would break your heart to see the great families… who were princes in the time of Elizabeth…deprived of their property… and yet with joy they accepted their spoliation for the sake of the faith." He was especially concerned about the total lack of educational opportunities for Catholics. As a young man Oliver had been well trained in acts of charity by his tutor Fr. Patrick Plunkett and also by Fr. Scarampi in Rome. Oliver wrote of Bishop Patrick after his death: "He died a poor man, because being a wealthy man in his lifetime he gave alms freely, his right hand did not know what his left hand did and he never denied alms to any poor person, he frequently gave secret help to the poor, ashamed gentlemen and widows, of whom we have many since the extermination carried out by Cromwell." Fr. Scarampi had organised

Oliver's apprenticeship in compassion in the hospital and in a home for the destitute in Rome, writing: "I also rendered special service with Mr. Marcantonio Odescalchi, often assisting him when he served the wretched beggars, needy and full of vermin, whom he gathered together in a house with all expenses paid by him, even to their clothing, often he cleaned and fed them with his own hands."

Marangoni, a famed Italian writer and Oratorian, wrote[1] sometime later of Oliver's time in Rome: "Here it is incredible with what zeal he burned for the salvation of souls. In the house itself and in the city he wholly devoted himself to devout exercises; frequently did he visit the sanctuaries steeped with the blood of so many martyrs and he ardently sighed for the opportunity of sacrificing himself for the salvation of his countrymen. He moreover frequented the hospital of Santo Spirito and employed himself even in the most abject ministrations, serving the sick poor to the edification and wonder of the very officials and assistants of that place." Oliver carried on that tradition as exemplified when he pawned two silver candlesticks and a silver cup during the awful famine of 1674. He did this, so as to be able to provide bread for the poor to the value of one pound each week. He recounted that even in his absence the poor would come to the cabin which was his home and they would say: "Where shall we find alms if not in our Primate's house." Most people would say: 'I'm very sorry, but I don't have any money.' Oliver on the other hand pawned his silver candle sticks which he had almost certainly brought with him from Rome, so as to provide food for the needy. Even on his journey home to his diocese as he travelled through England, he wrote on two occasions for a position to be found for Christian Coles a Catholic girl; again most people would say, 'it is not my concern, I'm only passing through on my journey' but not Oliver. There may be lessons there for us to follow in the twenty-first century.

---

[1] Ó Fiaich & Forristal 'Oliver Plunkett' Indiana USA 1976 Forristal. p.142

57. THE YEAR 1672

Viceroy Berkeley was replaced by Arthur Capell, the Earl of Essex and Oliver who was unsure of the attitude the new viceroy would adopt, wrote: "Until I see how the wind will blow I shall navigate very cautiously." Summoned to meet him, Oliver must have been relieved somewhat after the interview and the climate of toleration did not change a great deal for some time afterwards. The law was enforced with varying degrees of harshness and people today would be appalled at some of the statutes, for example Oliver relates: "There is the custom here that on the occasion of the baptism of Catholic infants, one shilling is offered to the priest, and two shillings to the Protestant minister as commanded by law, and although it was a heavy burden it was tolerated and the money was paid." The Protestant clergy while branding Catholic devotions and sacraments as idolatrous, nevertheless they seemed more than happy to accept or indeed to insist that the greater part of the offering would be received by them.

Oliver's extensive visitations continued, he held a diocesan synod in May 1672 and he travelled to Ardagh to settle the dispute about the new vicar. He deposes vicar Patrick McColyn of Clogher diocese, as a frequenter of taverns and he recalled an[1] incident concerning him: "I was in the palace of a distinguished knight named John Bellew, near Dundalk one day, having been invited to dinner, when along came this McColyn to speak to me about certain matters. There were some Protestant gentlemen present. He was so drunk that he could not stand up. Just imagine how embarrassed I was. The following day I reprimanded him severely. He promised to amend, but did not do so...I warned him not three but six or seven times...I removed him from office and appointed instead Edward Drumgoole." Fr. Edward Drumgoole was a key man in the diocese of Armagh and he was released from Clogher the following year when the newly appointed, Bishop Duffy came to his diocese.

Oliver's very high work rate continued and he wrote: "I shall not spare myself fatigue" elsewhere he wrote: "I labour night and day in the affairs of my calling, and I neither give rest to my brain nor sleep to my eyes, and may it be to the greater glory of God and the service of the holy see, which is the spreading of the holy faith." And at another time he wrote: "I did not give repose to brain, pen or even horses these four years, in a vast province of eleven dioceses." Many were worried about the effect all this hard work was having on his health, but from his own personal sea-going experiences, he wrote: "whenever a sailor has a fair wind he would set full sail." He certainly unfurled all sails as he could soon write: "I have not undertaken a single difficult assignment since my arrival in this country that God has not prospered," and elsewhere, he wrote: "All my undertakings so far, have been successful." Slowly but surely he was making progress on all fronts including the discipline of the clergy which had improved a great deal. The supporters of the Remonstrance were by then well on the wane and he often mentions them in his correspondence. He said that he used 'craft' to send them away from his province, by winning over pious and good gentlemen who proceeded to discredit them everywhere, until they were no longer welcome; imitating the patriarch he was able to direct the actors from the wings.

[1] Hanly 'The Letters' No.116

58. CLOUDS GATHERING

King Charles made a royal 'Declaration of Indulgence' in March 1672 which would have allowed freedom of religious worship to Catholics and indeed to Protestant nonconformists who were also harshly treated at times. Parliament was very unhappy with this and the Cavalier elements were strong enough to force the retraction of the declaration in the following year. Parliament then passed the Test Acts in that same year, forcing anyone in public office to take communion in an Anglican church and to explicitly deny the Catholic belief in the real presence of Christ in Holy Communion or the belief of transubstantiation. Although

Oliver was almost suffocated in a snow drift while on the run

King Charles II was receiving large sums of money from King Louis XIV of France each year, his lack of financial independence left him reliant on Parliament. He still wore the crown but was often powerless against his opponents, to whom he owed that crown in the first place. During his stopover[1] in London Oliver had written: "The King asked for two million pounds in order to pay his debts, but the parliament declared they would only grant him a quarter of a million and fifty thousand more, should France declare war against the Dutch. As the government has no money we shall continue neutral. The parliament often engages the King in foreign wars and then refuses to grant supplies, in order that in his need he may be dependent on them."

The puritans were gaining in strength and their attacks were becoming more and more focussed against the Catholics. The Stuarts already had a history of betraying their friends in order to appease their enemies. In order to placate parliament, the king ordered the expulsion of bishops and religious from Ireland. Father Howard wrote from London: "The King of England made his excuses to me in regard of the late edict against the Catholics. His intention in publishing this edict was to favour the Catholics. Had he not published it the parliament would assuredly have enacted a similar decree which would be an irrevocable law, whilst on the contrary when it was the king's doing, it was in his power to connive at the Catholics, and recall the edict when the occasion presented itself." Meanwhile Archbishop Oliver was at his busiest keeping four horses well exercised, and he knew neither rest nor comfort. He was not aware at the time, that he would soon experience some rest but certainly no comfort. It had become known that James the Duke of York, heir to the throne had become a Catholic and this fact was causing consternation in parliament. As a result, he was forced to resign as Lord High Admiral in 1673. Indeed some fourteen years later as the Catholic King James II, he would try to proclaim a similar Declaration of Indulgence and it would also provoke a major backlash, ultimately leading to the 'Glorious Revolution,' the Battle of the Boyne and his daughter and son in law, jointly ascending the throne as the Protestant Queen Mary II and King William III of Orange.

Towards the end of 1673, with the Test Act enacted, there was renewed persecution against Roman Catholics. Church leaders soon became hunted men and handsome rewards were offered for their capture. They were forced to flee to some quiet place in the mountains or woods until such time as the situation might improve. Each new meeting of the Parliament in London brought with it a foreboding of what new law might be enacted and a fear of which of the existing penal laws might be enforced more stringently. Oliver wrote in November 1673: "The bishops have all been put under the ban, so also the vicar generals and all the heads of the clergy. Only the parish priests remain, leaderless and like the scattered twigs of a brush. No Catholic may possess[2] or carry fire-arms, nor would they even be allowed swords were it not for our viceroy." Parish priests were allowed to function but only just, if a complete ban was introduced on all things Catholic, there was a danger that the Catholics might rebel, as they had done some thirty years earlier during the Confederation of Kilkenny. Archbishop Oliver was the only active bishop in his province of eleven dioceses for the greater part of the previous three years. Bishop Patrick Plunkett at this stage was getting on in years, having already carried the torch of faith throughout the whole country, as the only active bishop for some years previously.

Oliver wrote that the time had arrived: "To take down the sails and seek shelter in some safe harbour." This was a defining moment for Oliver, as previously he had been operating in a sort of twilight zone, functioning illegally, but by steering clear of politics and keeping a relatively low profile, he had been tolerated to a degree. While he was summoned to meet the viceroy on numerous occasions, these visits were all clandestine and he entered through the secret door on each occasion. Now, the law was to be strictly enforced, he was under the ban. All bishops were ordered to report to one of the larger ports and wait there for transport to the continent as exiles; the houses of the religious were also closed. By this time Oliver had yet again, destroyed all his papers, documents, files and his meticulous records. The religious houses also destroyed their records and as a result, many details of our history were lost yet again. This latest clamp down put a stop to all the petty feuding within the Church and indeed over the following century or so, the harshness of the penal laws were destined to put an end to many of the major cultural differences between the Catholics of Gaelic Ireland and those of the old Anglo Irish.

Oliver reported that the reward for the capture of a bishop had been increased to ten pounds. He emphatically refused to go into exile and he exhorted his fellow bishops to stay and weather the storm, otherwise most would have gone abroad as so many had done in previous generations. Taking the stand that he did, he copper fastened the idea for future generations that a bishop's place is with his people, writing: "Bishop Forstall of Kildare would have departed but I hindered him, for if the captains fly, it is in vain to exhort the single soldiers to stand in battle."

His old friend John Brenan then Bishop of Waterford and who later on became Archbishop of Cashel, hid with him in the hill country of South Armagh. Without lodging, he was left to his own devices in open countryside and to seek shelter in caves, huts or in abandoned shelters. Oliver wrote: "The Catholic laity are so much afraid of losing their property that nobody with anything to lose gives lodging to either bishop or religious, and although the secular priests have toleration and may remain on, the Catholic faithful are somewhat afraid to admit them to say Mass in their houses, and the priests give nothing to bishops or ordinaries, nor will they even approach them. I count myself fortunate now and again to obtain a little barley bread, and the house where Bishop Brenan and I are in is made of straw and is roofed in such a way that from the bed we can see the stars, and at the head of the bed every small shower of rain refreshes us, but we would rather die of hunger and cold than abandon our flock. It would be a shame if spiritual soldiers reared and trained in Rome should become hirelings." He concludes that letter by writing: "May the Lord God be ever praised and his most holy Mother." His reference to hirelings no doubt referring to the Gospel of St. John, chapter 10:13. "The hired man runs away because he is only a hired man and does not care about the sheep." In another letter he wrote: "If they come to me, praised be God, may they be welcome, either we shall suffer or we shall die, certainly we shall not be hirelings; with the halter around our throats they will drag us to the ship, otherwise we shall not abandon either lambs or sheep." He also reports: "In this country there is a fixed force of eight thousand soldiers between infantry and cavalry and these are now distributed throughout the counties and districts. It is thought that they will be ordered to help the police to hunt down the prelates and religious." One incident records them moving from one hiding place to a more secure one, having been informed that agents who were actively seeking them were getting closer.

The following is just a short extract from a letter dated 27th. January 1674 and describes their predicament: "Snow mixed with big hard hailstones was falling, a cutting wind was blowing into our faces and the snow and hail blew so strongly into our eyes and affected them so much that we are hardly able to use them even yet. Finally, after frequent danger of being suffocated by the snow in the valleys, we arrived at the house of a poor gentleman who had nothing to lose, but through bad fortune he had a stranger in the house, by whom we did not wish to be recognised, and so he put us in a fine room under the roof where we have remained without chimney or fire for eight days now, may it be for the glory of God and the good of our souls and of the flock committed to us. The cold and the hailstones were so rigorous that up to now the eyes both of my companion and myself have been trickling water, and I think I shall lose more than one tooth because they are giving me severe pain. My companion has several ulcers on his arm and can barely use it. It can be truly said that our flight was in winter and on the sabbath."

In the same letter, Oliver praises God for the grace they received to suffer on the feast of the Chair of St. Peter and he hoped that in the long run it would break the violence of the tempestuous waves. Oliver continues: "We shall not abandon our flocks unless compelled to do so, we shall first try out the prisons and other torments, already we have suffered so much on the mountains, in huts and caves, and have acquired the habit of suffering to the extent that it will be less inconvenient and difficult in the future…We shall flee to the mountains and caves in which these past fifteen months we have put in a very strict novitiate." Of that famine of 1674, he wrote: "The Bishop of Waterford and I would greedily gobble down a piece of oaten bread." And it must have given him no satisfaction at all to be able to report: "All the convents and novitiates have been destroyed; this last decree has put a stop to the quarrels between the Dominicans and the Franciscans." Oliver was to suffer greatly with his eyes subsequently and he wrote again about this problem with his eyes in August 1678.

Chair of St Peter, Apse, St. Peter's Basilica, Rome

By February 1674, he had received news from London and he sent reports to Rome, yet despite the ominous signs he stills displays a hint of humour and irony: "Parliament there has talked nothing but religion… A new oath has been drawn up to be presented to all the Catholic inhabitants of London, and among its fine clauses is one worthy of note, namely, that the pope is a heretic…It has also decreed that the sons and daughters of the Duke of York should have a Protestant tutor, and that they should be removed from the palace…in order that the children might not be Catholics. They also passed another law that for the future it should be unlawful for the king or anyone of royal blood to marry a Catholic without the permission and good pleasure of parliament. The king can pick servants as it pleases him, but not a wife. I believe that before long he will not be able to send away a footman without taking off his cap to parliament."

In May of that year he recounted another interesting situation which he had to endure: "I am all alone in an old granary which belongs to a farmer who brings me some bread and a little butter from the nearby town, and whenever this man drinks too much in town, I must fast for more than one day. Milk is the usual beverage and it is dear to buy, and when I get it fresh it seems to be as sweet and delightful as the wine of Albano or Genzano. I have however two consolations, one is interior, namely that I suffer for a good cause, and this will have its result, so I hope in the Divine Mercy, an eternal reward. The second consolation is in my books, which enable me to say that I am never less alone than when alone, never less solitary than when solitary." There were no half measures with Oliver and he now immersed himself completely with the Irish people, hiding in the Irish countryside and refusing the easy option of exile. Although he did not know it at the time, this decision would later cost him his life. Retiring to some hovel with his books and candles, would have been like the monks of old living in their cells, all the while praying, writing and developing their interior life. He had a great love of books and learning and he surely used this time wisely to catch up on his reading, prayer and study. He had taken another step on his journey to sainthood.

Elsewhere he writes that his diet on occasions consisted of just a little oaten bread. As a result of a wet autumn and a bad winter with ice and snow, he recounted that it was impossible to sow crops and consequently most of the cattle, horses and sheep, the wealth of the country had died. He reported that the resulting famine claimed the lives of five hundred people in the diocese of Armagh alone during the year 1674. His income was minimal, as the parish clergy were so poor themselves. As the persecution tightened its grip, he wrote in that same year: "As in the primitive Church, it was as if the persecutions of the early Church had returned."

He reports: "Sometimes it happens that a parish which one year has two hundred Catholic families will not have thirty the following year, as happened in various parishes of the diocese of Armagh this year, because the Catholics being as a rule, lease holders, often lose their leases." These leases would be given to families of other religions and he added: "When a new colony of them arrives, the poor Catholics are put aside." He recounted that one could travel twenty five miles in his area and only find a half a dozen Catholic families within that territory. He also noted that in the previous year his income was very small and that the priests were greatly harassed, not daring to appear openly by day, especially around Armagh. He reports one close call as follows: "One of the criminal justices along with some police came to the house where I have my hideout, to seek some thieves. I was standing ready for Mass, you can imagine what dread I was in. But the poor farmer who owned the house told them that the thieves were in the nearby wood and immediately they set out as fast as possible and we were free."

[1] Moran, Cardinal Patrick 'Memoir of Oliver Plunket' Dublin 1895. p.49
[2] Hanly 'The Letters' No.144

59. RESPITE OF SORTS

The political situation eased somewhat after about seven months and he was able to continue in his ministry. However, Oliver would never again have the freedom which he had experienced over the previous three years or so. Not at all impressed with Bishop O'Molony of Killaloe, Oliver informed Rome that Bishop Brenan was then the only resident bishop in the province of Cashel as: "Bishop O'Molony abandoned his flock and went to France." Determined not to do likewise, Oliver wrote of the great dangers of a leaderless church. He continued on his visitations for another four years or so, travelling from Meath to Donegal, from Ardagh to Antrim, constantly on the alert, often travelling after dark and keeping out of sight during the day. Staying in the woods, caves or in such shelter which might be offered to him, putting himself at risk and also those caught offering such shelter. He wrote: "I shall not spare myself fatigue," and also: "I did not give repose to brain, pen or even horses these four years, in a vast province of eleven dioceses."

Upon the death of Pope Clement X, Oliver recounted in a letter to Rome, "I wrote to the suffragan dioceses earnestly inviting all the clergy and people to beg the Divine Mercy for the eternal salvation of the deceased father of all Christians, and for a speedy election of a saintly successor to St. Peter. Now, at the instance of your Lordship and by the obedience which I owe my superiors I shall write again to all the dioceses, and I shall not for my part be wanting with my poor prayers in a matter of such importance." Sometime later Oliver could express his great joy at the election of his old friend Cardinal Odescalchi as Pope Innocent XI. He wrote: "While I was a professor of theology and controversies for many years in Propaganda College, I had first-hand experience of the saintly life led by his Holiness, and of the high reputation for wisdom, prudence and piety which all had of him. I also rendered special service with Mr. Marcantonio Odescalchi, often assisting him when he served the wretched beggars, needy and full of vermin, whom he gathered together in a house with all expenses paid by him, even to their clothing, often he cleaned and fed them with his own hands. There has arisen in me the duty of preaching to the people what I saw and experienced, so that they may raise their hands to heaven in thanksgiving to the Divine majesty and in supplication for long life to his Holiness." Pope Innocent XI was beatified by Pope Pius XII in 1956.

Fr. Luke Plunkett was appointed vicar of Derry diocese, he was a relative and Oliver wrote of him "He has suffered a great deal for his function as vicar, being twice imprisoned by the Protestants and put on trial, but his defence was so carefully prepared that he was released. Once he was taken at midnight and although ill was dragged two miles to prison, and his zeal is such that no persecution was sufficient to separate him from his flock, he has indeed borne the burden of the day and the heat." Oliver, who was determined to wear out rather than rust, continued to travel widely around the province and it is known that he had in earlier years visited Connaught and Munster. Perhaps his only holiday was a month long visit to meet relatives in Munster in 1676, although it must have been more akin to a busman's holiday as he soon reported to Rome

Archbishop Hugh MacMahon, brought the Relic of the Head of Oliver to Ireland in c.1720

on the state of the dioceses of Cashel and Waterford. To his credit, by visiting all four provinces of Ireland during his tenure as Primate of Ireland, Archbishop Oliver had shown himself willing to make considerable exertions and put up with any discomforts such long trips would necessarily entail. Earlier he had written: "I wander through the mountains even in the midst of the snow, often without fire, without bread." His eyes never quite recovered from all these hardships and in 1678 he wrote: "The distillation from my eyes has greatly increased because of the disastrous visitation of the northern mountains, I can hardly read or write letters even as big as headlines, but there was no check on my tongue from preaching in both the English and Irish languages." Despite these difficulties there was no check either on his letter writing, indeed that letter contained well over a thousand words and his next letter to Rome followed shortly afterwards is of equal length.

Oliver was interested to know about the prophecy of St. Malachy, a predecessor of his as Archbishop of Armagh. In particular with regard to what St. Malachy is supposed to have foretold about the Church in Ireland becoming clothed once again with beauty, after having to endure seven centuries of desolation and suffering. He received a detailed reply[1] from distinguished Benedictine, J. Mabillon, which is listed in Moran.

[1] Moran Cardinal Patrick 'Memoir of Oliver Plunket' Dublin 1895. p.240

60. RENEWED PERSECUTION

The Provincial Synod of Ardpatrick requested Oliver to undertake what was expected to be another arduous visitation of the whole province; while the Synod requested it, it may well have been at his own prompting. He completed a visitation of Meath and had barely finished a visitation of the diocese of Clonmacnoise when news arrived of the imprisonment of Archbishop Talbot. News also broke of new decrees emanating from London, ordering the banishment of all bishops and religious from the country. Oliver informed Rome: "And threatening fines and other penalties to any person who would give them food or drink, or assistance of any kind." Archbishop Talbot had returned to Ireland in May 1678, after a five year exile and was arrested a few months later. As he was quite ill, he was carried by sedan chair to be imprisoned in Dublin Castle. Later that same year the anti-Catholic plot of Titus Oates was hatched leading to increased persecution throughout the country and the price on the capture of a bishop was increased to ten pounds. This was an enormous sum of money at the time, particularly for the impoverished majority. London had seen hardship during the 1660's with plagues, fire[1] and wars, but the kingdom experienced mass hysteria in the latter part of the 1670's as more and more false revelations against the Catholics were coming to light.

At Oliver's suggestion, Rome had appointed Bishop John Brenan of Waterford and Lismore as the Archbishop of Cashel in 1677, in addition to looking after Waterford & Lismore. Bishop Brenan[2] wrote after St. Oliver's martyrdom: "The Catholics of the Kingdom for many years past, and particularly since 1678, lived amid incredible hardships – the laity, on account of their Catholic faith, being incapacitated for holding any office, public, military or civil, and the ecclesiastics, even more than the laity, being assailed by the fury of our adversaries. Notwithstanding the perversity of the times the Archbishop (Plunkett) remained always in his residence, and though concealed, he contrived to maintain correspondence with his vicar's general and with the leading gentry in the district, instructing and directing the former as to the due watchfulness and solicitude for the salvation of the flock and comforting the latter to remain firm in the ancient faith, and fervent in the practice of patience and the other Christian virtues amid such miseries and tribulations, and, through the grace of God, not one ecclesiastic of this district apostatized from the faith during the whole time, nor anyone of the laity, who all remained immovable in exalted patience and tolerance." Oliver recounted that police, soldiers and spies go hunting night and day and that he was morally certain of being captured. In spite of this he remained in his diocese and had absolutely no intention of leaving.

Throughout his ministry as Archbishop of Armagh, Oliver was forever on the lookout for potential leaders, either bishops or vicars for the various dioceses. For this reason he regularly sought training for priests as he was only too well aware of the consequences and dangers of a leaderless Church, writing: "Without leaders, without shepherds, the wolves will devour the sheep." Just as in 1674, Oliver decided he was not going anywhere and he declared his determination to remain with his flock. New edicts were issued which decreed that if the perpetrator of any illegality was not killed or caught within a fortnight then the local parish priest would be arrested and transported. Oliver was happy to work and comply with any benign Caesar when conditions allowed, but whenever the tide turned, Archbishop Oliver was not for turning or for complying. His example ensured that the days of the émigré or exiled bishop should be well and truly over. Often accused of being too conversant with the establishment, he repeatedly denied this, saying that any contact he had with the authorities was to the great advantage of priests and people; he proved his point by going on the run and becoming a wanted man. He wrote in 1679: "We are like sick persons, who when they commence to become convalescent, rise prematurely from bed, to fall with great impetus."

[1] See Chapter 21
[2] Power Canon P. 'A Bishop of Penal Times' Cork 1932. p.88

61. THE STUART KINGDOMS

As King Charles II had no legitimate children, his brother James, the Duke of York was next in line to the throne. James was a Catholic and there was huge and an ever growing opposition to the possibility of a Catholic on the throne. The Test Act which had been enacted by parliament in 1673 was strengthened in 1678, forcing all office holders to take oaths of allegiance and of supremacy. It also insisted that any office holder must receive communion according the rites of the Protestant religion and renounce completely any beliefs in the Roman Catholic doctrine of transubstantiation, the invocation of saints and of the Mass. At the instigation of Lord Shaftesbury, the House of Commons passed the Exclusion Bill in May 1679 which would prevent James ever succeeding King Charles to the throne, but the House of Lords rejected

King Charles II

it. Shortly afterwards Charles suspended parliament and on 12th July dissolved it. The Earl of Shaftesbury and some others in England had whipped up anti-Catholic feeling for political ends in their continuing battle with the Monarchy. The civil war may have been over but civil war politics continued unabated.

With the distinct possibility of a Catholic king and the great paranoia of those times came Titus Oates, 'the saviour of the nation,' with his extraordinary stories of plots by Catholics at home and abroad to foist their faith upon the people of the kingdoms. The finger of suspicion was pointed at many innocent people, who were jailed indefinitely and a score or so were martyred. In 1678, no priests had been executed for the previous eighteen years. Yet, eighteen were martyred over the following three years, culminating with Archbishop Oliver. A few others would have died a slow lingering sort of martyrdom during their stay in prison.

Interestingly and unknowingly to Archbishop Talbot, he may[1] well have had a small indirect part in Oliver's downfall. During his exile in France, Archbishop Talbot came to know an English secular priest, Fr. Sergeant who was also an exile. He later fell out with him and denounced a couple of Sergeant's books as heretical. A bitter war of words followed and the Archbishop of Paris imposed silence on both parties. This would have been the second time at least that silence was imposed on Archbishop Talbot, the first occasion after the squabble about the primacy with Archbishop Oliver. Fr. Sergeant was infected with many[2] of the modern ideas of the day and having been criticized himself, he denounced all and sundry, particularly the Jesuits who were seen as loyal to the Pope. He decided to return to England, undoubtedly thinking that he could both denounce his enemies and make a handsome profit at the same time. The Popish Plot was flagging slightly after the injustice of the martyrdom of the five Jesuits, but then it was reported that even more revelations were forthcoming from the well-known Fr. Sergeant. Going before the council, he told them of a great conspiracy and stated what the Jesuits taught: "That it was the duty of a good Catholic to kill the King." Fr. Sergeant had earlier been well known in England as a strong proponent of the Catholic faith and his fable was bound to hold some credence among the masses. As a result, Archbishop Talbot was also cited in the Popish Plot. This and other supposed revelations helped to revive the Popish Plot, which if left alone at the time, could well have died out before Oliver had ever been implicated in it.

[1] Major M.V.Hay 'The Jesuits and the Popish Plot' 1934
[2] McKee John 'A Martyr Bishop : The Life of St. Oliver Plunkett' Houston Texas 1975. p. 105

62. TITUS OATES

It was alleged by Titus Oates, that Catholics with the connivance of the Jesuits were plotting to kill the King, and the Pope was planning to organise an invasion of England. A thorough investigation was ordered and when Mr. Edmund Berry Godfrey an examining magistrate in London appeared to have been murdered, mass anti-Catholic hysteria ensued. Large demonstrations were held in the streets of the capital and effigies of the Pope were burned. Plots and rumours of plots were the order of the day, and within a period of about three years, King Charles signed the death warrants of twenty-three[1] innocent Catholics: 'I sign with tears in my eyes.'

Oates the son of an Anglican clergyman was expelled from two schools as a youth; he became a Baptist during the Puritan era, then reverted to Anglicanism and became a clergyman. Accused of perjury he absconded to become a chaplain on board ship. Coming back to England he was attached to the household of the Catholic Duke of Norfolk as an Anglican minister. He then converted to Catholicism and went to St. Omer's in France and Valladolid in Spain where he attended two Jesuit run colleges. However, he was soon expelled[2] in June 1678 from St. Omer's by Fr. Thomas Whitbread, one of the five Jesuit Martyrs of Tyburn. Within months, Oates was back in England, with stories of plots and he was able to give details of meetings, places, events and names, lots of names. Pointing the finger at many individuals, he gave his extraordinary account in great detail. It seemed as if any Catholic he had come across especially priests were woven into the plot and needless to say Archbishop Peter Talbot was also spun into his story. Oates even accused Queen Catherine of conspiring with the king's physician to poison the king. King Charles interrogated Oates and caught him out in some aspects of his story and ordered his arrest, but within a short time parliament forced his release and feted him instead. They provided him with a fine apartment in Whitehall, and an annual allowance of over one thousand pounds per year. In a rare and good year, Archbishop Oliver received fifty pounds from his diocese.

Titus Oates

Titus Oates was regaled as savour of the nation. His friend Israel Tongue and some other opportunistic discoverers also named scores upon scores of people who were supposedly involved in the plot, nearly all of them priests. Amongst those implicated was Fr. Dominic Maguire, a Dominican priest chaplain to the Spanish Ambassador; he was questioned[3] but released because he was attached to the Spanish embassy. Within a few years he was destined to become the next Archbishop of Armagh. Reports of conspiracies to kill the King were common because if such were to happen then James the Catholic Duke of York would automatically ascend to the throne. The exclusion crisis gathered momentum and James was obliged to go into exile in Edinburgh and Brussels for much of this period. Shaftsbury's party, the Whigs continued to whip up anti-Catholic feeling with annual marches and demonstrations. The aftermath of Titus Oates' life story is given in Chapter 95.

[1] Mc Kee 'A Martyr Bishop – The Life of St. Oliver Plunkett' Houston, Texas 1975. p. 141
[2] Kenyon John 'The Popish Plot' 1985
[3] Palmer C.F. 'The Life of Philip Thomas Howard, Cardinal of Norfolk' p.185

63. OLIVER'S ARREST

On 21st October 1679 the English Privy Council instructed Ormond to arrest Oliver, detailing vague information from Brussels that Archbishop Oliver along with the Bishop Tyrrell of Clogher and a Colonel John Fitzpatrick, were involved in the planning of a French invasion of Ireland. Colonel Fitzpatrick was a Catholic and was a brother in law of Ormond; he had been a friend and an important benefactor of Oliver but had since renounced his faith. Interestingly his mother, Brigid Darcy-Fitzpatrick from Platin near Drogheda, may appear on a list of Irish Catholic martyrs as she was burned at the stake[1] in Dublin in 1652 during Cromwell's commonwealth regime. Ormond was no doubt mindful that rumours of the involvement of his brother in law to bring the French into Ireland may have had repercussions against himself as viceroy. Civil war politics was also much in vogue amongst the higher echelons of society in Ireland and Ormond was seen as a royalist. Despite his possible misgivings, Ormond immediately followed his instructions from London by issuing a warrant to Sir Hans Hamilton in County

Armagh for the arrest of Archbishop Oliver.

Henry Jones the Protestant Bishop of Meath was in the opposing camp, having been involved some twenty years earlier as scoutmaster general with Cromwell's army. Ormond now appointed Jones to lead a commission of inquiry into the possibility of an Irish angle to the plot. Ormond believed that there was no real basis for the rumours, but by appointing a political opponent to lead the commission he felt that the matter might sooner be finished with. As in the case of possible plots and threats against the King, people might more readily believe a parliamentarian than a royalist like himself, particularly as his own brother in law was named as being complicit in the plot. Over the following months Bishop Jones was quite inventive and assiduous in discovering the Popish Plot from an Irish perspective; indeed he may have been the only prominent Protestant in Ireland who helped in the demise of Oliver Plunkett.

[1] Bennett Fr. Martin 'The Way of a Martyr' London 1974. p.78

64, IMPRISONED IN DUBLIN CASTLE

According to the registration of clergy records from 1704, Oliver ordained a twenty-four year[1] old Westmeath man to the priesthood, at Ardpatrick on 9th November 1679; Fr. Lewis Ferrall thus became Archbishop Oliver's last ordinand. Bishop Patrick Plunkett, Oliver's tutor of old died in Dublin a week or so later; this would have evoked many memories in Oliver. His teacher and advisor for many years, Bishop Patrick had entrusted the young Oliver into the care and patronage of Fr. Scarampi and both of his mentors were now dead. He had however learned a lot from both, particularly charity and compassion. Oliver secretly visited his cousin Bishop Patrick, who died on 18th November. A few weeks later on 6th December 1679, Oliver was apprehended and jailed in Dublin Castle. He was placed in a room close to that of

Archbishop Peter Talbot of Dublin. In disguise for this trip to Dublin, Oliver had shaved off his hair and beard and wore a light coloured wig. The authorities had become aware through the incaution of a priest that he was living near the Naul Co. Dublin as a Mr Meleady. Sir Hans Hamilton of Co. Armagh had simply informed a local priest that he needed to contact the primate urgently and the priest furnished him with Oliver's pseudo name, along with his disguise and the rough area in which he was based. The rest proved easy for a party of militia to track him down and arrest him. Oliver was kept in strict solitary confinement for six weeks in Dublin Castle while his papers were investigated, naturally nothing of an incriminating nature was found and he was then given a little more freedom. On 16th January 1680 he was allowed to have his servant James McKenna visit regularly, to bring him food, clothing and news from the outside. True to form, one of the first things

Dublin Castle - Prison

Oliver did was to write another fifteen hundred word letter to Rome. Sadly, much of this letter was taken up answering complaints which had been made against him and he wrote: "I console myself with patience on hearing the calumnies of that undisciplined friar, Anthony Daly…but I put up with these calumnies with I hope, spiritual profit, imitating my Saviour who suffered in the body and in His good name at the hands of opponents…" It seems from this, that Oliver even at the very beginning of his nineteen month prison term was already some way on his journey to sainthood. As was the custom of the time, Oliver was required to pay for his food and keep in prison and his poverty was such that he was forced to sell some property and to pawn his chalice and cross to help pay his bills.

King Charles II directed that all reports of a grand plot to bring in the French to Ireland should be kept secret and that Ormond should not have Oliver questioned about these matters. It was generally assumed, including by Oliver himself, that he was arrested because he had stayed on in hiding in Ireland, having refused to go into exile as directed by law. The King would not have put any great credence in a possible invasion of Ireland by the French, as he had already made a secret pact with the King Louis XIV in the Treaty of Dover and had received a very large grant from France each year for the previous decade. By July 1680 Oliver reported: "I am indebted at present to the extent of one-hundred and twenty five pounds. I have to pay one pound per week for a room for myself and two servants; not having the wherewithal to pay for my board, one of my servants brings food to me in a basket from the houses of two Catholic noblemen." James McKenna was reduced to going to pawn shops and scrounging food for the Primate and in order not to hurt Oliver's feelings on this or other occasions, he probably didn't relate the full story of his initiatives on his behalf or of any shame-faced refusals for help which he may have encountered at times.

---

[1] Concannon, Helena 'Blessed Oliver Plunket' Dublin 1935. Appendix V

65. PLOTTERS

It is a common and an erroneously held view that Archbishop Oliver was arrested only after a certain William Hetherington and a renegade priest, Fr. Edmund Murphy plotted against him. Oliver had in fact been arrested several months before Murphy and Hetherington had collaborated in a serious way as informers, but while they were not responsible for Archbishop Oliver's arrest, ultimately they greatly facilitated his demise. Fr. Edmund Murphy had been suspended from his parish by Archbishop Oliver in 1674 for his dealings with bandits and for drunkenness. As a Tory and a spy, Murphy had fallen out with Redmond O'Hanlon[1] the great Tory, who denounced Murphy and decreed that anyone who went to hear him would pay[1] one cow, on the second occasion, two cows and on the third occasion, lose his life. Murphy was later arrested and found himself in Dundalk jail on a charge of receiving stolen goods. Hetherington a Protestant, had been involved for several years in a quasi-military role to arrest Tories in various counties and had absconded from the Marshalsea debtor's prison in Dublin having faced the prospect of a long jail term until his debts were discharged. He also spent time in Dundalk jail where he met Murphy who told him that his own prosecutors, Lieutenant Baker and Ensign Smith were in alliance with the Tories. Murphy soon escaped from Dundalk jail and along with Hetherington they plotted how they could extricate themselves from their predicament. Hetherington badly needed money to pay off his debts. Murphy having already fallen out with the Tories was a wanted man in several quarters and was in desperate need to either prove his innocence or receive a pardon from government. He believed, proving his innocence would have been the easier option if his story was accepted that his prosecutors were in league with the Tories.

Having swapped stories with Hetherington, the pair soon became enmeshed as plotters and informers. Murphy went to viceroy Ormond in Dublin where he made a written deposition and stated his charge against his prosecutors; if proven, Murphy would be free. Ormond had no great sympathy for Murphy or for his story, writing that Murphy had made no mention whatsoever of a grand plot until he had placed him in prison and he was faced with the immediate prospect of a return to Dundalk Jail. Hetherington, who saw even greater potential than Murphy in the reporting of a conspiracy, went to Bishop Jones, whom he knew, both having served in Cromwell's army. Jones gave him expenses and a letter of introduction for Lord Shaftsbury in London, which was awash at the time with rumours of a Popish Plot and where Hetherington found many willing hearers of an Irish angle to the plot. Without delay, Lord Shaftesbury introduced him to the London Privy Council as coming from Ganderstown in County Louth; Hetherington, who knew that such a plot was all make believe, was somewhat cautious before the council, and stated that Edmund Murphy had the particulars of the plot in much greater detail than he. The council gave instructions that Hetherington should be given one hundred pounds and sent to Ireland to bring over witnesses of a grand plot. Corroborative evidence was needed from Ireland and who better to supply this than some of the suspended and renegade priests, whom Oliver had dealings with over the previous decade. Upon his return to Ireland, Hetherington had lots of dealings with Bishop Jones as he gathered Irish witnesses from within or without of prison, who were willing to give false evidence about a plot in Ireland.

Oliver's servant James, who was working on his behalf in dispelling such rumours in Dublin, became an anathema to the plotters. They reported him to the authorities and he was arrested in Dublin on 1st May 1680. He was sent to London where he was questioned before the Privy Council and the investigating committee. Denying all knowledge of a plot and unable to intimidate him, the council decided to send him back to Dublin where he could be interrogated before Moyer and Murphy. He was released shortly afterwards as they could not overawe him, nor get anything useful out of him in Dublin either.

Within weeks Hetherington was back in London with disgraced priests, Friar John Moyer (MacMoyer), Murphy and two more priests from the dioceses of Armagh, James Callaghan and Daniel Finan. These were examined at the Privy Council before the King on 7th May 1680, but they had difficulty making themselves understood. As Gaelic speakers their English like many of the other witnesses was often poor, although their difficulty in this instance may have been somewhat exaggerated at times. They were then ordered to write out sworn testimonies. Moyer said that he had seen a letter of Oliver's to the Secretary of Propaganda in Rome, stating that sixty-thousand men were ready but without arms in Ireland. King and council decided that Oliver should be tried in Ireland, arranging that the witnesses along with their depositions should be sent back to Ormond. The other two seemed more concerned about the Primate's jurisdiction and so Callaghan and Finan were not involved subsequently in the trial proper. Later, numerous villains were enlisted, priests and some lay people who were given various promises such as pardons, freedom from jail, land and money if they would testify against Oliver. With the exception of a couple of priests who were arrested and forced to travel, all of the remainder were

ready, willing and able to swear if need be, that black was white. Meanwhile in Dublin Castle, Oliver was able to brush past the prison guards in June 1680 where he reconciled with and absolved Peter Talbot the dying Archbishop of Dublin. In the interim, London had sent word to the Dublin authorities, stipulating that Oliver should be tried before an all Protestant jury.

[1] See Chapter 40
[2] Murphy Edmund 'The perfect State and Condition of Ireland etc.' London 1681. p.2

66. ARRAIGNMENT AT DUNDALK

Oliver was sent for trial to Dundalk assizes on 23rd July 1680. Two days earlier the English Privy Council had stipulated that the trial should only take place in Dublin, but the order arrived too late to be followed. At the arraignment in Dundalk, Oliver was not allowed any defence council and he raised no objection whatsoever to the all Protestant jury. Friar Moyer and Fr. James Callaghan had made depositions which were placed before the court in evidence. It seems that Callaghan, another parish priest of the divided parish of Killeavy, may also have seen a chance to get rid of Oliver, although in his case he may only have wished to see him found guilty of Premunire. In Oliver's first letter from prison, dated 17th January 1680, he refutes the allegation that he had summoned witnesses to accuse Callaghan of the crimes of treason; so it seems that Callaghan was already in trouble with the authorities, undoubtedly Tory related. It is therefore more likely that Callaghan had come forward to seize on an opportunity to get himself out of trouble. Shortly afterwards, he was deprived of his parish on the instructions of Oliver, but remarkably he was restored to it in[1] 1683. Prosecution witnesses, Murphy and Moyer did not turn up at the trial in Dundalk, being disreputable characters who were themselves wanted men in Dundalk, so the trial was aborted on the second day. By this time, it must have been finally dawning on Oliver that there was a determined effort afoot to convict him not on a minor charge such as Premunire, which amounted to foreign jurisdiction from the Pope or even of the lesser charge of refusing the command to leave the country, but that there may be much more serious charges pending. Even so, spending the four nights in Dundalk, Oliver could still joke: "I was conducted back to the royal castle of Dublin to my former cell, a very expensive one, but considering the shortness of the time, Dundalk was even more expensive." The old jail in Dundalk was situated at the corner of Yorke Street and Church Street.

He also wrote: "I had thirty-two witnesses, priests, friars and lay people, all prepared to contradict what the friar had sworn… that I had seventy thousand Catholics prepared to murder all the Protestants, and to establish the Catholic religion and popish superstition here, that I had sent agents to various countries to get help, that I had gone around and observed all the fortresses and maritime ports in the country, and that I had held a provincial council in the year 1678 with a view to bringing in the French." The friar mentioned was the same John Moyer who would travel to London in the following year along with Hugh Duffy and others to give evidence against him, these were the same two who had broken a bust of Oliver in Rome some years earlier and had many escapades in the meantime, including recent convictions for accessory to robbery. There were other religious also, but these had come forward in Dundalk to give evidence on Oliver's behalf.

He wrote at this time: "In accordance with the law here, I have to present myself before three criminal sessions before I can be released. The mode of procedure in criminal cases is strange to me. The accused knows nothing of the accusation until the day of his trial and he is not granted a lawyer to defend himself, nor is the oath given to the witnesses for the accused, and one witness alone is enough on the side of the King or the exchequer. Nevertheless they listen to what the witnesses for the accused have to say, even if they do not give them the oath."

The conspirators quickly sent word to London about Oliver's trial falling through in Dundalk, and the authorities in London decided that his retrial should take place in London rather that in Dublin. This was an extraordinary decision as it was a standard procedure at the time that trials should only take place in the district where the members of the jury would know the circumstances of the crime and have certain knowledge of the accused and of the witnesses involved. It was also the duty of jurists at the time to acquaint themselves with the facts of the case; this would not be at all possible in London.

1 Mac Phoil, An tAth. Donnchadh 'The Clergy of Oliver Plunkett' Seanchas Ard Mhacha 1957

67. Transferred to London

On 6th October, Ormond was ordered to send Oliver for trial in London. The 24th October 1680 was Oliver's last day in Ireland, barely over a year since instructions had first been issued in London for his arrest. He wrote from Dublin Castle: "They have taken pen, ink and inkstand from me, I write at cock-crow and secretly…I have been cited to appear before the King and Parliament in London and to-day I set sail. May it all be for the greater glory of God and the salvation of my soul. Another friar has popped up to give evidence against me. His name is George Codden, and he was jailed for I do not know what; to regain his freedom he has become an informer against me. A third friar, a certain Paul Gormley who was also in jail, in Derry, having been put there for theft, has also decided to become an informer in order to obtain his freedom." Oliver then realised that he was in a potentially serious situation, up to that time he had hoped for an acquittal even from any Protestant jury in Ireland, which might lead to a probable forced exile. He had already asked Rome for advice as to where he should go on the continent in such an event. A trial in London would be a great deal different and the outcome would be much less certain to go in his favour. His servant James could well relate to him the hateful atmosphere of London towards Catholics, having experienced it himself less than six months earlier. David Fitzgerald of Rathkeale was an active priest hunter who gathered up witnesses willing to give evidence backing up a Popish Plot in Ireland and travelled over and back to London. Bishop Peter Creagh of Cork was arrested as a result of his efforts and it was planned to send Bishop Creagh to[1] face trial along with Archbishop Oliver in London. Becoming very ill he escaped this fate. He remained in prison for two years and during his trial in Cork, the floor of the court gave way, killing a number of people including the perjured witnesses. He subsequently became Archbishop of Dublin in 1693.

Oliver was placed in the custody of an army captain along with four soldiers and needless to say, his recently freed servant James, also accompanied the party to London. They sailed out of Dublin on the twin masted, vice-regal vessel named the[2] 'Dogger.' Extremely anxious that the lines of communication between the Church in Ireland and Rome must be kept open at all costs, Oliver wrote from on board ship. He suggested that Bishop Forstall of Kildare and Leighlin might be the best person to keep the Internuncio informed of events in Ireland as he lives near Dublin, adding: "Please tell Canon Joyce that I received two letters from him, and ask him to send on the money in any case without delay to Mr. John Comyn, merchant in London. This man is my friend and he is Catholic. My expenses are intolerable. Communication by letter is both dangerous and difficult at present...If I can find a way, you shall hear from me in London. Meanwhile I commend myself to your prayers." He was not able to find a way to communicate and the next known letter from him out of England was not until 16th May. On 26th October while Oliver was still en route to London, the House of Lords empowered three messengers to travel to Ireland and secure extra witnesses, while the Privy Council promised pardon and payment from the treasury to all who would so oblige within a period of two months. Titus Oates had become a wealthy man because of his discoveries; surely there would be no shortage of takers in Ireland. This would bring an Irish angle to the conspiracy and so help to revive the plot which had lost momentum and was again flagging somewhat.

[1] Power Canon P. 'A Bishop of the Penal Times' 1932. p.70
[2] Stokes Mgr. John 'Life of Blessed Oliver Plunkett' Dublin 1965. p.65

68. NEWGATE PRISON

On 29th October, Oliver was lodged in strict solitary confinement in Newgate Prison, London. It was later reported back to Ormond that on 4th December, Oliver had made a good impression when brought before the Privy Council, this session was also attended by Edmund Murphy.

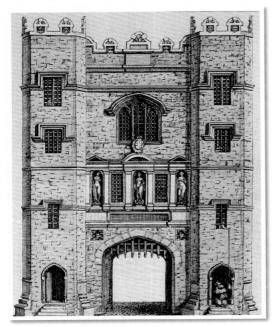

Newgate Prison London

Six days later, he was brought before a committee of the House of Lords, where he strenuously denied any correspondence or knowledge of plots with France. Oliver's faithful servant James was reported to the authorities by the conspirators. Shortly afterwards he was arrested when bringing a change of clothes for Oliver to Newgate prison and incarcerated there for the following four months.

Prisons were harsh places; inmates were required to pay[1] for everything, food, heat, light and even the mandatory shackles on their feet. Over the previous two years, five Jesuit priests had been martyred at Tyburn as a result of the Popish Plot. One of the martyrs, Fr. John Fenwick, suffered greatly from a gangrenous foot as a result of the shackles in Newgate. It had been thought that his foot should be amputated, sometime before his execution. Oliver was well aware that he was lodged in the same small cell which had been previously assigned to Fr. Thomas Whitbread, another one of the five Jesuit martyrs beatified by Pope Pius XI in 1929. This prison was a notorious place and was seen as a health hazard by Londoners; it was dirty, noisy, had no sanitation and was infested with many types of vermin. It has been said that more prisoners died of typhus than at the gallows. Oliver was about to spend another cold winter in jail when the first heavy snows were recorded by the middle of December of that year. His servant James was also lodged in the common felon's side, the worst wing of the prison.

Within a fortnight of his transfer to London, Oliver ran out of money and he was forced to send in the customary formal petition to be maintained at the Kings expense, which allowed ten shillings per week for each prisoner's support. The keeper's job was envied as it was a most lucrative one with the ability to charge the prisoners for everything. But, when a prisoner was maintained at the King's expense the keeper's attitude would undoubtedly be much less kindly. Oliver had absolutely no contact with anyone except his jailor, shackled as he was in a harsh prison cell of about eight square metres. Despite his many illnesses, it was reported that he was always in good form. In several of his letters he acknowledges his many sins and offences, yet it was while he was in strict solitary confinement in Newgate Prison that he quickly ascended the steps of sainthood, taking them two at a time by his frequent acts of mortification, regular fasting three or four days a week and constant prayer. Just like the time he spent hiding in huts, caves or attics, his prison cell enabled this man of sustained action to become a man of intense prayer. Over the following months, despite suffering from gall-stones, his other illnesses and many discomforts, his jailors could remark on his inherent good humour. Oliver had made a good impression on them.

Unknown to Oliver, his cousin Sir Nicholas Plunkett died on Christmas day 1680, just a few weeks after Oliver's transfer to England. Sir Nicholas was another benefactor unable to help him with either money or legal advice at this time. On 29th December, William Howard or Lord Stafford, was beheaded as part of the same plot; a member of the Howard family and uncle of Oliver's friend, Cardinal Philip Howard. Lord Stafford's family were one of the Catholic families whom Oliver would later write about as being most charitable to him at this time. Blessed William Howard was beatified by Pope Pius XI in 1929.

---

[1] Curtayne Alice 'The Trial of Oliver Plunkett' Ireland 1975. p.18

69. PROSECUTION WITNESSES

Meanwhile, the House of Lord's messengers had gone to Ireland with arrest warrants which had been issued for four priests, Brian MacGurk, dean of Armagh, Henry Hughes vicar general of Armagh, Manus O'Quinn PP of Creggan and Brian Holland (Hullan) PP of Mucknoo. The North of Ireland was also combed for further witnesses. London promised pardons and money and there was no shortage of takers. Professional informer and messenger, Owen Murphy, soon collected at least twelve villains most if not all, former jailbirds. In mid-January 1681, they were brought to London. Of the four arrest warrants, only Quinn and Holland were arrested as MacGurk and Hughes were in hiding. The twelve who arrived in London, added to[1] the four friars, Paul Gormley, George Codden, John Moyer (sometimes spelt MacMoyer) and Hugh Duffy along with Florence Weyer (MacMoyer but he preferred Weyer[2]) and Hugh Hanlon, making a grand total of at least twenty. The number of witnesses may have been greater than this as in a letter[3] from the Earl of Arran in London to his father, viceroy Ormond in Dublin, he writes: "There came the other day, about twenty–five witnesses out Ireland under the conduct of Owen Murphy."

The spelling of names in the seventeenth century varied quite a bit, it often depended on the writer. Names were frequently spelt phonetically and could even appear spelt differently in the same document. The prosecution witnesses were divided almost evenly between priests and laymen. The witnesses included four secular priests from Armagh; Murphy, O'Quinn, Callaghan and Finan of whom only Murphy would give evidence at the trial proper and rather reluctantly at that. Two priests from Clogher, John MacClave (sometimes spelt MacClane or MacLegh) and a Brian Holland who was later willing to give evidence on Oliver's behalf. There were four Franciscans, of whom three took part in the trial; Moyer and Duffy were the principal witnesses against Oliver while Gormley turned tack and gave some lame evidence in Oliver's favour. The laymen included Bryan Quinn, Cornelius Mac Girr, James Murphy,

Hugh O'Hanlon, Owen Murphy, Henry O'Neill and Phelim O'Neill with the last four giving evidence for the prosecution. With the exception of Holland, Gormley and O'Quinn all seemed most anxious to impose a great injustice on Oliver and all for pardons, freedom and a few pieces of silver.

Fr. Manus O'Quinn may have been one of those arrested in this group because of his knowledge of Patrick Fleming, a prominent Tory. Fleming was ambushed by soldiers from Ardee at an inn near Iniskeen, in February 1678. He was killed along with a few of his colleagues. On his person was found a letter from Oliver Plunkett to local parish priest, Manus O'Quinn, advising Fleming to leave the country and requesting Fleming to fulfil this promise which he had already made to Oliver in Jane Mekena's house[4] While it was somewhat controversial for Oliver, particularly amongst the remnants of the Tories, nothing further seems to have stemmed from it during the trial in London. O'Quinn, who was unlikely to testify against Oliver, took no further part in the trial. Another witness forced to travel to England, Brian Holland PP of Mucknoo, must also have been uncooperative as he did not appear for the prosecution either. He was then allowed home to Ireland and returned later to London in the unfulfilled hope of giving evidence in Oliver's defence.

The witnesses assembled against Oliver consisted mainly of two groups: Henry O'Neill was father to Phelim O'Neill and father in law to Hugh O'Hanlon. It was Fr. John MacClave of the diocese of Clogher who had encouraged their revelations. Friar John Moyer (MacMoyer) who had been a curate for a time to Fr. Edmund Murphy in Killeavy was a cousin of Florence Weyer and a foster brother of Friar Hugh Duffy who in turn had also been a curate to Fr. Murphy in Killeavy. James Callaghan, another priest of Killeavy had already been involved in Oliver's failed hearing at Dundalk. He went to London with the other witnesses, but seems only to have been interested in the Primate's papal jurisdiction. It is ironic how four priests who had served in the rather large parish of Killeavy, all became ensnared in the Popish Plot. Murphy,

Duffy and Moyer were certainly in collusion with the carry-on of the Tories in the area. Most, if not all of the witnesses were notorious characters and had spent time in jail for robbery, drunkenness, dealing in stolen goods, as highwaymen or dealing with the Tories. Living just for the moment, some of them would sell their souls for a bottle of spirits. Oliver wrote that John Moyer was always half drunk when he appeared before the councils. With the assembly of so many conspirators most of whom were resolute; it should have been obvious that there would be no escape for Oliver from an ever tightening noose.

Henry O'Neill had come forward on the promise that one of his sons would be freed from Mullingar jail. John Moyer, Edmund Murphy and some of the other suspended priests had hoped that they could minister at will in parishes, if only Archbishop Oliver could be removed from the scene. There was also the mindless idea that they might be allowed to minister officially by the state in parishes. If church authorities ever tried to suspend or interfere with them, they could then go to the civil courts where they would be secure under the law of Premunire. Moyer later complained bitterly in a letter to Hetherington that this promise of his was never fulfilled. Viceroy Ormond wrote of the witnesses going over and back to London: "Those that went out of Ireland with bad English and worse clothes are returned well-bred gentlemen, well coroneted, peri-wigged and clothed. Brogues and leather straps are converted to fashionable shoes and glittering buckles."

[1] Ó Fiaich & Forristal 'Oliver Plunkett' Indiana, USA 1976. Ó Fiaich. p.81
[2] Ó Fiaich Tomás 'Florence Weyer's Pamphlet against Blessed Oliver Plunkett' I.E.R. 1966. p.337
[3] Burke William P. 'The Irish Priests in the Penal Times 1660-1760' Waterford 1914. p.86
[4] Probably a relative of James McKenna or even a misspelling.

70. FAILED INDICTMENT

On 12th February 1681, the Bill of Indictment was presented before the grand jury of Westminster. Oliver was not allowed to see the indictment beforehand. The evidence of the witnesses was so haphazard and contradictory that the jury[1] rejected the bill. This was a major setback for the prosecution as it meant that their witnesses were not convincing and were not believed by the jury. The witnesses had disagreed strongly amongst themselves as each tried to be treated more favourably with promises of pardons and money. They had also fallen out with Hetherington who had been given money to look after them. They were not at all happy with his treatment of them. Among the witnesses were several distinct groups and each group tried to outdo the other. They earnestly sought complete pardons from Lord Shaftsbury and the prosecution, rather than the more restrictive pardons they had either received or were promised. The majority of the witnesses had very poor English and needed to be schooled in their evidence. Following this rejection by the jury the prosecution then set about training them more intensely. Nonetheless, things were looking hopeful for Oliver as he had already put up a good showing before the Council in early December.

[1] Curtis, Fr. Emmanuel 'Blessed Oliver Plunkett' Dublin 1963. p.144

71. DIPLOMATIC EFFORTS

During the early months of 1681, many letters were issued from Rome in the Pope's name to the Internuncio in Vienna and through many other diplomatic channels to various heads of state, pleading help for Oliver. Emperor Leopold was entreated to intervene on the side of justice. By mid-March he replied stressing prudence in any dealings with the English, lest the lot of Catholics be made even more intolerable. England and London in particular was still gripped in an atmosphere of mass hysteria about the imaginary plots of Catholics to usurp both king and state. It is rather doubtful if the circumstances of Catholics could have been made much worse than they actually had become. Oliver, who was in strict solitary confinement, fasted three or four days a week and spent his time well, in prayer and mortification. The Internuncio in Brussels reported to Rome that Oliver was guarded with exceeding rigour.

Interestingly, St. Claude La Columbière would undoubtedly have been active on Oliver's behalf at this time in France. As an earlier chaplain to the Duchess of York, he had been arrested along with his fellow five Jesuits as part of the Popish Plot and incarcerated in Newgate prison. As he was French and a chaplain to the wife of the heir to the throne, he was released and banished home to France. He thereby narrowly avoided becoming the sixth Jesuit martyr of the plot. Nevertheless, his health suffered considerably as a result of spending a harsh winter in Newgate prison. Some six years earlier, St. Claude had been appointed Spiritual Director to St. Margaret Mary Alocoque in France, shortly after the Divine revelations were made to her of the important devotion to the Sacred Heart of Jesus. St. Claude continued to correspond with her throughout his time in London.

St. Margaret Mary doubted the messages at first, but the Lord had promised to send her: "My faithful servant and perfect friend" who would help her promote the message to the world, of the unfathomable riches of the love of the Sacred Heart for mankind. As a young priest saying Mass in the convent, an interior voice told St. Margaret Mary that this was the man in question. St. Claude soon realised the validity of the messages and that it would be he, who would be instrumental in promoting this devotion to the Sacred Heart of Jesus. In former times he had also tutored the children of the Minister of Finance in France, and would have had prominent contacts in French government circles. All this was to no avail for Oliver however, as in England there was so much hatred of France, that any diplomacy from that quarter might only be counter-productive. Writing about Oliver in a letter, St. Claude wrote[1] about: "The travails of the Archbishop of Armagh." It seems appropriate that the Relics of St. Claude La Columbière which toured Ireland, were venerated in an all-night vigil in St. Peter's Church Drogheda, as they lay beside the Relics of St. Oliver Plunkett on the 14th-15th June 2006.

---

[1] Bellew Seamus 'The Seventeenth Century Reliquary of St. Oliver Plunkett at the Siena Convent, Drogheda' ref. 52. Seanchas Ard Mhacha 2011

St. Peter's Church, Drogheda.

72. Successful Indictment

On 25th February 1681, James McKenna while still in prison, petitioned to see Oliver. On the 9th March the Attorney General reported that James had been imprisoned solely on the grounds of being a Catholic found within the London area, a Catholic free zone. The Privy Council then allowed James his freedom[1] but only after substantial bail had been found; the date he was actually released is unclear. Undoubtedly some of the prominent Catholic families in the London area had again come to the rescue on Oliver's behalf. However, James was not yet allowed to visit Oliver who was still in strict solitary confinement.

On 22nd April the King and Privy Council decided that Oliver's conditions of imprisonment could be relaxed somewhat[2] and that he could be allowed visitors provided a jailor was present. On 27th April, after a further petition by Oliver; his private papers were returned to him having first been scrutinized by the Attorney General. After five months spent in solitary confinement, Oliver must have been glad to meet with visitors, including his servant James. He must have been even more delighted to receive a missal, a bible and a breviary which fellow inmate in Newgate, Fr. Maurus Corker the president of the English Benedictines had procured for him. Fr. Corker wrote later that Oliver had them in his possession for three months before his death, thus indicating a time some weeks before his arraignment on 3rd May. Oliver could now engross himself even more ardently in the official prayers of the Church, while on the latter stages of his journey to sainthood. Oliver was brought before the Westminster Grand Jury for the second time[3] on 29th April. On this occasion the witnesses against him were much better prepared and he was successfully indicted. The die was now cast and he was put forward to appear on trial before the Kings Bench on the most serious charge of high treason.

---

[1] Ó Fiaich & Forristal 'Oliver Plunkett' Indiana, USA 1976. Ó Fiaich. p.83
[2] Ó Fiaich & Forristal 'Oliver Plunkett' Indiana, USA 1976. Ó Fiaich. p.83
3 Curtis, Fr. Emmanuel 'Blessed Oliver Plunkett' Dublin 1963. p.145

73. ARRAIGNMENT IN WESTMINSTER HALL

On Tuesday 3rd May, Oliver stood arraigned in the dock. The harsh toll of imprisonment had by then taken its toll and although he was but fifty-five years of age, he looked like an old man, pale and emaciated after his prison ordeals and sicknesses. It must also be remembered that prior to his imprisonment, he had never spared himself during his period of active ministry in Ireland, which lasted for almost ten years. He had toiled ceaselessly in the vineyard of the Lord, in or out of prison and it showed. He listened attentively in Westminster Hall to the long indictment for high treason; planning to arrange the King's death by rebellion, collecting money for a war in Ireland and organising a sixty-thousand man army for this purpose, plotting to advance the Catholic religion in Ireland and conspiring to bring in a French army to Ireland via Carlingford. Oliver proclaimed that the court should have no jurisdiction over him and that his trial should take place in Ireland where the alleged offences took place. Lord Chief Justice Pemberton assisted by two other judges smartly over-ruled his objection and Oliver sought precedent for such action. The Chief Justice said they needed no such precedent as parliament had already decreed that his trial should take place in London and that his full trial must be so scheduled. Oliver was denied his request for extra time to assemble witnesses before his trial, which was set for Wednesday 8th June. The court granted a request, confirming that his servant James could in fact visit him, but denied him a visit by a priest. Assuming James was already free, it might be presumed that James could visit Oliver over the previous four[1] or five days, but this was undoubtedly discretionary and visits may not always have been allowed. By having it expressly allowed by the court it would have assured him of visitation rights.

The trial date, left only five weeks to assemble and bring over witnesses from Ireland for the defence. Oliver wrote to Rome requesting financial help and a sum of money was forwarded to him. Money was scarce and as he was totally dependent on the charity of relatives and some English Catholics. Oliver decided that only eight witnesses should be brought over. It was estimated that their expenses would be in the order of twenty pounds each and Rome agreed to provide financial assistance in this regard. John Plunkett a relative of Oliver who was then in London, along with McKenna, set off in haste for Ireland to accomplish their mission. They sailed from London, but while out at sea they were blown back to land losing two days as a result. They then travelled overland from London to Holyhead, where they were forced to wait a week as a strong westerly wind was blowing. They eventually landed in Dublin on 19th May leaving less than three weeks to complete their mission.

Interestingly, this was at least the eighth occasion that contrary winds at sea or difficulties on board ships would have an impact on Oliver; the last two indirectly as they impeded McKenna and Plunkett for the greater part of a fortnight on their important mission of procuring defence witnesses for him. The first occasion for Oliver occurred when as a young man he first set sail for the continent heading for the Irish College in Rome. He was delayed for several months awaiting a boat and a favourable wind in Waterford. On the second occasion they were chased by pirates. On the same voyage and the third occasion they were only saved from the pirates by the intervention of a severe storm, which greatly threatened their boat over a two day period, whilst being blown many miles off course. The fourth incident occurred when he was returning from Rome. The captain, who was drunk, ran the boat aground sailing down the river Rhine and the boat was in serious danger of capsizing. He was delayed at Ostend for twelve days awaiting a favourable wind as he travelled to London as the newly ordained Archbishop of Armagh on his way home to Ireland. While on the same journey home to his diocese in 1670, he experienced a sixth occurrence in Holyhead, where he waited for yet another twelve days for a favourable wind before setting sail for Ringsend. It is no wonder then that one of Oliver's favourite similes in his many letters is that of a ship at sea: "While the storm rages we will seek some quiet harbour to seek shelter...While we have the present viceroy we will set full sail...Until I see how the wind will blow I shall navigate very cautiously...To take down the sails and seek shelter in some safe harbour...whenever a sailor has a fair wind he would set full sail."

McKenna and John Plunkett's delays at sea, may not have been as decisive in Oliver's demise as they might seem. The authorities appeared determined to hinder at every turn their mission to bring over witnesses or to secure evidence. James McKenna set out for the familiar territory of Armagh and Derry, while John Plunkett toured Louth and Meath to muster together the eight witnesses. Assembling in Dublin, the witnesses sought safe passage to London which was still a Catholic free zone and a potential lion's den. They were justified in this as McKenna had already spent the winter in jail solely under the pretext that he was a Catholic, found in the city of London. They were also afraid because it was common knowledge at the time that witnesses denying the Popish Plot at the other trials were harangued, pelted and harassed regularly by the London mob. Heading into a lion's den such as this was not quite appealing to them. Principal amongst Oliver's defence witnesses was Edmund Fay from Co. Meath, who had been imprisoned with Murphy and Hetherington in Dundalk jail. He was willing to testify that the pair had totally made up the charges there and that he himself had been offered money if he should join them in giving false evidence against Oliver.

Safe passes were not immediately forthcoming and Oliver's witnesses were delayed until they finally procured them on 6th June, only two days before the trial date in London. Plunkett and McKenna were also denied by Irish court officials, copies of the criminal records of Moyer, Murphy and the other crown witnesses, unless expressly ordered to release them by the English court service. This was an organised blocking tactic, apparently as a result of collusion[2] between both privy councils. Yet another travesty of justice as these documents could normally be obtained upon the receipt of a standard fee. Meanwhile McKenna and Plunkett had rushed back to London, arriving on the same date. With only forty-eight hours to go before the trial, they relayed the sad news to Oliver. As a result of the enforced delays in Dublin, it would be some days before the witnesses could possibly arrive in London. While the pair failed in their mission, nevertheless it was a remarkable feat of endurance. It had taken them less than three weeks since the day they set sail from Holyhead, to tour Ireland in search for witnesses, persuade and assemble those witnesses in Dublin, try to collect the required documentation and arrive back in London. Oliver petitioned the Court of King's Bench for twelve day's grace, but his request was turned down on 7th June. This was supported with a sworn affidavit of the same date from John Plunkett, specifying how crucial the evidence of his witnesses would be for Oliver's defence.

---

[1] In his petition to the King, written shortly after the trial, Oliver states that he was a close prisoner until four or five days before his arraignment on 3rd May.

[2] Stokes Mgr. John 'Life of Blessed Oliver Plunkett' Dublin 1965. p.71

74. TRIAL

As far as the people of England were concerned, Londoners in particular, Westminster Hall was the centre of the universe. Parliament, both House of Commons and House of Lords took place there and trials before the King's Bench also took place there. It was also a great hub of activity for ministers of the realm, their officials or courtiers. As it was a great location to source all sorts of information, people would go there on a daily basis or to one of the newly introduced coffee houses in the vicinity to catch up on the latest rumour or gossip and to find out about latest happenings at home or abroad. Principal amongst these at the time was the newest discovery of plots by the 'wicked' Catholics.

Wednesday 8th June soon dawned and Oliver finally faced trial in Westminster Hall. Required to keep his right hand raised above his head while the long indictment was read out, he was not allowed any defence council as it was a trial for high treason. The defendant was not permitted to know the charges until the day of the trial and had no idea of who the witnesses might be or of the evidence that would be presented. Oliver had some inkling of the serious charges made against him, since his trial was aborted on the second day in Dundalk. He also knew a few of the witnesses as his friends or his recently released servant James McKenna, would have sussed some of them out. However, he had no idea of what surprise witnesses might be produced or of the dastardly lies they might tell.

He stood alone in the middle of the great hall and arrayed against him were five prosecuting council, including the Attorney General and the Solicitor General who had already scrutinised Oliver's papers before they were returned to him. As for all those people who packed into the hall, they were not only unbiased but were positively baying for a conviction. The hall was crammed with people who appeared scornful or mocking; all present eagerly anticipated another great and free spectacle, on a day when the outcome would surely go their way. The same type of crowd had packed into the hall for previous Popish Plot trials, when witnesses for the defence might often have difficulty making themselves heard above the din of the crowd. Even more frightening, defence

A Trial in Westminister Hall

witnesses often found themselves jostled or assaulted as they pushed their way through the crowd which congregated menacingly at the entrance to the court. Inside the hall, the witnesses against Oliver were also there and all appeared more than willing to perjure themselves for a few pieces of silver. The jury too, were not seen as unbiased. They were handpicked, even the jury foreman and another member had also been jurists in the trial of Richard Langhorne, an earlier plot victim and also in the trial of the five Jesuits, whom they helped to convict and have executed, some two years previously.

Seated high up on a dais under the great window of Westminster Hall were the three judges, who would shortly prove that they were not unbiased either. Led by Lord Chief Justice Pemberton and aided by Justices Dolben and Jones who were seated on either side. Also in attendance must have been John Plunkett, James Mc, Kenna, a priest or two, some Catholic friends and other supporters from the London area, all meekly keeping as low a profile as possible and undoubtedly praying silently for a miracle that true justice might somehow prevail. Undoubtedly, Oliver must have been heartened to see a friendly face or two, as everyone else there in the hall seemed to seek his downfall.

Westminster Hall, London

After the indictment, the prosecution laid out their case; Oliver had been appointed Archbishop solely to promote the plot; he used his high position to collect money and recruit men to stir up war and support rebellion so as to have the King put to death and promote the Romish faith throughout the land; he surveyed all the ports before selecting Carlingford to bring in the French. Oliver pleaded "not guilty." It was surely strange that Oliver who preached loyalty to the king and civil authorities and who had often been criticised for it, should now find himself put on trial for high treason against the same king. But of course the real reason why he was fighting for his life in Westminster Hall was his Catholic faith.

Oliver challenged the court rights to try him in England unless the particular English Statutes expressly mentioned Ireland, adding: "The case is rare and scarce happens in five hundred years." Pemberton interjected that it was all quite legal as Parliament had sanctioned the trial. Oliver then drew attention to the fact that several of the jurors had acted as jurors in two other of the plot trials and Lord Chief Justice Pemberton snapped "What if they have." The appointment of jurors was not by an open selection method but were the appointees of the sheriffs. Oliver again drew attention to his request for more time to assemble his witnesses. Pemberton replied: "For us to stay for your witnesses, or send you back to Ireland, we cannot do it. Therefore you must submit to your trial. We heard your affidavit yesterday and we did tell the gentleman that moved it, as much as we tell you, you are here to be tried."

Curtayne Alice 'The Trial of Oliver Plunkett' Ireland 1975. p.35

75. FLORENCE WEYER (MACMOYER)

First up was Florence Weyer, a schoolteacher of the illustrious clan which had proudly served for several centuries as keepers of the Book of Armagh. In medieval times, the 9th century book was seen as an important symbol of the Archbishop of Armagh and it was ironic that a member of a clan who were loyal for generations to successive Archbishops of Armagh should now turn against a holder of the office. Fallen on hard times, the family's large estate had been confiscated in the plantation of Ulster. After the trial, it became known that he had been deceived by the promise of "an estate as good as ever your grandfather had" if he gave evidence against Oliver. In order to be able to travel to London and give evidence in the trial, Florence had pawned the Book of Armagh for five pounds to a Protestant gentleman, whence it would be lost to the family evermore. The Book of Armagh is now housed in Trinity College, Dublin. Florence proclaimed to the court that Oliver in his peace agreement of 1670 had arranged for the Tory fugitives to go to France where they would organise an alliance with continental forces. He also claimed to have seen an order of Oliver's, for the collection of money and of his selection of Carlingford as a landing point. Challenged by Oliver, he was forced to admit that he never saw him in Carlingford nor did he report the information which he allegedly had in his possession for several years. This was a shrewd question by Oliver, as either Florence was making it all up as a lie or he himself was guilty of treason by not reporting it.

Curtayne Alice 'The Trial of Oliver Plunkett' Ireland 1975. p.55

76, THE O'NEILLS

Henry O'Neill was then put on the stand and he was followed by his son Phelim. Oliver must have looked intensely at them as he had never seen either of them before, not even at his failed trial in Dundalk the previous July. Both claimed in almost identical evidence that in the year 1678, meetings were held in Virginia and other locations in the diocese of Clogher, when oaths were taken to kill all the Protestants within one hour, from one end of Ireland to the other. They claimed that Bishop Tyrrell of Clogher arrived with forty horsemen and spoke at the meetings of having a good man in Lord Oliver Plunkett to assist them and that money had been already been sent abroad to contribute towards an army of men. Oliver followed the same line of questioning by asking "why did you not discover it before" and "why did you not tell it to some justices of the peace" Admitting that Oliver was not present at the meetings, their evidence against him was completely hearsay or gossip and like so much of the other statements presented at the trial should never have been admitted as evidence.

Curtayne Alice 'The Trial of Oliver Plunkett' Ireland 1975. p.93

77. OWEN MURPHY

Owen Murphy then took the stand and testified that Edmund Murphy had discovered the plot in Ireland and had relayed it to a Lieutenant Baker, that there was a design to bring in the French. Chief Justice Pemberton ordered him to speak up as he could not hear him. Murphy stated that he heard from Lieutenant Baker about the French. Speak what you know yourself, requested Pemberton. Murphy stated that he saw Edmund Murphy's evidence which he had produced in Ireland when Murphy was sent to jail there. Murphy had just let the cat out of the bag by stating that Edmund Murphy had been in jail in Ireland. The prosecutors quickly dismissed him before he could do any more harm for their case. Owen Murphy was an energetic, professional informer cum messenger and had gone over and back to Ireland a couple of times collecting information and informers. He had nothing material to say at the trial except what Edmund Murphy and others had told him. It is possible that Owen Murphy had already fallen out with Shaftsbury and company over his pay and conditions. Or perhaps, he had correctly sensed a change in the air that the King was in the ascendancy in his arguments with the Whigs of parliament and of Lord Shaftsbury's party.

Curtayne Alice 'The Trial of Oliver Plunkett' Ireland 1975. p.97

78. FRIAR HUGH DUFFY

The series of priest witnesses were then called. The discredited Franciscan friar, Hugh Duffy a former curate to Edmund Murphy in Killeavy parish, claimed to have obtained incriminating information against Oliver from the diocese of Clogher, especially about the collection of money. He knew Oliver and claimed that he saw him at meetings to raise money for the plot, money which was collected from all the priests of Ireland. He said that he could recognise Oliver's handwriting and he had seen a letter from him to Cardinal Bouillon in France, urging him to use his influence with the King of France not to wage war on Spain but rather to redeem Ireland from its heretical jurisdiction. He also claimed to have accompanied Oliver to Carlingford when it was selected as the chosen point of entry for an invading army. Oliver asked him to produce a letter of his for the collecting of money, Duffy replied "I could have brought them but thought it needless."

Curtayne Alice 'The Trial of Oliver Plunkett' Ireland 1975. p.98

Carlingford Harbour

79. Fr. Edmund Murphy

Next up was Edmund Murphy the only priest of the Archdiocese of Armagh who actually gave evidence. He seemed to have had a change of heart and may have regretted his former testimony against his former Archbishop. His evidence on the day was totally vague; he was wily in his answers: "I suppose he did...I can't say but it was...I forget it." He claimed that he could not remember many details, expressing the view that many of the witnesses never knew Plunkett. When he tried to slip out of Westminster Hall he was caught and put back on the stand. When brought back, he was cajoled through interrogation and the direct questioning by the prosecuting council to repeat what he had said and written in his earlier sworn testimonies before the council: 'Oliver had planned to raise an army of seventy-thousand men in Ireland and to raise money for that purpose.'

Over a year earlier, Lord Shaftsbury had introduced Hetherington as his informant to the Council. Hetherington, knowing that he was skating on thin ice with a lack of personal information, said that Edmund Murphy knew more than he. Now here was Murphy at the trial proper, trying to withdraw much of what he had previously said or written. Pemberton's jibe that the Catholics had got to him may well have had a ring of truth. Murphy had apparently hidden for a time in the Spanish embassy, a Catholic enclave in London who were working anxiously on Oliver's behalf. They may well have enticed Murphy to tell the truth, for once. Seeing Oliver his former archbishop, for the second time, looking old and sickly and knowing what he must have suffered in prison, it is hard to believe that his conscience would not have pricked him more than a little. Like James Callaghan, Murphy's arguments with his former archbishop may well have been regarding papal jurisdiction. During the trial he stated: "May it please your worship, first of all, I did not impeach Primate Plunkett, but the officers and justices of the peace." This was also backed up in his own pamphlet[1] which was printed at the time. On the other hand, Murphy was already a hunted man in several quarters.

He was wanted by the Tories under Redmond O'Hanlon, by the justices of Dundalk, by soldiers Lieutenant Baker and Ensign Smith, whom he had already testified against as being in league[2] with the Tories. If Oliver was to be executed on the strength of Murphy's evidence, then the whole of Ireland would be after him. He had already faced Oliver before at the Privy Council, the previous December, the occasion when it was reported that Oliver made a good impression. In the meantime, like thieves falling out, he had argued with many of the other witnesses. The Attorney General stated that Murphy had gone missing three weeks before the trial and could not be found for the earlier hearing. Asked, had he ever been a Protestant he answered that he was a priest: "I am indifferent whether I be a Protestant or a priest…yes I am a priest, but it makes me forget myself to see so many evidences to come in, that never knew Plunkett…I know not how these people come to swear this business, whether they had not malice against him." Serjeant Jeffries then speaks: "I desire that he may be committed, my Lord, because he has fenced from the beginning." Chief Justice Pemberton said that it was obvious that the papists had got to him and he committed him to Newgate prison.

[1] Murphy Edmund 'The perfect State and Condition of Ireland etc.' London 1681. p. 5
[2] Curtayne Alice 'The Trial of Oliver Plunkett' Ireland 1975. p.125

80. FR. JOHN MACCLAVE

Next up was Fr. John MacClave a deposed parish priest of the parish of Aughnamullen in the diocese of Clogher who gave evidence of attending meetings in Co. Monaghan where money was collected for the Primate, adding that he had also witnessed incriminating letters of Oliver's while in France. He stated that Oliver had been appointed archbishop at the behest of the King of France, so as to raise money and join with the French in destroying the Protestant religion. MacClave had fallen out with his own bishop, former Franciscan, Patrick Tyrrell of

Clogher and undoubtedly must have also belonged to the group of dissidents who would not accept Bishop Tyrrell as administrator of Kilmore. In his dispute with him he implicated Oliver. In court, Oliver asked him to produce written orders for the collection of money and he gave a similar answer to that given by Duffy: "Yes I can show them, but they are afar off. I did not expect to have them asked for." Oliver asked a few questions: "Have you no superiors of your own" the suggestion being that Oliver would not have had any involvement with MacClave as he had his own bishop. He also put it to him: "What is the reason you kept it so secret all this while" again like his question to Florence Weyer, either he was making it up as a lie or he was guilty of treason by not having reported it. There was no written proof of orders to collect money and as it was not even claimed that Oliver had attended any of these meetings, this evidence should not have been admissible either.

[1] Curtayne Alice 'The Trial of Oliver Plunkett' Ireland 1975. p.133

81. FRIAR JOHN MOYER (MACMOYER)

By far the most hostile witness against Oliver was the disgraced Franciscan friar John Moyer, who clearly had an obsessive hatred of him for the greater part of a decade. Moyer had returned from the continent in 1674 and in his own statement, he recalled that he called to Archbishop Oliver's house at Ardpatrick on 9th December of that year. He received faculties from him and was appointed a curate in the parish of Killeavy, where Edmund Murphy was parish priest. Sometime later, Moyer became vicar of the Armagh Friary under the guardianship of Anthony Daly. Both were hotheads and it was not long before Moyer was suspended by his provincial as an apostate. The Armagh community at the time lived at Brantry, Co. Tyrone and there is some evidence to suggest that this community was in the vanguard of opposition to Oliver as a result of his decisions in favour of the Dominicans over four disused convents and over the questing issue. Oliver published his sentence against Moyer throughout the archdiocese and requested that no Catholic should receive the sacraments from him. Moyer was also convicted of giving powder and shot to the Tories and his hatred of Oliver was such that he carried out a prolonged vendetta against him. Some five years earlier in 1676, he had given information to Sir Hans Hamilton, linking Oliver with a French invasion. Despite suspension by his superior and a subsequent prohibition by Archbishop Oliver, he defiantly continued to preach, administer the sacraments and of course to collect offerings.

In court, Moyer produced a handwritten translation of a copy of a letter, supposedly written by Oliver in 1672 to the Secretary of Propaganda in Rome. When he was in Rome he claimed he had come to know Oliver's handwriting well and when he saw the letter he immediately recognised that the letter was genuine and in Oliver's handwriting. He had been on his way home to Ireland and on the journey he met a Neal O'Neill whom he claimed was a page or messenger of Oliver's who was bringing his mail to Rome. Oliver interjected that he never had a page. Quizzed further, Moyer states that the original copy which had been in his possession had been taken by soldiers and Tories from his home. Amazingly, the translated copy of the letter was admitted in evidence, although it was not included in the written report of the trial. Assuming it followed Moyer's earlier depositions to the councils, the letter allegedly requested that the King of France be persuaded to make peace on the continent and instead to send his arms to Ireland, where many were ready to rise up in rebellion.

Moyer then claimed that on his visit to Oliver's home in 1674, Oliver had told him many such secrets. He then produced in court a copy of the widely distributed decrees of the Clones Synod of 1670, in which it was agreed to collect fifty pounds from amongst the Irish church leaders for the expenses of their agent in Rome. Oliver was asked if it was his and replying that it was, Sergeant Jeffries then pipes up: "He owns it" as if it were an incriminating document. However, this document had been altered and another zero was inserted after the fifty pounds to make up the number five-hundred pounds, the implication being that such a sum would be used to further the plot. Oliver challenged Moyer on both documents; the letter to Rome was a complete fabrication and the second document had obviously been tampered with. Oliver pointed out that it was easy to recognise that a zero had been added in with a different colour of ink. Pemberton exclaimed that it could be easily be explained: "leaving a blank for the sum, and then, may be, you put it in with ink." Adding: "Look you Mr. Plunkett, consider with yourself fifty pounds or five-hundred pounds in this case is not five farthings difference, but the money was to be raised by your order."

Oliver then produced letters sent by Moyer to Friar Anthony O'Neill, son of Eoin Roe, which proved Moyer's hostility towards the Archbishop. Moyer agreed that it was his handwriting, Oliver asked him to read it out to the court. In it, Moyer berates Oliver who had suspended his ministry, Oliver in turn tells the court that even if such things were true, was it likely that he would tell a man secrets whom he had already denounced throughout the diocese. Oliver again states that if his witnesses were only present, they would put a different light on the evidence presented. He continued by telling the court that the prosecution witness had been convicted and found guilty of giving powder and shot to the rebels and asks Moyer to confirm it. Pemberton states that he may not answer that and Justice Dolben instructs Oliver: "Produce the record if you have any such thing." The court were well aware of the facts of this, as John Plunkett had written in his affidavit only the previous day, that the criminal convictions of the witnesses would be made available if a deferment of the trial was granted. It was important for Oliver to undermine the credibility of the principal witness against him, so he tried again, stating: "He hath been convicted and found guilty, he will confess it himself." Moyer grimaces and replies: "It was a Tory swore against me that you did absolve." Oliver had won a major point so Justice Dolben jumps in: "Don't tell us a story of your Tories." Pemberton immediately pipes up: "Look you Mr. Plunkett, don't misspend your own time; for the more you trifle in these things, the less time you will have for your defence." Moyer's own confirmation of his conviction would ultimately make no difference to the prejudices of his hearers.

Curtayne Alice 'The Trial of Oliver Plunkett' Ireland 1975. p.144

82. HUGH HANLON

The last witness to take the stand against Oliver was Hugh Hanlon, son in law to O'Neill. He was put on the stand, solely to back up Moyer's earlier testimony of the existence of the incriminating letter supposedly written by Oliver. He confirmed in a short testimony that he had been on the continent where he met Neill(Neal) O'Neill and saw the unopened letter in question. When asked how he knew O'Neill was Oliver's servant he replied: "Because he showed me his letter." Oliver questioned him and asked where he seen the letter; he replied at Mant in France. Oliver again expresses his frustration to the court at not having time to bring his witnesses or records: "What can I say when I have not my witnesses against these people that may swear anything in the world. You cannot but observe the improbability of the thing in itself, and unto what condition I am brought." The witness stood down; the case for the prosecution thus ended having heard nine witnesses, five laymen and four renegade priests, two of whom were Franciscan friars and two secular priests, one each from the dioceses of Armagh and Clogher. The four suspended priests were all quite familiar with prison life.

Curtayne Alice 'The Trial of Oliver Plunkett' Ireland 1975. p.165

83. OLIVER'S DEFENCE

As defending council were not allowed in trials for treason; Oliver was required to put up his own defence. Downside Abbey have possession of the document which Oliver held in his hand throughout the trial. On this, he had written notes[1] to help him remember points relevant for his defence. These include references to notes from previous viceroys, Berkeley and Essex attesting to Oliver's character and stating that he had performed some service in the kingdom. His other reminders referred to Moyer's three letters to Friar O'Neill and some points Oliver had made previously during his arraignment at Dundalk court a year earlier. Two papers signed by Edmund Murphy, a letter of Collin Murphy, a copy of a petition to the council in Ireland, a letter of Patrick Donnelly stating that Moyer was abroad, an attestation from a foreign country that Moyer was beyond the seas,

a note of what his witnesses could say for him and his last point referred to the interrogation by him of Moyer and the other witnesses arrayed against him. It is interesting to note that the official trial notes, which had to be sanctioned by Lord Chief Justice Pemberton before they were printed, do not cover many of the points which Oliver had obviously intended covering in his defence. Primate Oliver, who was on trial for his life as head of the Catholic Church in

Ireland, it would be unthinkable that he would not have presented his case in its entirety, lest the Church in Ireland might be tainted in any way.

If Oliver's cousin, Sir Nicholas Plunkett, the leading Catholic lawyer in Ireland had still been alive, he would certainly have travelled to London to advise him from the wings. He would surely have noticed that the wrong[2] date was on Oliver's indictment, namely the two and thirtieth year of Charles II which referred to 1680. By this time Oliver was already in custody and therefore unable to commit any such crimes. Another point of law which was not followed in Oliver's case and which might also have helped to overthrow the trial if noticed; stated that in trials for treason, the accused should be prosecuted within[3] six months and arraigned within a further three.

Without defending council, Oliver pointed out how untenable his position was, his own witnesses had been unfairly delayed in Ireland and the Dublin court officials had delayed the issuing of documentation which would have clearly proven the criminal records and corrupt character of the opposing witnesses. Without council, Oliver was left to his own devices and he again challenged the court to try him in England, a good point in law, stating he would be happy to defend himself before any Protestant jury in Ireland where he and his accusers would be known. Pemberton had done his homework as he recounted a precedent by the name of O'Rourke. Oliver had also done his homework, stating: "He was arrested in Scotland." Pemberton interjected that he was getting as fair a trial there as if he were in Ireland. As further proof that he was well briefed, Oliver drew the courts attention to the precedent of the Sir Thomas Gascoigne[4] court case. Only the previous year, an elderly Yorkshire man, Sir Thomas Gascoigne, was acquitted by a jury in a popish plot trial after his request was granted that he should be tried in London by a Yorkshire jury who knew the accused and the accusers.

[1] Hanly 'The Letters' Appendix 1 p.583

[2] Curtis, Fr. Emmanuel 'Blessed Oliver Plunkett' p.147/148 Dublin 1963

[3] Curtis, Fr. Emmanuel 'Blessed Oliver Plunkett' p.147/148 Dublin 1963

[4] Curtayne Alice 'The Trial of Oliver Plunkett' Ireland 1975 p.190

84. FRIAR PAUL GORMLEY

Oliver then asked that three witnesses be called, David Fitzgerald, Eustace Cummins and Paul Gormley, all three had originally been assembled as witnesses for the prosecution. The only one to answer was Fr. Paul Gormley, a Franciscan friar released from prison in Derry; he lived for fifteen months in London and survived like the other witnesses on a twelve shillings weekly allowance from the secret service. Oliver asked whether[1] Moyer had ever enticed Gormley to swear against him. Answering no, he added: "Mr. Moyer and I were in discourse, and he said if there was law to be had in Ireland, he would show Mr. Plunkett his share of it. Pemberton then replied: "What of it." And Gormely replied: "My Lord, I did come out of Ireland to reveal what plans the Irish had against the king, and as for this Mr. Plunkett, as I have a soul to save, I never heard of any misdemeanour of him." Justice Dolben: "How come you are here today?" Gormely replied that he was summoned. Justice Dolben: "By whom, was it the Attorney General or Plunkett that summoned you?" Here is the summons replies Gormely and upon inspection Serjeant Jeffries states: "It is a common sup-poena." Oliver then tells the court that he never sent for him. Gormely adds: "It was not against you; they knew I had nothing against you. I thought you did more good in Ireland than hurt; so I declare." Pemberton asked Oliver: "Have you any more witnesses." Oliver replies: "My Lord, I have not any more witnesses." Oliver's friends on the outside were obviously trying their best for him by organising a witness, any witness, but the testimony of this surprise witness had descended to the same[2] level as much of the prosecution's case, namely hearsay and conjecture. Reports of the trial later stated that Oliver made but a weak defence; calling three witnesses, when only one appeared, who had declared in court that he had nothing to say for him, only that he sympathized with his case.

---

[1] Curtayne Alice 'The Trial of Oliver Plunkett' Ireland 1975 p.176

[2] Ó Fiaich & Forristal 'Oliver Plunkett' Indiana, USA 1976. Ó Fiaich. p.92

85. CONVICTION

Having no further witnesses, Pemberton summed up the full list of charges for the jury, but in a way which seemed to accept the guilt of the accused: "And these things do seem to be very plain by the witnesses, that he himself hath taken a commission to promote these things...I leave it to you it is very strong evidence, he does not say anything to it, but that his witnesses are not come over." The jury retired to make their decision and returned in the short space of a quarter of an hour. Pemberton: "Oliver Plunkett hold up thy hand, how say you, is he guilty of high treason or not guilty." The foreman of the jury replies: "Guilty."

Oliver then exclaimed in a joyous voice: "Deo Gratias" or God be thanked. The court which had sat for a mere three hours on a capital charge of high treason, then rose and Oliver was taken by the keeper back to Newgate prison.

A day or two afterwards, Oliver sent a petition to the King, pleading that his case should be looked into further. He requested that the papers and records of his witnesses should be examined and the findings of a report sent back to London. In essence, he wished that his trial would be reopened. As an act clemency, he also asks for a pardon or a reprieve. An affidavit was affixed to the petition, presumably a copy of the one written by John Plunkett, dated 7th June and heard before the King's Bench on the day before the trial.

The Habeas Corpus Act had formally become law just months before Oliver's imprisonment, entitling an accused to trial and disallowing arbitrary imprisonment. However the act could offer no protection against perjured witnesses, or judges who were more interested in playing to the gallery than to natural justice. The fact that so much hearsay evidence was freely submitted against Oliver must also leave the manner of conducting the trial highly irregular. The trial has since been studied by legal counsel and their impression of the way the trial was conducted could be summarised by a single word, shambolic. The trial has therefore been described as marking a low point in the history of the English

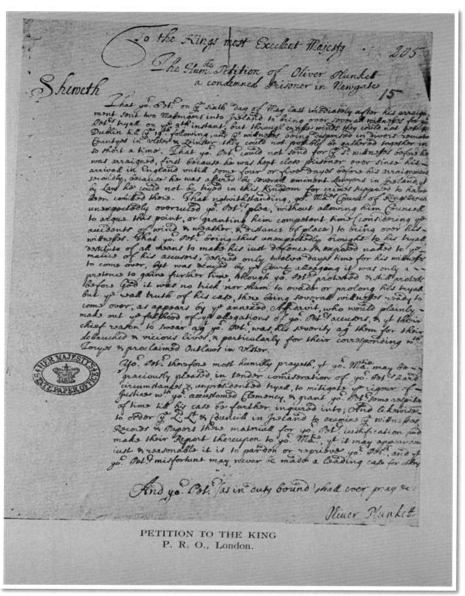

PETITION TO THE KING
P. R. O., London.

Petition Letter to the King

judicial system. Oliver had been friendly with a Colonel Fitzpatrick, who for many years had been a great benefactor to him, however he was a traitor and later renounced his faith. He had nothing incriminating on Oliver, neither word nor deed, proving yet again how Oliver was always straight in his dealings and would have nothing at all to do with politics, nor would he gossip or engage in any loose talk whatsoever.

In order to get a conviction, the prosecution were therefore forced to rely totally on concocted evidence at the trial. However, let us not forget that the witnesses who testified against him were all Irish Catholics, bought and brought over from Ireland. Among them were at least four suspended priests and five laymen, most and probably all of them with criminal records. The Duke of Ormond had already described them as: "scoundrels who found treachery safer than cow stealing and not even a schoolboy would entrust them with a design of robbing an orchard."

Oliver's trial was followed on the following day by another highly publicised trial for high treason, the case of Edward Fitzharris. After his discoveries of plots, he had gone way too far as he had tried to implicate the Duke of York and Queen Catherine in a web of treachery. King Charles had him removed from Newgate to the Tower of London so that Lord Shaftsbury's colleagues who had ready access to Newgate could not school him further. The King had got one over on the Whigs of parliament and after Fitzharris was convicted, the King was certainly not in any mood to commute the sentence, particularly as he had tried to implicate his own family in a plot.

Pope Innocent XI, who had known Oliver in Rome continued to mediate on his behalf with Emperor Leopold in Vienna, the Spanish ambassador in London and also the Duchess Modena, mother of the Duchess of York but all without success. Lord Essex, a previous Viceroy in Ireland who knew Oliver well, went to the King claiming that the charges against Oliver could not possibly be true, but the King retorted: "Why did you not say that at the trial, it might have done him some good then, I dare pardon no one. His blood be upon your head, not mine." Like Pilate, King Charles washed his hands of all responsibility for the execution which was about to take place in his name. Weak and duplicitous as ever, King Charles II whose wife, mother, brother and sister in law were all Catholic, was determined to die in his bed and not beheaded like his father, King Charles I.

[1] Curtayne Alice 'The Trial of Oliver Plunkett' Ireland 1975 p.177

86. SENTENCING

On 15th June, a week after his trial and conviction, Oliver was brought back to Westminster Hall for sentencing. When asked if he had anything to say before sentence of death would be passed on him, Oliver again went over his main points; stating that he was innocent of all the crimes of which he had been accused. However he would declare that he had exercised the functions of a bishop and if he had been accused of premunire, there would have been a case to answer but of these charges he was as innocent as a child born yesterday. Documentation had been denied to him, his witnesses were deliberately delayed, adding that they were in Coventry on the previous day. Pemberton in an attempt to justify the trial verdict, spoke about the prosecution witnesses: "For consider here were persons of your own religion, the most of them priests…I think almost all of them in orders." Oliver replied: "There were two friars and a priest, whom I endeavoured to correct seven years, and they were renegades from our religion and dastard apostates."

Chief Justice Pemberton nodded to Jack Ketch the hangman who approached Oliver and tied his thumbs together, while Pemberton donned a black cap[1] and pronounced sentence: "And therefore you must go from here to the place from which you came, that is to Newgate and from there you shall be drawn through the city of London to Tyburn; there you shall be hanged by the neck, but cut down before you are dead, your bowels shall be taken out and burnt before your face, your head shall be cut off, and your body be divided into four quarters, to be disposed of as his majesty pleases, and I pray may God have mercy on your soul." Oliver was given leave to have his servant James given unlimited access to his cell and also to have friends visit. He asked for the services of a priest, adding that there were some in prison who were never indicted or accused of any crime. This request was denied by Chief Justice Pemberton who offered him instead the services of a Protestant minister, to which Oliver answered: "I am obliged for your good intentions, but such a favour would be wholly useless to me." Oliver adds: "…I might have saved my life, for I was offered it by divers' people here, so I would but confess my own guilt and accuse others, but my lord… I had rather die ten thousand deaths, than wrongfully take away one farthing of any man's goods, one day of his liberty, or one minute of his life."

Later Oliver in his last speech from the gallows would expressly forgive everybody who had anything to do with his death, including the judges. In his last words to Chief Justice Pemberton, Oliver offers what can only be described as a most forgiving prayer: "God almighty bless your worship." Oliver's witnesses arrived in London on the day after the trial. Writing in a letter to Rome: "Sentence of death was passed against me on the 15th without causing me any fear or depriving me of sleep for a quarter of an hour." Oliver was a man of high morals, also very courageous, he was never afraid to take the action which was required, irrespective of the consequences for himself. Previously he wrote: "Let the world perish, but let justice be done" and one of his regular quotes was: "If the whole world should come crashing down the ruins will strike an undaunted man." A lesser man might have compromised along the way and lived a longer life, but a lesser man would never have become a canonised saint. The keeper stepped forward and took Oliver out of Westminster Hall and brought him back to his prison cell.

Three hundred and twenty-nine years later, St. Oliver must have smiled broadly on Friday 17th September 2010, as Pope Benedict XVI during his papal visit to Britain, gave a memorable address in Westminster Hall to the members of both Houses of Parliament and many other dignitaries of Church and State. It was the first time a Pope ever visited Westminster Hall, scene of a great injustice on Archbishop Oliver Plunkett, St. Thomas More and so many other innocents of the time. A packed hall was often the scene during sixteenth and seventeenth century trials, when a cross section of English society would acclaim the guilty verdicts pronounced upon so many blameless Catholics.

Just to broaden St. Oliver's smile a little more on that day in 2010, among the attendance in the Hall to hear the Holy Father's address as an honoured guest, was Cardinal Seán Brady, the Primate of all Ireland and St. Oliver's successor as Archbishop of Armagh. Most of those three hundred and twenty-nine years were extremely difficult for Catholics in these islands and the papal visit marked another milestone for the laudable objectives of reconciliation and mutual respect between our peoples.

[1] Curtis, Fr. Emmanuel 'Blessed Oliver Plunkett' Dublin 1963. p.171
[2] Curtayne Alice 'The Trial of Oliver Plunkett' Ireland 1975 p.189

87. CONDEMNED MAN

As a condemned man, the regime in prison was relaxed for the last sixteen days or so of his life and he was allowed free access of visitors. Fr. Maurus Corker, the Benedictine monk who had already been in regular communication by letter with Oliver, got the opportunity through influence and perhaps a little bribery of the guards to meet Oliver and so hear each other's confession on the evening of 23rd June. Fr. Corker had been acquitted two years earlier as part of the popish plot, but was condemned to death in January 1680 because he was a priest; granted a reprieve he remained incarcerated in Newgate until freed on the accession of King James II in 1685. Fr. Corker wrote in a private letter that he and Oliver did in fact meet and that Oliver was able to celebrate Holy Mass in his prison cell. This letter was copied and distributed among Catholics but those two[1] references were omitted in the copies, in case they might cause difficulties or lead to tighter restrictions for those priests and some others who were still imprisoned. During this time, they were in regular communication with each other; Fr. Corker wrote that since Oliver's arraignment on 3rd May they could write to each other in prison: "But our letters were read, transcribed and examined by the officers before they were delivered to either of us."

After sentencing on 15th June, James McKenna had free access to Oliver's cell and could deliver letters and messages between cells. Fr. Corker and Oliver had not yet met, but they had already developed a deep bond of friendship and as Oliver's anam-chara, Fr. Corker was destined to maintain a lifelong devotion to the martyred Archbishop of Armagh. Oliver made an earnest appeal to all, including Fr. Corker to pray for him. Oliver was also conscious of the importance of having his confession heard and he wrote to Fr. Corker: "Your prayers I desire, the passage is but short yet tis dangerous, tis from time to eternity, it can never be repassed or reiterated, your prayers I say I beg, and your brethren's." Conscious of his sinfulness, and placing himself at the mercy of God; he professed his hopes in the fairness of the great Court of God, stating that there he could be sure of an absolutely fair trial, where no false witnesses could appear. Oliver was destined to follow the path of so many others and was especially aware of the five Jesuits who preceded him on the last legs of his own journey to sainthood. His prison cell had previously been occupied by one of those five Jesuits, Blessed Fr. Thomas Whitbread. Oliver endured a similar type of trial with the same unjust outcome, quickly followed by an identical type of martyrdom and at Oliver's request he would soon occupy the same grave as the five Jesuits.

His servant James visited him daily and brought Mass requisites and letters to him from Fr. Corker. To his great joy, Oliver could once again celebrate daily, the Holy Sacrifice of the Mass and so become a real priest once more. James, more often in the prison than not, was allowed stay in the cell with his master for the last couple of days of Oliver's life. Teacher to the last, Oliver wrote at this time: "Being the first among the Irish, with the grace of God I shall give good example to the others not to fear death. To exhort others to die stoutly is easy and not difficult, but to instruct them by example and by practice is more efficacious." In one of his few known letters written in English, using the spelling of the time: "I am as innocent of all treason as a child borne yesterday as for my caracter, profession and function I did owne it publickly and that being alsoe a motive of my death I dye most willingly." In the same letter written to a relative, Fr. Michael Plunkett, his former secretary then living in Rome, he mentions by name several of his relations including his brother, his nephews and nieces and shows warmth and concern for their wellbeing. With remarkable candour and with more than a trace of humour, Archbishop Oliver could write only a short time before his death: "Those who once beheaded my statue[2] have now achieved the same object in the case of its prototype." While Oliver firmly believed that it was prosecution witnesses, Friars Moyer and Duffy who knocked over his statue, there is some doubt about this. One of the pair may have been involved along with another culprit or perhaps Oliver was correct in what he wrote. His sentiment stands however.

[1] Curtis, Fr. Emmanuel 'Blessed Oliver Plunkett' Dublin 1963. p.178
[2] See Chapter 34

88. ARCHBISHOP OLIVER'S WILL

Fr. Corker and others organised a collection among some of the prominent Catholic families for Oliver's many expenses. Oliver wrote of a separate bequest of £38, which was made to him by 'Fallon.' Added together, it enabled him to make a will in which he left a few small bequests, not forgetting one of ten pounds for his servant James: "Who served me faithfully these past eleven years." Worried for so long about his intolerable and crushing debts, Oliver thanked God that so many good people had come to his aid and perhaps he realised that he should have trusted a little more in the great providence of God. Oliver had not yet attained sainthood, but he had very nearly reached the last step of the journey and he ultimately succeeded in reaching that goal through his lifelong practice of spiritual development. Finalising his financial affairs, he wrote[1] to Fr. Corker: "If I be able I am I think bound in conscience to remunerat some servants, who served me in hope, that I might do them good, served me gratis but that hope vanished for stipend but smale and suffered with me in prisons of Ireland. Of it can be spared I desire that the thirty-eight pounds of Fallons[2] may be distributed thus."

To my man James MacCanna	*£10*
To one James Nugent who served me gratis	*£10*
To one Joseph Plunkett who served gratis	*£10*
To one John Mortagh	*£3*
To one Robert Plunkett	*£3*
To one Hugh Ward	*£2*

"Mr Rely doth deserve much from me for he ventured, and was extremely well disposed for those knaves might out of theire wicked humors doe him some mischeefe. I think you may give him £10 of the £62 and the rest to be for the other expenses and my soule. &c I see your great charity that you are desireous to be careful of my unworthy carcas after my death which being a work of mercy in high degree I ought not to deprive you of its reward being most precious Vidz everlasting glory I ought not to forget Mr. Pinkard."

Some of the same families also promised to show James charity after Oliver's death. In a letter written the day before his death, he prays in thanksgiving for all his benefactors: "I desire that you be pleased to tell all my benefactors, that for all eternity I shall be mindful of them and that I will pray for them until they come where I hope to come soon and then also will thank them in the sight of the supreme master. I beseech my Saviour to give all the good Catholics perseverance in their faith and good works and to grant me grace to be tomorrow where I shall pray for them not in obscurity but face to face."

[1] Hanly 'The Letters' No.222

[2] Fallon, was undoubtedly Fr. Gregory Fallon, a former professor of theology in Bologna. Oliver knew him well, having recommended him on several occasions to become a bishop or a vicar apostolic and he referred to him in five of his letters. Oliver probably stayed with him on his stopover in Bologna some twelve years earlier while on his journey home to Ireland. In 1681, Fallon was living in London as a chaplain in the Spanish embassy.

89. OLIVER'S FINAL DAYS

Oliver then had to bear the uncertainty of when the end might finally come, so as to get all his affairs in order, both spiritual and temporal. Sentenced on 15th June, he was informed on Saturday 18th June that his execution would take place on Tuesday 21st June. That day came and went as the execution had been postponed until Friday 24th; this in turn was postponed for the third and final time to Friday 1st July. He expressed disappointment at the last postponement as he would have been happy to suffer on the eve of the feast of St. John the Baptist, but expressed satisfaction that it would still be within the octave of that feast and would take place on a Friday. The one and only time Oliver met Fr. Corker his anam-chara, was on the evening of the 23rd and it was to leave a lifelong impression on Fr. Corker.

Oliver fully understood that his speech from the gallows would be of great importance, as it would be widely reported and commented upon. Some of his correspondence at this time with Fr. Corker dealt with this topic, he was concerned that the speech should be detailed and specific and not just general in terms, writing: "because of the danger that equivocation can often be hidden in such generalities." Drafts went to and fro as Oliver was anxious that it should not be too severe or uncharitable in content but yet should address each and every charge for which he had been convicted. Oliver was very calm all during this time and never lost any sleep; indeed on the morning of his execution he was awakened early by his servant James, to pray and to celebrate Holy Mass. The letters he wrote from his prison cell at this time are very revealing, as they show clearly the depth of his spirituality and holiness. This is much more evident in this series of letters than in his earlier ones, which could be classed in general as his reports to Rome and as such, they would be expected only occasionally to show warmth or personal insights. Because of the general hysteria about the plot and the importance of the accused, there was considerable talk and publicity surrounding the trial. Much of Europe was aghast at the outcome. Diplomatic efforts continued to be made in various countries to obtain a pardon. To be hung drawn and quartered was a horrible death and gruesome spectacle, Oliver surprised himself by his total lack of fear or concern of it, having no fear whatsoever of those who can only destroy the body. He believed it was his Saviour who had merited him with this grace and compared to what our Lord suffered, he believed his own death would be but a flea bite in comparison. Oliver was very conscious of his past sins and prepared himself earnestly for death. He expressed his faith in a baptism of another sort, that of blood spilled upon the ground.

Throughout his lifetime, Oliver had led an exemplary life, it is documented that as a young man he had been a well behaved, excellent student. As a priest he was devout and very compassionate as witnessed in the Spirito Santo Hospital. As a professor in Rome, even the Pope had admired his work and as archbishop and primate, his record speaks for itself. Yet it was in those last months, in the dark unheated dungeon of Newgate, that his sanctity had fully developed and shone forth for all to see. Many English Catholics came to visit him in prison, to spend time with him and comfort him, however they came away comforted and edified by his demeanour and his blessings and his holiness was quite apparent to them. He was also impressed and very grateful to them for their kindness and great charity towards him, he described them as "rare

Catholics." Writing in thanks, he listed many of the families who had helped him, including the Sheldon's, Stafford's and he also mentions a Mrs. Chavers, née Ann Sarsfield sister of the famous Patrick. During the last fortnight of his life as a condemned man in Newgate Prison, he was allowed countless visitors including children and he almost certainly confirmed at this time.

Some eleven years before his death, on his way home to Ireland as the newly consecrated Archbishop of Armagh, Oliver undoubtedly confirmed during the few months that he spent in England. It is highly likely then, that Archbishop Oliver's first and last exercises as a bishop were performed in the London area. Renowned for his confirmation ceremonies, this might altogether be quite appropriate. The endless stream of visitors throughout each day was such that it left Oliver desiring just one full day to recollect himself before death. Even some Protestants came to visit him and it is recorded that along with everyone else, they were impressed by his apparent holiness. It was no wonder that he had so many visitors, Catholic bishops were actually extinct in England and quite miraculously, here was an archbishop readily accessible, right in the heart of London, a Catholic free zone. Many, who already saw him as a martyr for the faith, came on account of this to visit him and to receive a bishop and a martyr's blessing. It was truly an amazing scene and a blessing from heaven.

Undoubtedly, the martyr's most revealing letters about himself were ones he penned at this time from within his prison cell. Amongst these were letters and notes to Fr. Corker, each of which display a deep spirituality. Teacher to the last, he wrote: "And since I exhorted others by word in Ireland, it is only fitting that I should strengthen them by example." This series of letters are all well preserved and among the cherished possessions of the Benedictine Community at Downside Abbey. Just a few hours before his execution, Father Corker gives him a cap, handkerchief and two guineas for the executioner. Oliver quite remarkably, in perfect and steady handwriting makes out a receipt. This author felt highly privileged to hold this letter/receipt in Downside Abbey, and to take the attached photo.

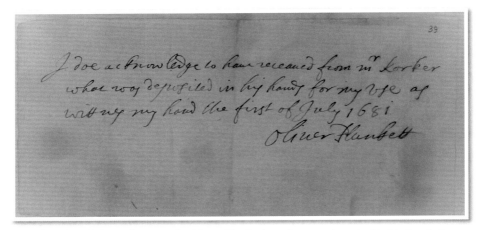

I do acknowledge to have received from Mr. Corker what was deposited in his hands for my use as witnes my hand the first July '81. Oliver Plunkett

It is often said that Fr. Corker possibly enrolled St. Oliver as a confrater[1] of the Benedictine order. Indeed another Benedictine priest imprisoned with St. Oliver at this time, Fr. Cuthbert Wall alias Mr. Marshall, a monk of Lamspringe Abbey, Germany, lent Oliver a 'shift' to wear on his way to Tyburn. This garb may well have been a form of habit or scapular[2] to represent the Benedictine order. In any event, St. Oliver saw himself as coming under the obedience of Fr. Corker, who was President of the English Benedictines at the time. St. Oliver left all decisions in his hands, even such small ones as; how the barber would attend to him, whether or not to have a fortifying drink on the day of execution, the drafting of his final speech and finally he left his clothes, possessions and his body to be at Fr. Corker's 'will and pleasure.' Oliver sent James to Fr. Corker's cell to ask whether he should accept the glass of sac, a type of sherry, which was offered to him an hour before leaving Newgate. The answer being in the affirmative; Oliver readily obeyed.

Likewise when the barber came, Oliver inquired of Fr. Corker how he should have his moustache cut, as he was not at his own disposal.

In a letter to Mrs. Sheldon, Fr. Corker wrote[3] of Oliver's time in Newgate: "After his transportation hither he was as you know close confined and secluded from all humain conversation save that of his keepers until his arraignment, so that here also I am much in the darke, and can only informe you of what I learnt as it were by chance from the mouthes of the said keepers. That he fasted usually three or four dayes a week with nothing but bread. That he appeared to them always modestly cheerful without any anguish or concern at his danger or strict confinement. That by his sweet and pious demeanour hee attracted an esteeme an reverance from those few that came to neare him. When he was arraigned, it is true I could write to him, and he to mee, but our letters were read, transcribed and examined by the officers before they were delivered to either of us, for which cause wee had little other communication than was necessary in order to his tryall."

[1] Cramer Dom Anselm 'Lamspringe an English Abbey in Germany' Ampleforth Abbey 2004. p.124
[2] Cramer Dom Anselm 'Lamspringe an English Abbey in Germany' Ampleforth Abbey 2004. p.125
[3] Curtis, Fr. Emmanuel 'Blessed Oliver Plunkett' Dublin 1963. p.178

90. MARTYRDOM

Before dawn on 1st July 1681, James awoke[1] Oliver at 4am who had slept soundly since 11pm. A loyal servant for eleven years, it must surely have been the longest and saddest night of James's life. Oliver then celebrated an early morning Mass in his cell, his last before meeting his Lord face to face. After writing some short notes in his usual firm handwriting and bold signature which indicated no signs of strain, he said his final goodbyes. It would have been around 9am when Oliver got ready to leave the prison and as he was led out of the priests yard, his sledge was turned around to face the cell windows as described by Fr.

Corker: "With a pleasant aspect and elevated hand, gave us his benediction." The keeper of Newgate when asked how the prisoner was, replied that he had slept soundly and that he was as unconcerned as if he was going to a wedding.

Placed lying on a sledge face upwards, stretched and bound tightly with rope, Archbishop Oliver was dragged by a horse from Newgate prison to Tyburn, a distance of three kilometres, before a pressing and noisy crowd. James McKenna, faithful servant to the last, kept close by. Edward Fitzharris was taken from the Tower of London that morning for the double execution at Tyburn; both sledges were dragged together from Newgate. Hangings were often seen as carnival events and it was not uncommon for a fife and drum band to accompany a parade of thousands of people. Archbishop John Brenan wrote that the procession to Tyburn was accompanied by: "A multitude of spectators, numerous guards of militia and royal officers." Archbishop Oliver must have felt quite sore and faint as the sledge was dragged over the bumpy roads on its slow convoy. Crowds had gathered along his via dolorosa while a multitude waited at Tyburn, many of whom were on the stand. From the three cornered gallows at Tyburn, which was capable of hanging over twenty people at a time, Archbishop Oliver delivered his speech. It is ironic that as he did so, he was standing over or close to the pit into which Oliver Cromwell's disinterred body was ignominiously thrown some twenty years earlier, the same Oliver Cromwell who had come, conquered, planted and subjugated. It was almost a century since a Catholic bishop had been publicly hanged at Tyburn and interest was high. As a result the crowd was undoubtedly larger than normal for that day's double execution. Many Catholics were also in attendance, secretly and silently praying, as they fully realised that a martyr for the faith was before them.

His final speech would have taken at least fifteen minutes to deliver; Oliver refuted his accusers point by point and forgave all of them. It was reported that he delivered as powerful a sermon as he had ever done before, which was noteworthy because he would only have had a poor

Tyburn Scene Painting at Shrine

weather beaten cart for a pulpit. Showing great sincerity of heart, forgiveness and humility, without the slightest hint of any caginess or ambiguity, Oliver had won over the crowd, who listened to him throughout. In a clear and strong voice, he stated: "If these points of seventy-thousand men, etc. had been sworn before any Protestant jury in Ireland, and had been even acknowledged by me at the bar, they would not believe me, no more than if it had been deposed, and confessed by me, that I had flown in the air from Dublin to Holyhead." He then forgave the judges and those who had given evidence against him at the trial: "I beg of my Saviour to grant them true repentance, I do forgive them with all my heart.... But you see how I am requited, and how by false oaths they brought me to this untimely death; which wicked act, being a defect

221

of persons, ought not to reflect upon the order of St. Francis, or upon the Roman Catholic clergy. It being well known, that there was a Judas among the twelve Apostles, and that among the deacons there was a wicked man called Nicholas."

Oliver's theme of reconciliation continued, by his asking forgiveness of all those whom he had ever offended by thought, word or deed. He prayed: "I beseech your Divine Majesty by the merits of Christ and the intercession of his Blessed Mother and all the holy angels and saints to forgive me my sins and to grant my soul eternal rest." Edward Fitzharris then spoke and this gave Oliver the opportunity to pray. Kneeling he recited an act of contrition, the miserere psalm and he repeated before his death: "Into Thy hands, O Lord, I commend my Spirit." He gave his rosary beads to his servant James, most likely having used them as he was dragged on the journey to Tyburn. The cart was moved away and at least three priests[2] were present to give a final absolution to Archbishop Oliver. Among them were two Carmelites, Fr. Gasper from Belgium who was attached to the Spanish Embassy and Lucian Travers an Englishman; also there was Fr. Petre, a Jesuit. Fr. Petre declared that Oliver's countenance was angelic and that he had a profound effect on many who were there. Fr. Corker wrote something similar of Oliver's demeanour while he was in

Martyr's Altar - Tyburn Convent

Newgate: "But I neither can nor dare undertake to describe unto you the signall virtues of this blessed martyr. There appeared in him something beyond expression, something more than humane. The most savage and hard hearted people were mollifyed and attendred at his sight. Many Protestants in my hearing wisht their soules in the same state with his. All believed him innocent, and he made Catholics even the most timorous in love with death."

Oliver worked tirelessly as Archbishop for ten years, paying the ultimate price of martyrdom without seeing the fruits of his labours. His crowning glory was the manner of his death; humble, heroic and holy. For some considerable time, Oliver had already given his all, now he was being asked to give his life blood as well and he was happy to do just that. Jack Ketch the hangman placed the noose around his neck, the cart pulled away and Oliver who had at long last ascended all of the steps of sainthood, could now meet his Divine Savour face to face.

He was almost certainly dead when taken down and the further mutilation began. His bearing and his speech from the scaffold were well received and it was patently obvious to many that he was innocent, as the plot had already shown signs of crumbling. In the previous few years, many innocent individuals had been hanged at Tyburn, mostly priests. None had tried to gain their freedom by pleading guilty or condemning others and this had exposed a major weakness in the plot. Oliver's trial, conviction and his eventual martyrdom on 1st July 1681, was such an outrageous episode that it greatly discredited those who had brought it about. The credibility of the plot and of its advocates collapsed completely thereafter. Lord Shaftesbury, the principal promoter of the plot was arrested and imprisoned on the following day and Titus Oates was arrested soon afterwards on a charge of perjury.

It was a shrewd move to have a copy of his speech set aside for the printers, as it became widely available afterwards. Indeed it has been reprinted several times over the centuries. Archbishop Oliver had been greatly maligned and misrepresented during his life; by having his speech printed and made widely available, ensured that this should not happen after his death. The speech was exceedingly well crafted and among other points he stressed over and over again that he spoke without any equivocation whatsoever. It was widely reported and generally believed that Catholics could speak with forked tongues, i.e. equivocation, although in truth they were no better at lying than any other group. While not true, it was what people believed and the lie had to be confronted. Oliver left no one in any doubt with regard to the veracity of his denials of any involvement whatsoever in any such plots: "For a final satisfaction of all persons, that have the charity to believe the words of a dying man, I again declare before God, as I hope for salvation, what is contained in this paper, is the plain and naked truth, without any equivocation, mental reservation, or secret evasion whatsoever, taking the words in their usual sense and meaning, as Protestants do, when they discourse with all candour and sincerity. To all which, I have here subscribed my hand the first of July."

Oliver Plunkett

His two and a half thousand word speech is well worth a read in Appendix IX p. 289 and may be downloaded from the Saint Oliver Plunkett[3] website. Oliver's willing sacrifice both in life and in death, his dying prayers as bishop and primate, his courageous and strong witness, his deep holiness through prayer and fasting which shone ever brighter over two harsh winters while in prison and his loving and absolute forgiveness of anyone who may have brought about his downfall; all of this had a profound effect and the Lord answered his prayer. As a result, St. Oliver became the last of the one hundred and five Catholic martyrs of Tyburn who had given their lives over the previous one hundred and fifty years. It must be highly significant that he was also the very last of the Catholic martyr's condemned by the state in these islands. Deo Gratias.

[1] Curtis, Fr. Emmanuel 'Blessed Oliver Plunkett' Dublin 1963. p.181
[2] Ó Fiaich & Forristal 'Oliver Plunkett' Indiana, USA 1976. Ó Fiaich. p.106
[3] www.saintoliverplunkett.com

91. FUNERAL

The execution of those convicted of high treason was a thoroughly horrific event; the usual fire had been prepared beside the gallows to consume the viscera. Oliver's Head was thrown into it, but it was quickly recovered, probably by James who was close by. Scorch marks may still be discerned on the left cheek and upper lip of the Relic of the Head in Drogheda. Oliver's body which was quartered on the block at Tyburn was retrieved with great courage and forward planning by his friends. Like Joseph of Arimathea and Nicodemous who arranged for the taking away and the burial of the Body of Jesus with Pilate, Mrs Elizabeth Sheldon an English Catholic lady had already received permission from the King for the body of Oliver. Along with James McKenna, a few priests and some Catholic friends, they collected his remains. While Oliver had willed his body into the care of Dom Maurus Corker, in actual fact it might be true to say that it was Mrs Sheldon who thus became the first custodian of the precious Relics, albeit for a short time. Surgeon John Ridley, a Catholic placed the Forearms and Head in tin boxes and along with Mrs Sheldon signed and dated a document of authentication. This document may be seen at the shrine in Drogheda beside the Head and is in itself a valuable witness to the courage and foresight of all those involved. Fr. Travers wrote[1] joyfully: "I had the honour of holding the sacred head and quarters of the venerable martyr in my own hands and placing them in the chest after the cruel sentence had been carried out in all its gruesome details."

Undoubtedly, the valiant James McKenna would have carried the boxes containing the remains of his earthly master away from Tyburn, the scene of the tragedy. The Body was buried in St. Giles in the Fields graveyard with the five Jesuits, as it was Oliver's wish to be buried with them. It must have been a poignant funeral ceremony for all those who attended, including John Plunkett, James McKenna and many of his loyal English friends. An inscribed copper plate[2] which is now in the possession of the Siena sisters in Drogheda, was placed on the coffin.

After the funeral, James McKenna disappears again into the shadows, something he had become quite expert at over the previous eleven years; but one can be sure that he always carried the rosary beads and a relic of his beloved master Oliver, even if only a lock of hair. It is commonly believed that it was Oliver's relatives who originally choose James as his servant. He remained faithful until the very end, never leaving his masters side irrespective of adversity; it seems that Oliver's relatives choose well, very well indeed. Utterly dependable, Oliver had entrusted James with the most important and delicate of tasks over his eleven years of service. St. Oliver willingly gave his life for his faith and his servant James had shown his willingness to risk his own life on countless occasions for the very same cause. James had also shown himself willing to suffer the harshness of prison life for six months and to experience the inside of at least five prison cells in both Dublin and London. For the rest of his undocumented life, James had countless memories to sustain him, a rosary to pray on and of course, a saint to watch over him. In the company of a saint for eleven years, James must have a taken quite a few steps on his own journey to sainthood within that time; without doubt, he and St. Oliver have met a few times since.

[1] McKee John 'A Martyr Bishop - The Life of St. Oliver Plunkett' Houston Texas 1975. p.171
[2] For Inscription see Chapter 93

92. AFTERMATH IN THE CHURCH IN IRELAND

For a short time there was a little respite; everyone in Ireland knew of Oliver's innocence and Archbishop John Brenan wrote in 1682: "Since the death of the Primate matters have changed for the better. That happy soul receives every day, greater veneration from the faithful." There was however consternation at home and abroad about the great injustice inflicted upon Archbishop Oliver by some people of his own religion. Bishop James Cusack of Meath led the charge, writing to Rome that there must be some punishment inflicted on Armagh and at the very least, let the diocese of Meath be cut off from the province of Armagh and subject directly to the Apostolic See. He expressed his indignation at the repeated injuries of the wicked men who brought down the 'illustrious Oliver of Armagh.' Bishop Cusack added that these men were adding evil to evil by their attempts to seek new warrants to procure the death of Patrick Tyrrell, the Bishop of Clogher, along with Father's Drumgoole, Hughes, Maguirke and several other priests of Armagh. He wrote that because of the conduct of some within the archdiocese, it should be stripped of its privileges and should be taught a salutary lesson. It is interesting to note that Bishop Patrick Tyrrell of Clogher, the Franciscan with Meath origins, was translated to Meath early in 1689 after the death of Bishop Cusack in 1688.

Before the end of 1681, or within six months of St. Oliver's martyrdom, Fr. Edward Drumgoole a native of Killartry, Clogherhead, who according to Oliver was 'the ablest and best priest I have,' was appointed by Rome as vicar apostolic of Armagh and acted in this role for about two years. It was not a happy time for him as the diocese was much divided in its loyalties. He was followed by Archbishop Dominic[1] Maguire, a Dominican in 1683, who went into exile in 1691, the year after the battle of the Boyne. After his death in Paris in 1707, the See became vacant for eight years, during which time Patrick O'Donnelly, the Bishop of Dromore, who was ordained by Oliver in Dundalk in 1673, provided for the needs of the Northern Province. Archbishop Hugh MacMahon was appointed to Armagh in 1715, becoming the first of three MacMahon bishops, who were consecutively translated from Clogher diocese to Armagh. Since c.1720, the archdiocese of Armagh has been blessed by God with a continuous and unbroken line of resident archbishop's, right down to the present day. The archbishops of Armagh continued to reside in the Drogheda area until the mid-nineteenth century, when they moved to Armagh upon the construction of Armagh cathedral. While the diocese was blessed with resident archbishops, nevertheless, conditions were quite often appalling for Catholics and their pastors.

Indeed, of the three archbishops[2] buried in St. Peter's church, Drogheda, two died of dreadful diseases. Archbishop Richard O'Reilly (born1746, Archbishop 1787-1818), Archbishop Patrick Curtis (b1747, 1819-1832) died of cholera and Archbishop Thomas Kelly (b1793, 1832-1835) died of typhus after administering to a sick soldier. The living conditions would undoubtedly have been much more severe for the general populace.

The cultural differences between Catholics of the Anglo-Irish tradition and the Gaelic tradition soon became purely academic as the penal laws tightened their grip. Suffering great hardship together helped to fuse many of their diverse views. For a time the priest hunters were back in vogue; all arguments between the religious were soon forgotten, as all sought pure survival in both body and in spirit. Of course the family rosary helped preserve the Catholic faith in no small measure. Following the penal laws, Catholic religious education among the laity became a huge concern for the Church in Ireland.

[1] See Chapter 62
[2] Carr Patrick 'St. Peter's Church - A Quasi History' 2001/2014 Appendix I

93. RELICS OF THE BODY

Two years later in 1683 and shortly after the crop-eared plot, Fr. Corker while still in prison in Newgate, arranged that Oliver's remains be exhumed and smuggled the following year to the English Benedictine Abbey in Lambspringe, Germany. The removal of the body would have been an illegal act in itself, made all the more complicated as a green[1] woman had since been buried there. Organising a few body snatchers from inside Newgate prison, seems not to have presented any great problem to the resourceful Fr. Corker. Archbishop John Brenan in a letter written in April 1684 stated that the translation of the Body to Germany had taken place shortly beforehand. The Body was interred with great

Lamspringe, Abbey Church, Germany

ceremony in the crypt of the church with a plaque placed overhead in 1693 by Maurus Corker the then abbot. The new Abbey Church was almost completed by this time. Fr. Corker sought permission from Rome to have a perpetual lamp lit before the shrine and his petition was supported at the time by Archbishop Brenan. Fr. Corker had a great veneration for the Primate, his anam chara and felt honoured to have been his faith friend in Newgate prison; he viewed him not alone as a martyr, but as a great saint, referring to him as: "My perpetual intercessor and patron." The inscriptions on the coffin plate and the original shrine in the crypt at Lamspringe both refer to Oliver Plunkett, Archbishop and Primate as a martyr. Fr. Corker had no compunction in calling Oliver a

Monument in Crypt, Lamspringe Abbey

martyr and undoubtedly had a hand in composing both inscriptions. Likewise, for the same reason, the Head and Arms were not buried but retained as relics.

The inscription on the coffin plate, now with Siena convent reads as follows: "In this tomb rested the body of the Most Rev. Oliver Plunkett, late Archbishop of Armagh and Primate of all Ireland, who, when accused of high treason, through hatred of the faith, by false brethren, and condemned to death, being hanged at Tyburn, and his bowels being taken out and cast into the fire, suffered martyrdom with constancy, in the reign of Charles the Second, King of Great Britain, on the 1st July, 1681."

The inscription[2] at Lamspringe reads as follows: "In Holy

Remembrance, here lies the body of Oliver Plunkett, Archbishop of Armagh and Primate of all Ireland. He was hanged by a rope in hatred of the Catholic religion, his internal organs ripped out and thrown into the fire. He died as a glorious martyr in London on July 1 in the year of our Lord 1681. This memorial was built for him by the most venerable Maurus Corker, Abbot of this Monastery in the Lord 1693."

About 1840, Bede Polding[3] wished to acquire the relic of the body for his new church in Sydney, writing: "There is another quasi-relic which I am desirous to have, the remains of Oliver Plunkett, the Catholic Archbishop of Armagh, who received the Benedictine habit from Abbot Corker in the prison of Newgate." It is interesting to note that Cardinal Moran a former student and vice-rector of the Irish College in Rome,

Coffin Plate - Siena Convent

who wrote three famed biographies of St. Oliver later became the Cardinal Archbishop of Sydney and died in 1911.

The Relic of the Body which had lain in Lamspringe Abbey for some two hundred years was translated to the Benedictine Abbey at Downside near Bath, England in 1883 by Dom Aidan Gasquet, later Cardinal Gasquet. St. Oliver's Body rests today in a fine tomb erected on the north aisle of the large community church at Downside Abbey. Lamspringe Abbey and the Cathedral of Hildesheim Diocese held onto some Relics at the time and since the year of beatification in 1920, Lamspringe have been faithful in holding each year an annual procession and celebration in honour of St. Oliver, an adopted patron of the Hildesheim diocese.

New Bell Dedicated in 2014 to St. Oliver, Hildesheim Cathedral, Germany

Even during the Nazi era, when members of the congregation were accosted as they entered the church in Lamspringe, the St. Oliver celebrations continued with the congregation processing with the Relics around the inside of the very large and ornate abbey church. The one thousand year old Cathedral at Hildesheim which reopened in 2014 after major renovation work, has incorporated a fine new peal of bells, one of which is dedicated to St. Oliver.

When the Tomb at Lambspringe was opened before the Body was translated to England, it was noticed that the Relics had a distinct fragrance and were in an unusually good state of preservation. There is a long saga about St. Oliver and boat trips, in this instance perhaps the ninth such boating incident involving Oliver. In January 1883, while the Relics were at sea en-route from Hamburg to London, there was a storm which pitched the ship and when the relics arrived in Downside it was noticed that some of the fleshy parts had turned to dust, although traces of blood and the knife marks after the quartering could still clearly be discerned on both the ribs and other bones. Undoubtedly the exposure to the atmosphere, along with the handling of the Relic on the rest of the journey, would also have contributed to deterioration at this time. At the time of the canonisation in 1975, Downside Abbey kindly donated quite a number of relics to Cardinal William Conway, Archbishop of Armagh; these relics may be venerated at the National Shrine in Drogheda, Oldcastle Parish Church, Dromore Cathedral and some other relics were also given out at that time. The generosity of the community of Downside was seen as an important gesture[4] of promoting Christian peace between England and Ireland, which St. Oliver had sought in life and death.

Archbishop Brenan of Cashel was given a Relic of his arm, which is now in St. Patrick's Church, Rosario[5], Argentina. The Poor Clare Convent in Arundel, Sussex has major Relics and important reliquaries, including blood stained cloths retrieved from Tyburn. Appendix IV lists the locations of other major shrines and reliquaries.

---

[1] Green as in a fresh grave or perhaps Greene by name.

[2] Kronenberg Axel 'The Monastery of Lamspringe and the Irish Martyr Oliver Plunkett' p.16

[3] Cramer Dom Anselm 'Lamspringe an English Abbey in Germany' Ampleforth Abbey 2004. p.128

[4] Murphy, Martin 'Saint Oliver Plunkett and Downside' Downside 1975. p.12

[5] Formerly in the Dominican Convent, Cabra. Picture with explanation on p.275

94. RELIC OF THE HEAD

Shortly after Fr. Corker's release from Newgate in 1685, it is believed that it was via Lamspringe that he brought the Relic of the Head to Rome; giving it to Oliver's old Dominican friend and correspondent, the Cardinal of Norfolk, formerly Fr. Philip Howard, who had hidden Archbishop Oliver in St. James' Palace in London some fifteen years earlier. Fr. Corker became abbot of Lamspringe monastery in 1690. The Relic of the Head was in Cardinal Howard's possession in Rome until his death in 1694; it stayed at Santa Sabina and later with another Dominican community at S.S. John and Paul. Sometime later, about the year 1720, the Archbishop of Armagh, Hugh MacMahon took possession of it. He was a student in the Irish College in Rome when the Relic of the Head of the former past pupil of the college first arrived in the city. This would have had made quite an impact on the students and undoubtedly Hugh MacMahon would have venerated the Relic over the

Old Siena Convent, Cord Road

Siena Convent

years. Archbishop MacMahon, the second successor of St. Oliver as Archbishop of Armagh, brought the Relic back to Ireland shortly afterwards and gave it into the care of the Siena nuns whose first superior was Sr. Catherine Plunkett. Born in 1690, she was certainly a close relative of Oliver and is recorded in the annals of the community as a grandniece[1]. Her father was Thomas Plunkett of Drogheda and her mother's name was Rose. Oliver's brother Edward did not appear to have any children by the name of Thomas or Rose, but perhaps one of his sisters, Catherine, Anne or Mary may have had a daughter called Rose who could have married a Thomas Plunkett of Drogheda and in turn a daughter called Catherine, the first prioress of the community.

Alternatively, one of his sisters may have married a Plunkett and had a son Thomas, father of the said Catherine.

It is generally believed that the Siena community became custodians of the Relic of the Head shortly after they moved to Dyer Street in 1725, but certainly quite some years before Archbishop MacMahon's death in 1737. The religious sisters were living surreptitiously as a group of women friends and lodgers, at a time when the oppression of the penal laws was quite severe. This community of Dominican sisters was founded in 1722 and they originally resided in a mud cabin, probably on the south banks of the river Boyne, as it is recorded that a Dominican priest would travel to them by boat. The community subsequently moved to a large convent off the Cord Road in 1796. Following the tragic fire in 1994, the community moved into their fine new purpose-built convent at the Twenties in 1997.

[1] Forristal, Rev. Desmond. 'The Siena Story' Drogheda, 1999. p.10

95. FATE OF WITNESSES

Shortly after Oliver's martyrdom, the witnesses who swore against him were not at all happy with the pardons they had received. Having been involved in so many crimes, it seems a pardon for some crimes was not a pardon for all. Subsequently, nearly all of the witnesses spent time in jail. However, it appears that Oliver's prayers of forgiveness from the scaffold were largely answered by God. Cardinal Tomás Ó Fiaich in his biography of St. Oliver and Alice Curtayne in her book, 'The Trial of Oliver Plunkett,' record most of the following.

Henry O'Neill was subsequently hanged in Mullingar for robbery. Before his death he retracted completely, the evidence he had given at the trial, stating to a priest that Archbishop Oliver was completely innocent of all crimes and that the witnesses had completely made up the false evidence against him.

Friar John Moyer (MacMoyer) was solemnly declared an apostate and excommunicated from the Church by the Sacred Congregation of Propaganda. He languished in prison for some time in Ireland, as people were not inclined to give food to him or provide for any of his other needs. Imprisoned again and in danger for his life he sought reconciliation with the Church through the offices of Bishop O'Donnelly of Dromore in 1709.

Florence Weyer also languished in prison for some time unprovided for. He never reacquired the Book of Armagh. He died in 1713 and was buried in Ballymoyer, where his headstone was defaced and broken. Passers-by would throw stones or pebbles at his grave as a sign of disapproval.

Fr. Edmund Murphy was discharged from the secret service payroll on 27th September 1681, he served two periods of prison in England and he worked as a farm labourer making hay in Kent. He lived in poverty in London and disappeared soon afterwards from history.

Friar Hugh Duffy was also solemnly declared an apostate and excommunicated from the Church by the Sacred Congregation of Propaganda. Imprisoned for a time, he later lived with the Tories. In 1721, some forty years later, Duffy an old man, called to Archbishop Hugh MacMahon seeking forgiveness, pleading: "Is there to be no mercy for me? Am I never to make my peace with God?" Dr. MacMahon opened the door of a shrine revealing the Relic of the Head of Primate Oliver. Duffy recognised it at once and was quite overcome. This event probably took place in Drogheda. Pardoned, he died at peace with God.

Friar Paul Gormely died in London, a year after the trial.

Hugh Hanlon returned to Ireland, after he received a note that his evidence was not material to the trials of Dr. Oliver Plunkett and others.

Owen Murphy retracted his evidence some six months after Oliver's martyrdom, he admitted he was persuaded by Titus Oates and Hetherington to take money for the swearing of false evidence.

William Hetherington was accused of treason. He spent time in prison and was later acquitted. He disappeared into obscurity after the accession of King James II in 1685.

The following individuals were not witnesses per say, but deserve a mention nonetheless.

Titus Oates was arrested just a few months after Oliver's martyrdom. In 1685, upon the accession of King James II, he was retried and convicted of perjury. Imprisoned for life, he was publicly whipped on several occasions; the hangman whipping him all the way from Newgate to Tyburn, the journey of so many of his innocent victims. He was also pilloried a few times and pelted by passers-by with eggs. During the subsequent reign of Protestant monarchs, King William and Queen Mary, Oates was pardoned, released from prison and given a pension of between two and three hundred pounds per annum. The 'Savour of the Nation' later disappeared into obscurity and died in 1705; the place of his burial is unknown.

The Earl of Shaftsbury was arrested and placed in the Tower of London the day after Oliver's trial. Upon his release, he felt so threatened in England that he died in Holland within eighteen months of the trial.

The Earl of Essex was arrested in 1683 and he committed suicide in the Tower of London shortly afterwards.

King Charles II was forever fearful of a gruesome death like that of his father. He did get his wish, as he died in his bed after all, although not entirely peacefully. Less than four years after Oliver's martyrdom, he developed a sudden fit and died some four days later. The evening before his death, he was received into the Catholic Church. The lives of King Charles II and St. Oliver were both cut short at fifty-five years of age. The first person to forgive King Charles II was Oliver. He had already sincerely forgiven him and all others involved in his death, while standing on the cart at Tyburn: "I do forgive them with all my heart, and also the judges, who by denying me sufficient time to bring my records and witnesses from Ireland, did expose my life to evident danger. I moreover forgive all those who had a hand in bringing me from Ireland, to be tried here, where it was morally impossible for me to have a fair trial. I do finally forgive all who did directly or indirectly concur, to take away my life, and I ask forgiveness of all those whom I ever offended by thought, word, or deed." Without doubt, Oliver was on the very last step of sainthood.

96. INITIAL CAUSE OF ARCHBISHOP OLIVER

For several centuries, Oliver Plunkett, Archbishop and Martyr, was almost completely forgotten about in Ireland as a result of the harsh penal laws and the difficult famine times. The Siena convent in Drogheda, the Irish College in Rome, Lamspringe Abbey and the Benedictine

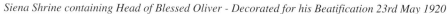

Siena Shrine containing Head of Blessed Oliver - Decorated for his Beatification 23rd May 1920

communities never forgot, and Oliver's memory has been faithfully venerated in these communities right down to the present day. A great debt of gratitude is therefore owed to these communities for the way they venerated and kept alive the memory of St. Oliver down through the centuries. Centuries which were difficult ones for Ireland, as the Irish people continued to struggle and scrape for bare survival, in body and in soul. At the request of the Irish hierarchy, Pope Leo XIII sanctioned that the cause of Oliver Plunkett could be separated from the English and Welsh martyrs and he declared him Venerable on 9th December 1886. He was confirmed a martyr for the faith on St. Patrick's Day 1918 and declared Blessed on the Feast of Pentecost, 23rd May 1920 by Pope Benedict XV. For background information on the centenary of the beatification in 2020 see Appendix VIII p.277.

97. TRANSLATION OF THE RELIC OF THE HEAD

Cardinal Michael Logue, Archbishop of Armagh, while in Rome in 1920 for the beatification ceremony requested that the Sacred Congregation of Rites give permission for the Relic of the Head to be translated from the Siena convent to the fine new parish church in Drogheda. It was felt that the Relic could be placed in an impressive new shrine in the church where it would be more accessible for veneration by parishioners and pilgrims, both in terms of centrality of location and hours of opening. The foundation stone of the new parish church of St. Peter's in Drogheda was laid in 1881 on the bi-centenary of Oliver Plunkett's martyrdom and was dedicated as the memorial church of Oliver Plunkett. Consecrated in 1914, this beautiful church of God was still undergoing internal decoration to the highest of standards at the time. After a second approach shortly afterwards by Cardinal Logue to the Scared Congregation, permission was granted.

The Siena nuns and the wider Dominican order were quite upset at losing this priceless Relic and immediately appealed the decision to Pope Benedict XV. To the great disappointment of the nuns, the Pope while

Relic of the Head of St. Oliver, National Shrine, St. Peter's Church, Drogheda

sympathetic to their case let the decision stand, as when they were given the treasured Relic by Archbishop MacMahon some two hundred years earlier, he had stipulated in his will that it could remain in the custody of 'Mrs Mary Reilly and ye gentlewomen in Deer Street, Drogheda' until such time as an Archbishop of Armagh should ever wish to reclaim it. He was unable to mention the community by name in his will as it would undoubtedly have caused trouble for them. The sisters could well be excused from thinking that the Relic would never be requested of them, as for two hundred years the community had proven themselves more than capable of protecting, preserving and venerating the priceless Relic over those most difficult of centuries for the Church in Ireland. The sisters had even drawn up plans which were at an advanced stage to build a new shrine for the Relic at their Cord Road convent, but this was not enough to sway the decision in their favour. It must have seemed in this

Authentification Certificate, at Shrine in Drogheda

case that possession was not nine-tenths of the law, as Cardinal Logue the Archbishop of Armagh and successor of Archbishop MacMahon was now requesting the return of the Relic.

The Holy Father instructed in his communique that the Siena sisters must be given another major Relic of Blessed Oliver in its place and as there were no relics readily available, the Bishop of Hildesheim through the good offices of the Canon of Hildesheim Cathedral, presented a Relic of a Rib from the Cathedral to the Siena community in Drogheda. This Relic was carried for many years on the annual procession held on the first Sunday of July each year in Drogheda. The Siena sisters also possess other major relics of the saint along with the reliquary of the black ebony box, topped with a tiny silver mitre, which housed the Relic of the Head. This reliquary sat perfectly camouflaged on top of their grandfather clock during penal times. The community also possess the inscribed copper coffin plate which had been exhumed with the Body from the graveyard of St. Giles in the Fields. Another treasured possession of the Siena community is the purple zucchetto which rested on the Relic of the Head for over a hundred years and it is firmly believed by the community that it was Cardinal Howard who placed his own zucchetto on the Relic upon first receiving it in c.1685. Over the years, several miraculous cures and favours have been attributed to the wearing of this zucchetto, yet another holy item, owned and cherished by the sisters of the Siena community.

During the debate about who should be the custodian of the Relic of the Head, there was much talk and publicity about it locally and a lot of attention was drawn to the Relic during what were very troubled times. In a story told to this author by Mr. Seán Mullaney, a veteran of the war of independence: "Because of a fear that Black and Tan forces might steal the Relic of the Head of St. Oliver, armed republican forces were often positioned in the locality of the Siena Convent in order to prevent a possible desecration of the Relic, this being in an era of attack and reprisal."

The Relic of the Head was translated in 1921 from the St. Catherine of Siena Convent, and was installed on 29th June of that year in a shrine in St. Peter's Church Drogheda, the memorial church of the martyred Archbishop of Armagh. The Siena community while greatly disappointed at having to hand over the Relic, were most gracious in their loss and continued to work and pray as hard as anyone, for the promotion of Blessed Oliver's cause to full sainthood. At the translation ceremony, Cardinal Michael Logue presided, Dr. Joseph MacRory, Bishop of Down and Connor and later Cardinal Primate, sang a Pontifical High Mass and Bishop Hugh McSherry of Port Elizabeth, South Africa delivered the homily. It is interesting to note that the first of many church's named after the Martyr Primate, was in Port Elizabeth, S.A.

Monsignor Patrick Segrave parish priest of St. Peter's in Drogheda,

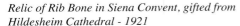

Relic of Rib Bone in Siena Convent, gifted from Hildesheim Cathedral - 1921

who organised the decoration of the new church to a very high standard, wrote: "The Relic of the martyr's head is now enshrined on one of the altars but the whole church forms but his worthy shrine, which it was meant from the beginning, being called the Oliver Plunkett Memorial Church." The Relic of the Head of St. Oliver was translated from a side altar to an imposing new shrine in St. Peter's church dating from 1995. The Head is heavy and not just a bare skull and is in remarkably good condition considering that it is open to the air and has never been hermetically sealed. A doctor who examined the Relic in the late twentieth century was surprised to see the spinal marrow[1] intact and in quite perfect condition. Perhaps one should not be too surprised at the inexplicable preservation of even soft tissue such as his spinal marrow, because above all else, St. Oliver had a backbone like very few others!

Thousands of pilgrims visit the National Shrine in Drogheda each month and the Head preserved as it is, must surely be one of the most important relics of the Irish Church. Of noble bearing, it is a visual and an eloquent expression of the faith and loyalty, practised by St. Oliver in troubled times and is an inspiration to all of us to follow his example of loyalty to the Lord, even unto death. Many notable pilgrims and visitors

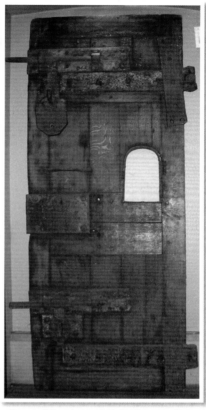

Door of Condemned Cell, Newgate Prison

have prayed at the shrine in Drogheda over the years. During its time in Siena Convent it was venerated by Daniel O'Connell, Cardinal John Henry Newman, Cardinal Logue, Bishop Patrick Moran of Dunedin N. Z. and the Earl of Fingall. Since the translation of the Relic to St. Peter's church in 1921, the stream of visitors has been almost constant, including innumerable people of note, certainly too many to name. On 4th November 1998, there was a well-attended ecumenical service for peace and reconciliation at the National Shrine which was graced by the presence of Mary McAleese, Uachtarán na hÉireann. Mgr. Montini, who later became Pope Paul VI, venerated the Relic at Drogheda, and of course St. John Paul II venerated the Relic on his papal visit to Killineer, Drogheda in 1979.

Beside the National Shrine of St. Oliver, is the door of the condemned cell of the Newgate prison, London, behind which Oliver would have spent the last sixteen days or so of his life. The Mayor of Wrexham in Wales, Mr. W. Clarke and his wife visited Drogheda in 1949; his wife[2] had picked up a booklet at the Shrine and having given it later to her husband, he recognised immediately the strong connection of Blessed Oliver and the door which was in his family's possession. He had been told some years previously, that it was the door behind which, Oliver Plunkett spent his last few days in Newgate; the Mayor offered the door to the Shrine and it has been at St. Peter's since 1951.

Over the National Shrine is the four meter tall canonisation picture which hung from the balcony of St. Peter's Basilica in Rome during St. Oliver's canonisation ceremony in 1975. Subsequently, it hung for some twenty years in the refectory of the Irish College, Rome. The canonisation picture was painted by Professor Alfred Missori, under the guidance of Mgr. John Hanly, postulator for the cause of St. Oliver. It is a highly symbolic picture, which tells the story of St. Oliver and is described in Appendix V. This author was delighted to receive an email in late 2001 from Mgr. Liam Bergin, Rector of the Irish College in Rome, wishing to know if we would like to have the canonisation picture in Drogheda; within twenty minutes he had received a reply in the affirmative and within months it was situated in a highly suitable location over the Shrine. A return letter to Rome within the hour and free at that; if only St. Oliver had use of the internet, it would have saved him so much effort and expense, as his voluminous correspondence helped in no small measure to drive him into poverty.

[1] Donnelly Mgr. Frank 'Until the Storm Passes St. Oliver Plunkett' Drogheda 1993/2000. p.20
[2] Matthews Deirdre 'Oliver of Armagh' Dublin 1961. p.113

98. MIRACLE

The 1932 Eucharistic Congress in Dublin - the fifteenth centenary of St. Patrick bringing Christianity to Ireland, saw huge crowds travel to Drogheda to venerate Blessed Oliver. A special[1] ceremony was held at the Shrine attended by the Papal Nuncio and many other dignitaries, Pope Pius XI sent his blessing. Following the Eucharistic Congress there was renewed interest in Blessed Oliver and a league of prayer was initiated to pray for his canonisation; many people recited a prayer daily for this intention. The cause of Blessed Oliver resumed after the Second World War in July 1951. In 1958 an Italian woman, Mrs. Giovanna Martiriggiano who was gravely ill in hospital in Naples, was

Giovanna Martiriggiano, the lady who was cured in 1958. Photo taken in 2006 with Mgr. John Hanly, Postulator of the Cause

Sr. Cabrini Quigley M.M.M.

unexpectedly cured of her illness. A sister of the Irish Medical Missionaries of Mary, Sr. Cabrini Quigley from Donegal who was working in the hospital, prayed regularly throughout the night with the lady's husband Nicola to Blessed Oliver, for a cure of the patient who was expected to die overnight. The lady, who was expecting a child and was full term, had been found unconscious in her home. After many hours in this state, she was brought to hospital where it was found that she had lost the baby girl and that some of the mothers internal organs were severely damaged and almost non-existent as a result. The surgeon attending her, knowing that death was imminent, did not spend too long as he quickly stitched her up in theatre. He arranged that she should be placed in a side ward, stating that he did not wish her to die in 'his' theatre. Overnight, surprise was expressed on several occasions that she was still alive and hospital staff were astonished the following day when the patient revived. She soon made a complete recovery without the need of any further medical intervention whatsoever. Within a month, some of the sisters from the Medical Missionaries of Mary went to visit Giovanna at her home, but missed her as she was out shopping. She subsequently lived a healthy life for a further fifty years. This cure was thoroughly investigated by several panels of independent doctors, seven doctors in Naples and nine others on the medical board; all gave a unanimous verdict in favour of the miraculous. Giovanna Martiriggiano was interviewed on film for the first time in 2006, during the making of the DVD on the life of St. Oliver. The DVD is available from the Shrine in Drogheda.

[1] Matthews Deirdre 'Oliver of Armagh' Dublin 1961. p.122

99. CANONISATION

Oliver Plunkett was declared a saint by Pope Paul VI in a canonisation ceremony held in St. Peter's Square Rome on 12th October, in the Holy Year of 1975. Pronouncing him a saint, completely reversed the court judgement which had found him guilty in Westminster Hall all those years earlier. Many Irish dignitaries from Church and State attended the canonisation along with an estimated twelve thousand Irish pilgrims who had travelled out from Ireland. Pilgrims also travelled in large numbers from Downside, the Diocese of Hildesheim and from the USA. A combined choir from Dundalk and Drogheda had the privilege of a lifetime by performing at the ceremony. Signora Giovanna Martiriggiano the lady cured some seventeen years earlier took part in the offertory procession; also present at the canonisation was her husband Nicola and their son Enzo. The Plunkett family were represented by Lord and Lady Fingall and Lord and Lady Dunsany, with members of the Plunkett family travelling from at least ten countries across the globe so as to be present for the memorable occasion.

During the canonisation ceremony, Archbishop Bafile, Pro-Prefect of the Sacred Congregation for the Causes of Saints, and Mgr. John Hanly, Postulator of St. Oliver's Cause, formally requested the Holy Father to place the name of Oliver Plunkett on the list of saints.

The Holy Father, during his address at the ceremony said: "And so we exhort dear sons and daughters of Ireland, saying with immense affection and love. Remember your leaders who preached the word of God to you, and as you reflect on the outcome of their lives, imitate their faith. Jesus Christ is the same today as he was yesterday. Let this then be an occasion on which the message of peace and reconciliation in truth and justice, and above all the message of love for one's neighbour, will be emblazoned in the minds and hearts of all the beloved Irish people. This message signed and sealed with a martyr's blood in imitation of his master. May love be always in your hearts, and may St. Oliver Plunkett be an inspiration to you all."

To mark the occasion of the canonisation; The Irish Episcopal Conference issued a pastoral letter which included the following excerpts:

"We thank God for having given him to us to show us an example in these troubled times and to be our Patron in Heaven."

"He travelled the country for ten years, often in disguise and sometimes barely ahead of his pursuers, until his capture and imprisonment put an end to his labours. During these ten years he had done as much as any man since St. Patrick to strengthen and preserve

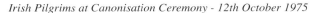

Irish Pilgrims at Canonisation Ceremony - 12th October 1975

the faith in Ireland."

"We ask him today for all the graces we need for ourselves and for our country. We ask that we may be as he was, steadfast, courageous and devout, untiring in our work for peace and reconciliation, loyal to the Church and firm in our faith even unto death. St Oliver Plunkett pray for us."

The following extracts are taken from the sermon given in Rome by His Eminence Cardinal Manning, Archbishop of Los Angeles, on 14th Oct. 1975.

"Whenever some doctrine is proclaimed a dogma of faith, it is usually in order to counteract a heresy or because the doctrine has special relevance at the time of its definition."

"In the same way, when saints are canonised, they are often felt to have a particular relevance to the era of their canonisation; they can serve as a means to overcome crises and to heal wounds in the Church. So it is with Oliver Plunkett."

"St. Oliver is placed before us as a model for his loyalty to Rome and for his dedicated work on behalf of the Irish people. Loyalty to Rome is essential for the Church."

"The martyr's dedication to duty, his courage in the face of death, his efforts to restore peace in his country at a time of troubles, all these have a special relevance to Ireland at the present time."

Ceremonies were also held around the time of the canonisation in Lambspringe, Downside, Oldcastle, Drogheda and other locations, and many memorable homilies were delivered at that time. The Irish Episcopal Conference asked the Irish government to consider an amnesty for prisoners to mark the occasion and the government acceded to the request by releasing eighty four prisoners on the 11th. Oct. 1975.

An Taoiseach, Mr. Liam Cosgrave, who led the Irish government delegation to Rome for the canonisation, broadcast a message on radio. In it he expressed a wish that the Irish people would pray to the new saint to intercede for peace in Ireland.

100. Patron for Peace and Reconciliation

Archbishop Oliver brought peace to the church, when he settled countless disputes in each of the dioceses that he visited; he also brought peace to the province by brokering a peace agreement between the government and the Tories. It is surely appropriate that St. Oliver has been adopted as Patron of Peace in Ireland and more particularly in recent times he is acknowledged more and more as the Patron of the Northern Ireland Peace Process. Writing about the Feast of 'Blessed' Oliver, which was celebrated a year after his beatification, Cardinal Tomás Ó Fiaich in his biography of St. Oliver states: "It is worthy of note that the Truce, which brought to an end the War of Independence, came into force on the Feast of 'Blessed' Oliver in 1921." Catholics in England must also have recognised the role of Blessed Oliver in this event, as the inscription[1] on a reliquary containing a Relic of the Martyr Primate in Westminster Cathedral, states: 'From Irish English Clients of Blessed Oliver in the year of the Truce 1921.'

More recently, a national campaign of prayer began in Drogheda in 1997, entitled, 'St. Oliver Plunkett for Peace and Reconciliation.' Hundreds of thousands of prayer cards have been distributed, at home and abroad and many people recite this prayer daily for Peace and Reconciliation in Ireland. The prayer is reprinted at the back of this publication. A relic of St. Oliver has also visited hundreds of parishes around the country where numerous Masses for Peace and Reconciliation under his patronage have been celebrated. One of St. Oliver's great charisms was undoubtedly his letter writing; the committee have tried to emulate this gift by posting over twenty thousand letters to every parish and religious community in Ireland, publicising the 'National Days of Prayer' for peace and reconciliation, held each year. A saint of reconciliation, this devotion has also inspired the committee to form an Ecumenical Peace Group and many ecumenical services have also been organised for peace and reconciliation in Ireland. Bishop Gerard Clifford, while paying tribute in 2012, to Drogheda's role in the peace process stated: "The prayer movement for peace in Northern Ireland under the patronage of St. Oliver Plunkett has become one of the great achievements of our time."

It has been noted and it is certainly more than co-incidence that the momentous first meeting of the new Northern Ireland Assembly took place on the 1st July 1998, the Feastday of St. Oliver. It must also be significant that the Good Friday Agreement of 1998 has many important similarities with St. Oliver's brokered peace agreement with the Tories, namely the decommissioning of arms and the release of prisoners, without which, a deal would not have been agreed in either case. We give thanks to God that so much has been achieved for peace and reconciliation in recent years, symbolised by the broken pike in the

Mass of Thanksgiving for Peace Process - The Author, Mgr. Francis Donnelly,
Cardinal Seán Brady, Mgr. John Hanly, Mgr. James Carroll

Cardinal Seán Brady breaking a Pike – Mass of Thanksgiving - 12th October 2007

canonisation picture, which is located above the Shrine in Drogheda. We are also most grateful to God for the fact that we can now repeat St. Oliver's words when he stated: "The province has not had greater peace in thirty years." We must not relax our efforts however at this time, as our peace is always fragile, so we must work, strive and pray that this peace may continue and grow in the future. There is still an immense need for reconciliation in our midst and St. Oliver would no doubt be quick to point out, that true peace and reconciliation can only be attained when the Peace of Christ enters all hearts, an ideal he spent his lifetime in the service of God, constantly working to achieve. At a ceremony held on 12th October 2007 in St. Peter's Church, Drogheda, to give thanks for the progress made through the intercession of St. Oliver in the Northern Ireland peace process, Cardinal Seán Brady symbolically broke a pike as depicted in the canonisation picture.

Present at St. Oliver's canonisation in 1975, was Cardinal Karol Wojtyla from Kraków, who was leading a pilgrimage to Rome from Poland. Less than four years later, as Pope John Paul II he received a hearty, céad míle fáilte on the first ever papal visit to Ireland. Unable for security reasons to travel north of the border during that important papal visit in 1979; Killineer, Drogheda, was chosen for the keynote homily of St. John Paul II to the province of Armagh, which took place on 29th September 1979. Drogheda while south of the border is in the Northern Province of Armagh. Less than five weeks earlier, Lord Mountbatten and eighteen British soldiers were killed in separate explosions on the same day and with tensions running high, the continuing security situation in the north of Ireland looked bleak indeed. Before preaching at Killineer, his Holiness, St. John Paul II, knelt and venerated the Relic of the Head of St. Oliver Plunkett, our adopted Patron for Peace and Reconciliation. He then delivered his unforgettable homily of peace to an estimated three-hundred thousand people.

St. John Paul II's earnest appeal to the men and women of violence that afternoon left a lasting impression on all present. His solemn and prayerful words: "On my knees I beg you to turn away from the path of violence and return to the ways of peace," will forever be remembered at home and abroad and those words echoed around the world for days afterwards. Another of the abiding memories of pilgrims on that day was the throngs of people walking good-humouredly for long distances to and from Killineer, as there was a restricted cordon of three or four miles around the event. Great importance is attached to that visit by the Holy Father to Drogheda, and in a future era, its true significance for peace and reconciliation will be more fully appreciated. Undoubtedly and

St. John Paul II giving a blessing at Killineer

unbeknownst to us at the time, the very first seeds of peace and reconciliation through the intercession of St. Oliver Plunkett in the modern era, were sown among us on that day, becoming as it did, the source of a great desire to commence and implement a peace process throughout the province.

As he was unable to go north of the border during that important visit in 1979, Pope St. John Paul promised that he would return. Although huge progress has been made for peace and reconciliation in the interim; this much desired visit by a Holy Father to the North of Ireland has so far proven elusive. We give thanks for the wonderful visit by Pope Francis to Dublin in 2018 for the 9th World Meeting of Families. Unfortunately, due to time constraints, the Holy Father was unable on that grace filled visit, to travel to locations other than Dublin and Knock.

Image © Courtesy of Maxwell, Dublin & WMofF 2018

Pope Francis preaching in the Phoenix Park, Dublin, 9th World Meeting of Families 2018
Pope Francis' homily in the Pro-Cathedral, Dublin 2018 'Never forget this brothers and sisters; faith is passed on in everyday speech. The speech of the home, everyday life, life in the family... So it is important to pray together as a family; speak of good and holy things, and let your mother Mary into your life and the life of your family. Celebrate the feasts of the Christian people; let your children see what it is to celebrate a family feast'

The St. Oliver Plunkett for Peace and Reconciliation Committee, are of the view that the time is ripe for a visit by the Holy Father to Northern Ireland. All the building blocks necessary for such a visit seem to have been put in place, including a hugely successful visit by Queen Elizabeth II to Ireland and a positive return visit by President Michael D. Higgins to England. Much symbolism went into both of those visits, which have created a great sense of friendship and a deep feeling of mutual respect between our peoples, all of which is essential between good neighbours. Unfortunately in more recent times, tensions and divisions have increased again across these islands because of the uncertainties and divisions about Brexit. A papal visit to the North of Ireland would do so much real good. It would strengthen the laity in their faith, reach out to the marginalised in our society and promote ecumenism in our midst. It would also build bridges between our peoples and greatly help the peace process at this time. A return visit by a Pope to Ireland, incorporating a pastoral visit north of the border has certainly been one of the ultimate objectives of our peace committee, since our formation in 1997 and has often occupied our thoughts. We pray through the intercession of St. Oliver Plunkett and St. John Paul that such a visit may soon take place.

[1] Bellew Seamus 'The Seventeenth Century Reliquary of St. Oliver Plunkett at the Siena Convent, Drogheda' ref. 130. Seanchas Ard Mhacha 2011

101 EPILOGUE

When St. Oliver arrived in Ireland, the Church was wavering and in the throes of virtual collapse. By the time he was put on board ship as a prisoner almost ten years later, the Church was largely united and had re-asserted its authority. His strategies brought hope, regularity and a much needed peace. As a result of his efforts, the Church in Ireland was much reformed from its earlier state and many of its former abuses rooted out. Importantly, its lines of communication had been re-established and its diocesan personnel and structures although still under much harassment, were functioning and had become fit for purpose. They later proved themselves capable of withstand the next wave of persecution which was already coming down the tracks. As a successor to St. Patrick, St. Oliver possibly accomplished more than anyone in all the intervening years to help reform and fortify the Catholic faith in Ireland for future generations. As a teacher, he helped instil fervour and loyalty into succeeding generations of bishops, clergy and laity. Many of these became missionaries, some voluntary and many others as exiles, enabling St. Oliver's influence to stretch over time and even over continents. God is always very close to his people and during a critical time in Irish history and by Divine providence, St. Oliver changed the face of Roman Catholic Ireland. By his work and example and in less than a decade he truly preserved the faith which has been passed down to us.

Oliver was a man both of intense prayer and untiring action and as such he would certainly invite us today to be loyal to Jesus and to his Church in all things. He would strongly encourage loyalty to the Vicar of Christ, knowing that this loyalty would guarantee faithfulness in the true faith. As a man of deep prayer he would surely recommend, that we should take some quiet time for themselves in contemplation and regular prayer, just as he practised in caves, huts, attics, prisons, catacomb, shrines, churches or basilicas. We have many opportunities and places, such as in our own fine churches or lovely Blessed Sacrament Chapels, or even in the tranquillity of our own special place. As a man of extraordinary action, he would assuredly encourage us, to become ever active and willing helpers in our parish communities and organisations.

Deo Gratias for the life,
example and intercession of
St. Oliver Plunkett.

APPENDIX I
LOCATIONS ASSOCIATED WITH ST. OLIVER

Loughcrew near Oldcastle was his home place he also spent much of his youth with his cousin tutor, Fr. Patrick Plunkett at Killeen Castle or in the area of Kilcloon. He lived for several years in both Ballybarrack and Ardpatrick, the locations of his pro-cathedrals and of course his schools in Drogheda took up much of his energy and time in the early years of his ministry. All of these had very strong associations with St. Oliver. Castletown Castle near Dundalk (St. Louis Convent) was the home of Sir John Bellew a prominent Catholic who regained land after the Restoration; Oliver made several references in his letters to visits there. Oliver would have recognised every tree and hedgerow in that area of north Louth. He held meetings with his priests at Blyke's Inn, Dorsey and Pierce's Inn Dunleer. He stayed with the Marquis of Antrim at his castle at Dunluce, Co. Antrim.

Oral tradition hands down to us a huge number of locations associated with St. Oliver, almost all are probably true because there must have been very few parishes or mass-rocks in the Northern Province which were not graced by his presence at one time or another. He also visited the other three provinces of Ireland over the course of his ministry. During his time on the run with Bishop John Brenan in 1674, all agree that they stayed in the area of the Mullabawn valley close to Sliabh Gullion in the area of Doctor's Quarters. Hugh A. Murphy[1] states: "There is a very strong oral tradition linking Oliver Plunkett with the house that stood on the site of what is now known as Sally Humphrey's house, the place where Patrick Donnelly was later to spend the last twenty odd years of his life as Bishop of Dromore. This link is quite significant and not easily ignored. The well which supplied water to the various families occupying this house down through the generations including in the time of Patrick Donnelly, is to this day known as Oliver Plunkett's well."

While many of the mass-rocks in the province have associations with Archbishop Oliver, strong oral tradition points to a Mass-rock in Mullaghbawn, Co Armagh. It is well worth a visit, particularly at the time of the annual celebration of Holy Mass. Members of the Knights of St. Columbanus process with a Relic of St. Oliver to the celebration which is held at 7pm. on the Thursday which precedes the first Sunday of July each year.

Lord Louth (Plunkett) took Archbishop Oliver under his wing for a time; he had his home at Louth Hall and up until the buildings collapse in the mid-twentieth century, locals could point to a room where it was believed Oliver stayed and the stone staircase leading up to it. It is also believed that he had occasion to hide in the ice-house and thick undergrowth near the main house. Ned, Oliver's brother settled on some of Lord

Louth's land at Ardpatrick, where Oliver also lived for a time, and where the St. Oliver oak tree is located, in which he hid on occasions.

Cardinal Ó Fiaich[2] mentions caves at Killeavy and Faughart, the Cairn on top of Slieve Gullion, the Cadger's Pass between Ravensdale and Omeath, a grove at Forkhill and a secluded spot near Lislea and other areas such as East Donegal. He also states that there is some evidence that Oliver took up residence on the estate of Sir John Bellew and that he lodged for a time with a Sylvester MacMahon or Mathews in the townland of Haggardstown. Members of the MacMahon family leased land in Ballybarrack and Rossmakea and he surmises that it was under their protection that he set up his little chapel at Ballybarrack and several ordination ceremonies were carried out there and at Rossmakea.

Mgr. John Stokes[3] refers to Slieve Gullion along with Craigagh Wood in the Glens of Antrim and in the mountains of Donegal. In one of last letters, St. Oliver[4] refers to Acarne, presumably referring to Athcarne Castle near Duleek.

Cardinal Moran wrote[5]: "In the parish of Termonfeckin where the Primate generally resided, the site of the hut wherein he dwelt is still traditionally pointed out, and the inhabitants vividly cherish the memory of the orchard wherein he was accustomed to assemble the little children for instruction in the rudiments of faith and of the rude loft formed of branches of trees, on which he used to seek concealment by day and repose by night."

Canon Francis Carolan[6] recorded all of the following oral traditions regarding Oliver's associations with south Louth in the early 1940's. Oliver lived in Hagarty's House, Brownstown and Monasterboice, two or three fields away from the ruins of an ancient church at Drumshallon. In Kearneystown, he said Holy Mass regularly in an old quarry or in a cavity of the rocks. He hid in an old house on the lane which leads from the Drogheda – Dundalk road towards Stonehouse, south of Mullary. He was arrested at one time near Fieldstown. He preached near Clogherhead, standing on a rock along the roadside, in the garden of a neat farm house owned by a Mr. Bernard McKenna at Parsonstown; this was pointed out to Canon Carolan in 1903 by Fr. John Greene c.c. who was living in the house at the time. Oliver hid under the bridge in Termonfechin while soldiers marched past; the latter is also recorded in Cardinal Moran's book number 5 which was printed about fifty years earlier.

The Plunkett's of Beaulieu had relocated to Carstown Manor (Cartown House) and at nearby Ballymakenny and it is believed that Oliver spent time in these locations. Fr. Patrick Plunkett a native of Termonfechin parish and no near relation, was parish priest of the parish throughout Archbishop Oliver's active ministry; Oliver appointed him vicar general of Louth in 1671 and as such, he attended the important Provincial Synod of Ardpatrick in 1678. Along with visiting so many other areas, Oliver must have been a frequent visitor to the parishes around Termonfechin. Fr. Edward

Drumgoole, who took over the archdiocese as vicar for a period two years after St. Oliver's martyrdom, was from Killartry, Clogherhead, which may well have provided Oliver with another reason to visit the area.

[1] Murphy Hugh A. Culture Northern Ireland Website: Article: 'Dr Patrick Donnelly - The Bard of Armagh'
[2] Ó Fiaich & Forristal – 'Oliver Plunkett' Indiana USA 1976. p.121
3 Stokes, Mgr. J F. – 'The Life of Blessed Oliver Plunkett' Dublin 1965. p.42/43
[4] Hanly, Mgr. John 'The Letters of Saint Oliver Plunkett' Dublin 1979. No. 224
[5] Moran Cardinal Patrick 'Memoir of Oliver Plunket' Dublin 1895. p.435
[6] Carolan Canon Francis - Blessed Oliver Plunkett and Louth Drogheda c.1943. p.1/2

APPENDIX II
QUATRAINS ATTRIBUTED TO OLIVER

Priests of gold and chalices of wood
Were Ireland's lot in Patrick's time of old;
But now the latter days of our sad world
Have priests of wood and chalices of Gold.

Sagairt Óir is cailís chrainn
Bhi le linn Phádraig I n-Eirinn;
Sagairt chrainn is cailís Óir
I ndeire an domhain dearÓil.

*

Tara of the Kings, how strange for thee,
In Cormacs Mac Art's far distant day,
To feel upon thy back the fist
Of some rough peasant cutting hay.

A Theamhair na Rí, dob annamh leat,
Re linn Chormaic mhic Airt mhic Cuinn,
Alt riabhach do bhodach bhoct
Bheidh ag gearra guirt ar do dhruimm.

Appendix III
St. Oliver Timeline

England and Ireland refused to adjust from the Julian calendar (old style) to the Gregorian calendar (new style) until 1752 and were ten days behind the continental calendar at the time.

All dates marked * are in 'old style' and are ten days behind 'new style' dates.

*1st November 1625: Born on all saints day, Loughcrew

*February 1647: Sailed from Waterford for the Irish College, Rome

4th March 1651: Received tonsure and minor orders in St. John Lateran's

20th December 1653: Ordained sub-deacon in St. John Lateran's

26th December 1653: Ordained deacon in Propaganda College

1st January 1654: Ordained priest in Propaganda College

November 1657: Appointed professor in Propaganda College

1st December 1669, 1st Sunday of Advent: Consecrated Archbishop in Ghent

*7th March 1670: Lands at Ringsend, Dublin

*6th December 1679: Arrested and jailed in Dublin Castle

*23rd July 1680: Arraignment and failed trial at Dundalk

*24th October 1680: Sailed from Dublin, imprisoned Newgate prison

*12th February 1681: Failed indictment

*25th February 1681: Successful indictment

*3rd May 1681. Arraignment Westminster Hall

*8th June 1681: Trial Westminster Hall

*15th June 1681: Sentencing Westminster Hall

*1st July 1681: Martyrdom at Tyburn

9th December 1886: Declared venerable and his cause was separated from the English and Welsh.

17th March 1918: Declared a martyr

23rd May 1920: Beatified on Pentecost Sunday by Pope Benedict XV

1st April 1958: Miraculous cure of Mrs Giovanna Martiriggiano

12th October 1975: Canonized by Pope Paul VI

1st July: Feastday

APPENDIX IV
SHRINES OF ST. OLIVER

The National Shrine of St. Oliver: St. Peter's Church, Drogheda. St. Oliver's Head and Major Relics and Reliquaries

Downside Abbey, Somerset, England: Tomb and Body of St. Oliver, Major Relics, Letters and Reliquaries.

Monastery of St. Catherine of Siena, Drogheda: Major Relics and important Reliquaries.

Irish College, Rome: Relics and important Reliquaries. Picture p.54

Oldcastle, Co. Meath: Major Relic housed in Church of St. Brigid the parish of St. Oliver's birth.

St. Patrick's Cathedral, Armagh: Shrine and Major Relic. Archbishop Eamon Martin dedicated the shrine with a large bronze statue of St. Oliver on 9th July 2019, 350th anniversary of the appointment of St. Oliver by Pope Clement IX as Archbishop of Armagh.

Lamspringe Abbey, Germany: Major Relics and important Reliquaries.

St. Patrick's Chapel, Rosario, Argentina: Shrine and Major Relic. 'The Cabra Relic' See p.275

Poor Clare Convent, Arundel, Sussex: Major Relics and important Reliquaries. Pictures Appendix IX

Westminster Cathedral: Relic and Letters.

Relics are also housed in numerous other churches around the world, with many small Relics in the possession of churches and individuals.

APPENDIX V
THE CANONISATION PICTURE.

Refer to picture inside front cover

The canonisation picture displayed over the Shrine is the original one which hung from St. Peter's Basilica in Rome during the canonisation ceremony in 1975. Full of symbolism, it was painted by Professor Alfovino Missori, a noted artist and was commissioned by Mgr. John Hanly, postulator for the cause.

St. Oliver is depicted as bishop: Born in 1625 near Oldcastle Co. Meath, he went to Rome in 1647 and returned to Ireland after a period of twenty-three years, in March 1670 as Archbishop of Armagh and Primate of Ireland. A student for the priesthood at the Irish College he was unable to return home after his ordination because of the Cromwellian Conquests, which had peaked around that time. He then undertook further studies, gaining a doctorate in canon and civil law, becoming a professor for twelve years in the famous Propaganda College where it is said he helped to improve standards a great deal. He was ordained Archbishop of Armagh at a quiet ceremony in Ghent, Belgium on his way back to Ireland, lest a well-publicised ceremony in Rome might antagonise the government back home. As spies were on the lookout for him upon his return, he travelled for some months in disguise as a Captain Brown complete with wig, sword and pair of pistols as befitted an officer.

With a halo and rays of light: This signifies that he is holy and a canonised saint of the Church.

A father is seen on the right presenting his son to the Archbishop to be educated: He built and equipped from the foundations up, a school in Drogheda, which catered for one-hundred and fifty boys, also a college in the same building for the education of priests. This was badly needed after the turmoil of the Cromwellian persecutions, barely twenty years earlier. No Catholic schools were allowed at that time, and he was called before the Council in Dublin on nine occasions to defend them. Three and a half years later, they were knocked to the ground by the authorities and this action caused St. Oliver considerable sadness.

In the foreground a newly ordained priest is shown holding a chalice: St. Oliver probably ordained about two-hundred priests in total and he went to great lengths to ensure that they were all properly trained and educated, before and after ordination.

The kneeling figure represents the great loyalty of the Irish people to the Catholic faith over the centuries: The Irish gave up their land, property and positions, rather than give up the great treasure of their Catholic faith. On several occasions he wrote of his admiration for the deep faith of the Irish people.

A confirmation scene is portrayed outdoors under a tree and is set close to a ruined church: For several years, St. Oliver was the only active bishop in the eleven dioceses of the Northern Province and he performed countless confirmation ceremonies, over forty-eight thousand in his first three years as Archbishop. They were usually held at mass-rocks, as there were only a handful of Catholic churches allowed in the whole of the province at that time. He wrote shortly after his return to Ireland: "There are bearded men of sixty who have not yet received the sacrament of confirmation."

This ruined church to the left of the tree, contrasts greatly with St. Peter's Basilica Rome, which is in its background: This symbolises St. Oliver's strong loyalty to Rome. He willingly came back to help the Church in Ireland which was impoverished, and in quite poor shape with no church buildings.

The broken pike at the bottom of the picture: This symbolises the decommissioning of weapons at his request by the Raparees or Tories, having negotiated a peace agreement between them and the Government. Interestingly, this has some similarities with the more recent Good Friday Agreement as it also included the laying down of arms and the release of prisoners. Without leadership for several decades, the Church in Ireland was often divided and there were very strong divisions and disagreements within it. He also brought peace to each diocese in turn on his visitations.

The gallows scene recalls his death as a martyr: During his nineteen months in jail on false conspiracy charges against the government, he prayed and fasted, yet all the while he remained cheerful, despite suffering from various illnesses, during two incredibly harsh winters. His trial in Westminster Hall, London was a travesty of justice, where the packed jury returned a guilty verdict after only fifteen minutes deliberations. St. Oliver replied: 'Deo Gratias' or 'God be Thanked.' His Martyrdom took place on 1st July 1681 at Tyburn, where he was hung drawn and quartered. In a moving speech he forgave all those who had any part in his downfall. His holiness was plain for all to see and as a result he became the very last Catholic martyr of Tyburn.

The tower on the top right hand corner of the picture: This a motif of the Plunkett family.

The shamrock on the top left hand corner of the picture: This symbolises the Faith of St. Patrick, which St. Oliver as his successor, helped to preserve and to hand down to the present day. In a pastoral letter from the Irish Bishops to mark St. Oliver's canonisation in 1975 they wrote: "He travelled the country for ten years, often in disguise and sometimes barely ahead of his pursuers, until his capture and imprisonment put an end to his labours. During these ten years he had done as much as any man since St. Patrick to strengthen and preserve the faith in Ireland." Deo Gratias.

Zuccetto placed on the Relic of the Head of St. Oliver in Siena Convent

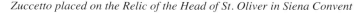

Appendix VI
Bibliography

All biographies in the 'List of Biographies of Oliver Plunkett' in Appendix VII may be added to this bibliography.

Bellew Seamus. 'The Seventeenth Century Reliquary of St. Oliver Plunkett at the Siena Convent Drogheda' Seanchas Ard Mhacha, 2011

Burke, William P. 'The Irish Priests in the Penal Times 1660-1760' Waterford, 1914

Brady, Rev. John. 'The Arrest of Oliver Plunket' Irish Ecclesiastical Record, 1953

Brady, Rev. John. 'Why was Oliver Plunket Arrested' Irish Ecclesiastical Record, 1955

Brady, Rev. John. 'Oliver Plunket and the Popish Plot' Irish Ecclesiastical Record, 1958

Burns, Tommy. 'St. Oliver Plunkett - Deo Gratias' Drogheda 2000

Burns, Tommy. 'St. Oliver Plunkett – Episcopal Ordination and Journey to Ireland' Drogheda 2008

Civil Survey for Meath. Vol. V pp. 264-72

Collegio Hibernorum De Urbe, Rome, 2003

Corish, Patrick J. 'The Irish Martyrs' Dublin, 1989

Corish, Patrick J. 'The Catholic Community in the Seventeenth and Eighteenth Centuries' Dublin, 1981

Forristal, Rev. Desmond. 'The Siena Story' Drogheda 1999

Gasquet, Cardinal. 'Blessed Oliver Plunket - The Martyr's Body' Downside Review, 1921

Gibney, John. 'Ireland and the Popish Plot' Palgrave MacMillan, 2009

Hanly, Mgr. John. 'An Unpublished Letter of Saint Oliver Plunkett' Seanchas Ard Mhacha, 1975/6

Hay, M. V. 'The Jesuits and the Popish Plot' London, 1934

Horne, Dom Ethelbert. 'The Last Speech of Blessed Oliver Plunket and other Papers' Downside Review, 1921

Horne, Dom Ethelbert. 'Blessed Oliver Plunket – His Prison Letters' Downside Review, 1921

Hughes, A. 'The History of Drogheda with Memoirs etc' Drogheda, 1893/2003

Hughes, Fr. Philip. 'Blessed Oliver Plunket' The Irish Way – F. J. Sheed, London 1932

Kane, Dom John. 'Blessed Oliver Plunket - The Translation Ceremony' Downside Review, 1921

Kenyon, John. 'The Popish Plot' London, 1972

Lane, Jane. 'Titus Oates' London, 1949

Ó Fiaich, Tomás. 'The Fall and Return of John Mac Moyer' Seanchas Ard Mhacha, 1958

Ó Fiaich, Tomás. 'Blessed Oliver's Report on the Diocese of Armagh' Louth Archaeological Journal' 1957

Ó Fiaich, Tomás. 'Florence Weyer's Pamphlet against Blessed Oliver Plunket' Irish Ecclesiastical Record, 1966

Ó Fiaich, Tomás. 'Canonisation of St. Oliver Plunkett' Seanchas Ard Mhacha, 1975/6

Ó Fiaich, Tomás. 'Documents Connected with the Canonisation of St. Oliver Plunkett' Seanchas Ard Mhacha, 1975/6

Ó Fiaich, Tomás. 'Consecration of Blessed Oliver Plunket' Irish Ecclesiastical Record, 1958

MacLeod, C. 'Bonaventura' 1939

MacPhoíl, An tAth. Donnchadh. 'Blessed Oliver and the Tories' Seanchas Ard Mhacha, 1959

MacPhoíl, An tAth. Donnchadh. 'The Clergy of Oliver Plunkett' Seanchas Ard Mhacha, 1957/8/9 +1983/4/6

Millet Fr. Benignus. 'Ancient altar-plate and other furnishings of the church of Armagh' Seanchas Ard Mhacha, 1958

Mooney, Re. Canice. 'Accusations against Oliver Plunkett' Seanchas Ard Mhacha, 1956

Moran, Anne. 'New Light on the Family of Blessed Oliver Plunket' Seanchas Ard Mhacha, 1959

Murphy, Edmund. 'The perfect State and Condition of Ireland etc.' London 1681

Murray, L. P. 'Lament of Patrick Fleming' Louth Archaeological Journal, 1933

Murray, P. G. 'A Previously Unnoticed Letter of Oliver Plunkett's' Seanchas Ard Mhacha, 1975/6

Newton, Diane 'Papists, Protestants and Puritans 1559 – 1714' Cambridge, 1998

O'Callaghan, Seán 'To Hell or Barbados' Brandon Books, 2000

Ó hAnnracháin Tadhg. 'Catholic Reformation in Ireland' Oxford, 2002

O'Reilly, M. 'The Plunkett Family of Loughcrew' Riocht na Midhe, 1958

Palmer, C. F. Raymund. 'The Life of Philip, Thomas Howard O.P. Cardinal of Norfolk' London, 1867

Phillipson Rev. Dom Wulstan. 'Blessed Oliver Plunket - Historical Studies' Dublin, 1937

Plunkett, Oliver. 'Jus Primitiale' O.A.T.H.P. Dublin, 1672

Power, Rev. P. 'A Bishop of the Penal Times, Letters of John Brenan' Cork, 1932

Rafferty, Oliver P. 'Catholicism in Ulster 1603 – 1983' South Carolina, 1994

Ronan, Rev. Myles. 'Blessed Oliver Plunkett' Irish Ecclesiastical Record, 1920

Sister Francis Agnes. O.S.F. 'Blessed Oliver's Relics at Goodings' Seanchas Ard Mhacha, 1969

Wall, Maureen. 'The Penal laws, 1691 – 1760' Dublin Historical Society, 1976

Wall, Thomas. 'The Primatial Controversy' Irish Ecclesiastical Record, 1939

Walker, Rev. Breifne. 'Blessed Oliver Plunkett and the Popish Plot in Ireland' Irish Ecclesiastical Record, 1968

Weyer, Florence. 'The Honesty and True Zeal of the King's Witnesses...' London 1681

APPENDIX VII

LIST OF BIOGRAPHIES OF ST. OLIVER PLUNKETT

It is a testament of St. Oliver's international status that biographies have been written by nationals of seven countries and printed in six languages. Oliver Plunkett invariably spelt the name Plunkett with two t's, although it may be noticed that many of the earlier biographers used just one. Those interested in further study of St. Oliver should certainly start with book number 50: 'The Letters of Saint Oliver Plunkett by Mgr. John Hanly', although each book listed below has something unique to offer the reader. For those wishing further research on the myriad of articles and research papers written about St. Oliver, there is an excellent bibliography at the back of book number 31 by Emmanuel Curtis and together with the list of biographies printed here will provide a pretty comprehensive list of sources of information about the martyred Archbishop of Armagh.

1:	Challoner Richard -The Life and Martyrdom of the Most Rev. Doctor Oliver Plunket	Dublin 1835
2:	Crolly, G. - The Life and Death of Oliver Plunkett	Dublin 1850
3:	Moran, P.F. - Memoirs of the Most Rev. Oliver Plunket	Dublin 1861
4:	Moran, P.F. - Life of Most Rev. Oliver Plunket	Dublin 1870
5:	Moran, P. F. - Memoir of the Ven. Oliver Plunket	Dublin 1895
6:	Anon. - Life and Death of Ven. Oliver Plunket	Dublin 1896
7:	Fleming, Dean - Oliver Plunkett	Dublin 1897
8:	Duggan, Michael T. - Ven. Oliver Plunket	Dublin 1904
9:	Powell, F. J. - The Ven. Oliver Plunket	Drogheda 1918
10:	A Sister of Notre Dame - Sr. Mary Grehan - Blessed Oliver Plunket	London 1920
11:	Salotti Mons. Carlo - Oliviero Plunket (In Italian)	Rome 1920
12:	O'Connell, Rev Sir John - The Blessed Oliver Plunkett	Dublin 1921 / 1944
13:	Callery, P. - Blessed Oliver Plunkett	Dublin 1922

14: Segrave Mgr. - Blessed Oliver Plunkett – (Irish Messenger Publication) — Dublin c.1931

15: Macardle Peter L. - Local Associations with Bl. O. Plunket — Dundalk Democrat 1934

16: Concannon, Mrs. T. - Blessed Oliver Plunket — Dublin 1935

17: Mary St. Thomas - The Story of Blessed Oliver Plunket — Dublin 1936

18: Ed. Anon - Blessed Oliver Plunket Historical Studies — Gill, Dublin 1937

19: Dease, O. - With Blessed Oliver in Ireland — Dublin 1939

20: Collier, Most Rev. P. - Blessed Oliver Plunket — Dublin 1941

21: Carolan Canon Francis - Blessed Oliver Plunkett and Louth — Drogheda c.1943

22: Various - Devotion to Blessed Oliver — Gill, Dublin 1945

23: O'Higgins. - Oliver of Ireland — Dublin 1945

24: Gaffney, H. - Oliver — Dublin 1946

25: Curtayne, Alice - The Trial of Oliver Plunkett — London 1953 / 1975

26: Stokes, Mgr. J. F. - Booklet based on Radio Talks On Bl. Oliver — Dublin c.1955

27: Blessed Oliver Plunkett - Shepherd of Shamrock Isle - Benedictine Convent Clyde. — Missouri, USA 1956

28: Stokes, Mgr. J F. - The Life of Blessed Oliver Plunkett — Dublin 1954, 1956, 1965

29: Roberto, Bro. - Now Comes the Hangman - Bl. Oliver Plunkett. Notre Dame, — Indiana USA 1956

30: Matthews, Deirdre - Oliver of Armagh — Dublin 1961

31: Curtis, Fr. Emmanuel - Blessed Oliver Plunkett — Dublin 1963

32: De Miserey Marie. - Bienheureux Olivier Plunkett (In French) — Paris 1963

33: Carty, F. X. - Blessed Oliver Plunkett — Dublin 1972

34: Kennedy H.P. & Early H. Barry - Oliver Plunkett — Dublin 1974

35: Bennett Fr. Martin - the Way of a Martyr — London 1974 / 1975

36: Hanly Mgr. John - Canonisation Commemorate Booklet — Rome 1975

37: Hanly Mgr. John - Saint Oliver Plunkett — Dublin 1975 /1984

38: Gleeson, John - Oliver Plunkett, The Resolute Shepherd — Melbourne 1975
39: McKee John - A Martyr Bishop : The Life of St. Oliver Plunkett. — Houston Texas 1975
40: Murphy, Martin - Saint Oliver Plunkett and Downside — Downside 1975
41: Faul, Mons Denis - St. Oliver and Louth Village — Louth 1962 / 1975
42: Tigar, Clement - Saint Oliver — London 1975
43: Meagher, Rev. John - Saint Oliver Plunkett — Dublin 1975
44: Nowak, Josef. - Oliver Plunkett (In German) — Hildesheim 1975
45: Ó Fiaich Mons. Tomás - Oliver Plunkett, Ireland's New Saint — Dublin 1975 / 1981
46: Forristal, Fr. Des. - Oliver Plunkett - In His Own Words — Dublin 1975
47: Ó Fiaich & Forristal - Oliver Plunkett (Both books in same edition) — Indiana USA 1976
48: Ó Fiaich Mgr. Tomás. - Oilibhéar Pluincéid (As Gaeilge) — Baile Átha Cliath 1976
49: Hanly, Mgr. John. - Oliver Plunkett (In Italian) — Rome 1977
50: Hanly, Mgr. John - The Letters of Saint Oliver Plunkett — Dublin 1979
51: Oliver Plunkett - Gebete Und Gesänge - Lamspringe Parish — Lamspringe c.1990
52: Donnelly, Mons Frank - Until the Storm Passes St. Oliver Plunkett — Drogheda 1993 / 2000
53: Donnelly, Mons. Frank - Oliver Plunkett in a Broken Church — Drogheda 1995 / 1999
54: Collins, Donal - Oliver Plunkett — Chigago 1995
55: Burns, Tommy - St. Oliver Plunkett, Deo Gratias — Drogheda 2000
56: Burns, Tommy - St. Oliver Plunkett - Episcopal Ordination and Journey to Ireland — Drogheda 2008
57: Axel Christoph Kronenberg - Kloster Lamspringe und der Irishe Märtyr Oliver Plunkett — Lamspringe 2010
58: Axel Christoph Kronenberg - Monastery of Lamspringe & the Irish Martyr Oliver Plunkett — Lamspringe 2013
59: Gaeil Uladh – Naomh Oilibhéar Pluincéad - Pictiúr Maitiú Ó Cathain As Gaeilge — Na Doire Beaga
60: Downside Abbey – Saint Oliver Plunkett — Downside 2016
61: Tracey Fintan – St. Oliver Plunkett - Witness - (Book in Comic Format) — Drogheda 2017
62: Rafferty Sr. Veronica - San Oliverio Plunkett de Irlanda (In Spanish) — Rosario, Argentina 2017
63: Burns, Tommy - St. Oliver Plunkett - Journey to Sainthood — Drogheda Rev. 2019 / 2014

Reception of St. Oliver Relic by Fr. Pablo, St. Patrick's Chapel, Rosario, Argentina 1st July 2016 With Rodolfo Plunkett on left of picture and Patricio O'Sullivan, President of St. Patrick's Catholic Association on right

After St. Oliver's martyrdom, this Relic was given into the care of his best friend, John Brenan, Archbishop of Cashel. Handed down to successive Archbishops of Cashel, it was eventually given to Fr. Patrick Moran, nephew of Cardinal Cullen. Fr. Moran had already published the first of his three books on Oliver Plunkett. Shortly afterwards, he became Vice-Rector of the Irish College in Rome, the bishop of Ossory and in 1884 the Cardinal Archbishop of Sydney. He gave this important Relic in 1869 into the care of the Dominican Sisters, Cabra, Dublin, expressing the following hope in his book: "I trust it may one day, with the solemn sanction of the Holy See, receive that honour and veneration which are due to the martyrs of the Church of Christ." Memoir of the Ven. Oliver Plunket Moran 1895 p.451

In 2015, the Cabra Community gave the Relic to the Siena Sisters, Drogheda who in turn gave it the following year into the care of the Dominican Sisters, Argentina. We give thanks that this ardent wish of Cardinal Patrick Moran has finally been achieved and that after three centuries this important Relic is now venerated publicly. It is especially pleasing that this new Shrine to St. Oliver is on the other side of the world, in Rosario, Argentina. Deo Gratias.

17th Century Reliquary, Siena Convent

A beautiful and important reliquary which was specially made within a couple of years of St. Oliver's martyrdom, to house the Relic of the Head. Topped with a small silver mitre, a silver plate on the front has the Plunkett coat of arms along with those of the Corker, Sheldon and Cotton families. It is recorded that Archbishop Hugh McMahon, the second successor of Archbishop Oliver as Archbishop of Armagh brought it back from Rome and gave it into the care of the Siena Sisters in Drogheda shortly after they moved to Dyer Street in 1725. Their first superior was Sr. Catherine Plunkett, a grandniece of St. Oliver. The community also record in their annals that it came through customs disguised as a clock case. Indeed, for two hundred years during penal times, it housed the Relic of the Head, sitting perfectly camouflaged on top of their grandfather clock. The religious sisters were living surreptitiously as a group of women friends and lodgers, at a time when the oppression of the penal laws was quite severe, but behind closed doors they lived as a regulated community of nuns.

For a full description of the Ebony Box Reliquary: Bellew Seamus 'The Seventeenth Century Reliquary of St. Oliver Plunkett at the Siena Convent Drogheda' Seanchas Ard Mhacha 2011

Painting of St. Oliver in St. Patrick's Church, Rosario by Rodolfo Plunkett, Rosario, Argentina

APPENDIX VIII

BEATIFICATION OF BLESSED OLIVER IN CONTEXT

Archbishop Oliver Plunkett was beatified in Rome by Pope Benedict XV on Pentecost Sunday 23rd May 1920. The Irish gave thanks to God and the great event was celebrated joyously by the Irish diaspora across the world. Thirty-four years earlier, Oliver had been declared Venerable Oliver Plunkett by Pope Leo XIII on 9th December 1886 and while his cause advanced slowly it progressed steadily. For two centuries after his death, Archbishop Plunkett was almost completely forgotten about in Ireland as a result of the harsh penal laws and the difficult famine times. During this period, the Irish people struggled and scraped for bare survival in body and in soul. The Siena Convent in Drogheda, the Irish College in Rome, Lamspringe Abbey in Germany, along with several other Benedictine communities never forgot, and Oliver Plunkett's memory has been faithfully venerated in these communities right down to the present day. Bishop Challoner, Dr. Crolly of Maynooth, Cardinal Moran and other biographers had made Archbishop Oliver's life and work more widely known, and his last speech delivered from the gallows at Tyburn was reprinted on several occasions during the nineteenth century. The speech is a must read and printed in the following chapter, Appendix IX.

Over the following years, the minutest examination took place of Archbishop Oliver's life; his reputation, his virtue, his writings and above all his sanctity were all considered and debated in depth. All possible objections raised by the 'devil's advocate' appointed to oppose the cause were answered creditably. Three tribunals of inquiry were set up to hear evidence from the various disciplines, one in Armagh, another in Dublin and a third in Sydney, where Cardinal Patrick Moran had much evidence and paperwork to offer. Even the legalities of Oliver's case had to be gone into, in the greatest of detail. Oliver had after all been convicted in a court of law of the most serious charge of high treason, and had been sentenced to a gruesome death because of that 'guilt'. The Dublin tribunal looked at the original trial in great detail. Christopher Pallas, the Lord Chief Justice of Ireland and a team of lawyers had much to say about the serious shortcomings of Oliver's trial in Westminster Hall and in particular of Lord Chief Justice Pemberton's inept handling of the trial and of the false evidence produced at it. The tribunals completed their work and submitted their findings to Rome.

All appeared in order and there seemed to be no reason why a declaration of martyrdom should not be soon forthcoming. In the interim, World War I intervened and this slowed the whole process down. Archbishop Oliver's case was undeniably good; he had lived a good life and the manner of his death was virtuous beyond any shadow of doubt. And so, on St. Patrick's Day 1918, Archbishop Oliver Plunkett was duly declared a 'Martyr for the Faith' by Cardinal Vico in the presence of Pope Benedict XV. Many Catholics who had observed the tragedy at Tyburn in 1681 already believed that they had witnessed a martyr's death. The arms and head of Oliver's mutilated body were not buried with the rest of his body but kept as relics because of this commonly held belief at the time. Also, Dom Maurus Corker the Benedictine monk, who had befriended Archbishop Oliver in Newgate Prison, had inscriptions made for the coffin and the tomb, both of which clearly indicated a martyr's death. For translations of the texts and pictures of the inscriptions, see p.230 and p.231. All of this was unofficial however, Archbishop Oliver's martyrdom could not be proclaimed publicly, certainly not until the decree of martyrdom would be declared by the sacred congregation in Rome and sanctioned by the Pope. The declaration of his martyrdom when declared in 1918 was rightly seen as a major step forward in his cause. There was much rejoicing at home and abroad as it was anticipated that the beatification of Oliver Plunkett was imminent and could soon take place.

A year later it came to pass and Irish people across the globe celebrated with great joy when Blessed Oliver Plunkett was beatified by Pope Benedict XV on Pentecost Sunday 1920. Although journeys were expensive and travel times long and difficult, many hundreds of Irish made the journey to Rome to witness this great event. While many more were unable to travel, it was arranged that every facet of Irish Catholic life would be represented at the ceremony. The Irish were led by Cardinal Michael Logue the Archbishop of Armagh who was accompanied by the majority of the Irish Bishops. Many Cardinals and bishops were also in attendance and the English speaking world was particularly well represented. Cardinal Francis Bourne of Westminster, Cardinal William O'Connell of Boston, Cardinal Bégin from Canada, Archbishop Michael Kelly of Sydney and many others. The Benedictines were well represented, led by Cardinal Francis Gasquet, along with the Abbot of Downside Abbey. As Vatican archivist, Cardinal Gasquet was already in Rome and was quite knowledgeable about the life of Oliver Plunkett. In 1883 he brought the body of Archbishop Plunkett from Lamspringe Abbey in Germany to Downside Abbey in Somerset,

St. Oliver Statue, Kilcloon Parish Church, Co. Meath

where he was prior at the time.

Civic society was also well represented at the beatification ceremony in Rome. The rejoicing and celebrations were tempered somewhat because so many tragic events were taking place in Ireland, mid-way through the War of Independence. The freedom of nationhood and the freedom to worship, which had been denied for so long in Ireland had become inextricably linked. The right to nationhood and faith were causes which many countries had struggled for over the centuries. This point was not lost by those in Rome; St. Joan of Arc had become a talking point that very week as she had been canonised only seven days previously by Pope Benedict XV. While the right to nationhood and faith may often be inextricably linked; in the case of the Irish, they had also proven much to their material cost, that faith was a great deal more important

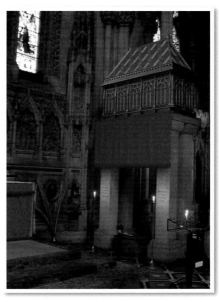

St Oliver's Tomb, Downside Abbey

to them than nationhood. The Cromwellians had given Catholic Ireland an unenviable choice, either give up the Roman Catholic faith and convert to the new strands of religion or become dispossessed of land, property and positions. Almost unanimously, Catholics refused and were made to suffer severely for holding onto the beliefs of the ancient faith. As a result of their loyalty and steadfastness in this belief over succeeding generations, their misery and sufferings were destined to continue even beyond the period of the penal laws.

The civic representatives in Rome were led by Seán T. O'Ceallaigh, representing Dáil Éireann and the National Executive. Count George Noble Plunkett who had promoted Oliver Plunkett's cause at every opportunity and his wife the Countess were present and would not have missed such a momentous event in the history of the Plunkett clan. Laurence O'Neill, Lord Mayor of Dublin, the Mayor of Drogheda, along with mayors and councillors from many cities and towns in Ireland were also present. One lord mayor not present in Rome was Tomás Mac Curtain, Lord Mayor of Cork. He had been murdered in his house in Cork, barely five weeks before the beatification by two Royal Irish policemen out of uniform. They had gained entry to his home and shot him there at one o'clock in the morning.

Pitched battles between Sinn Fein supporters and Unionists had taken place in

Derry, less than a week before the beatification. This was a time of real tension in Ireland and much darker clouds were already appearing on the horizon. The first of the Black and Tans were arriving and before July was out, serious rioting and violent attacks in Belfast would claim fourteen lives. Prisoners were on hunger strike in various prisons while their relations and supporters held demonstrations and recited the Rosary outside. Dockers were refusing to handle military supplies. The police were ostracised and Dáil courts were in the process of being set up around Ireland. The War of Independence which had begun the previous year was intensifying; it was a worrying time all round and no one knew how it would all end. Atrocities were committed by both sides.

In Drogheda, armed republicans would soon locate themselves in the vicinity of the Siena Convent to protect the precious Relic of Blessed Oliver's Head, lest the Black and Tans might steal or desecrate the Relic as an act of reprisal for acts committed against crown forces. In Rome, many prayers were offered that week by the pilgrims as they prayed for a troubled Ireland, whenever they would visit St. Peter's Basilica or the other locations in Rome which had associations with Ireland. Oliver Plunkett too, had often offered prayers for a troubled Ireland in these very same locations, during his twenty-two years in Rome, whether as a seminarian, deacon, priest or teaching professor.

The Beatification Ceremony of Blessed Oliver Plunkett, 23rd May 1920

Beatification ceremonies are full of splendour and ceremony. On the outer balcony of St. Peter's Basilica hung a large canvas depicting Archbishop Oliver addressing the judges at the trial. The apse of St. Peter's, located in the area at the back of the high altar was beautifully decorated for the occasion and a huge number of lights were installed. Afterwards it was said that the multiplicity of lights were like the stars in the heavens. A reminder perhaps to all present, that Archbishop Oliver usually ministered outdoors, often travelling and ministering under the stars of the heavens. The majority of the Irish present had certainly never seen the likes, as most of them were probably more used to the dimness of old oil lamps. Within five years, a free

Chair of St Peter, Apse, St. Peter's Basilica, Rome

Dáil would make the decision to spend huge amounts of money and build the largest hydro-electric scheme in the world of its day at Ardnacrusha, which began to power increasing areas of the country before the end of the 1920's. The lighting in the St. Peter's Basilica can clearly be made out in the picture which was taken on the day of the beatification.

Very high up over the Chair of St. Peter, hung a large veiled picture of the martyr primate. The apse is the traditional location for ceremonies of beatification and it was an entirely appropriate location for the beatification of Archbishop Oliver. While he was a teaching professor in Propaganda Fide College in Rome, he would have witnessed in 1666, the dedication of a monumental work by Bernini in the apse, the Shrine of the Chair of St. Peter. Exactly eight years later on the feast of the Chair of St. Peter in 1674, Archbishop Oliver who was then caught out in a savage snow storm while on the run in south Armagh, wrote: "God be praised that he gave us the grace to suffer for the Chair of St. Peter and on the feast dedicated to the chair founded upon the rock, which will, I hope in the long run break the tempestuous waves". Archbishop Oliver's love and loyalty to the See of Peter has been written about frequently over the centuries. At 10am on the morning of the beatification, the solemn procession wound its way to the apse where Mass was celebrated by Monsignor Pietroppoli, Archbishop of Chalcis, and Assistant to the Pontifical Throne. Following custom, Pope Benedict was not present

Cardinal Seán Brady blessing the St. Oliver, Irish Oak Tree, Lamspringe - 2013

at the beatification ceremony. The Papal Bull was read and relics of new Blessed were venerated. The veil covering the picture of Blessed Oliver was withdrawn and Te Deum sung. In the afternoon, Pope Benedict XV arrived and he too knelt in prayer before the relics of Blessed Oliver before giving benediction. There he was presented by Mgr. John Hagan, Rector of the Irish College, with a Relic enclosed in a large reliquary, modelled on the reliquary containing the Bell of St. Patrick, which is housed in the National Museum, Dublin.

The following day, the Irish assembled at the Church of San Pietro in Montario for Mass celebrated by the Bishop of Clonfert with a discourse by the Bishop Patrick O'Donnell of Raphoe, destined to become Cardinal O'Donnell and successor of Cardinal Logue in Armagh. He spoke in memory of O'Neill and the O'Donnell, Irish princes of old and their relations, who were buried in tombs close to the altar in Montario, some thirty years or so before Oliver's arrival in Rome. They too had fought for faith and country in their day. There followed prayers as Gaeilge and a short talk by Cardinal Logue as the national flag hung overhead. A short talk was given by Seán T. O'Ceallaigh; Count Plunkett then spoke as did the Lord Mayor of Dublin. As this meeting broke up, hearty cheers were raised for their Lordships and for the national cause. During the week, the Holy Father, Pope Benedict XV, held private audiences with Cardinal Logue along with many of the Irish Bishops. He also received Count and Countess Plunkett. At the general audience on the Wednesday, Pope Benedict XV met four hundred of the Irish pilgrims and told them of his affection for the Irish nation, and recommended Blessed Oliver to them as patron.

One topic very much in the thoughts of Cardinal Logue at that time was the Relic of the Head of Blessed Oliver. While in Rome for the beatification ceremony, he repeated his request that the Sacred Congregation of Rites give permission for the Relic of the Head to be translated from the Siena convent to the fine new church of St. Peter, already dedicated as the Memorial Church of Dr. Oliver Plunkett, since the foundation stone was laid on the bi-centenary of his martyrdom in 1881. This request was granted and not withstanding an appeal by the Dominican order, the Relic of the Head of Blessed Oliver was translated from The Siena Convent to St. Peter's Church, Drogheda, Memorial Church of Blessed Oliver Plunkett on 21st June 1921. To the great disappointment of the nuns, the Pope while sympathetic to their case let the decision stand, as when they were given the treasured Relic by Archbishop MacMahon some two hundred years earlier, he had stipulated in his will, that it could remain in the custody of 'Mrs Mary Reilly and ye gentlewomen in Dyer Street, Drogheda' until such time as an Archbishop of Armagh should ever wish to reclaim it. See chapter 97 on p.240.

The representatives of the Dáil, who were present in Rome for the beatification, held a reception in the Grand Hotel. Seán T. O'Ceallaigh welcomed in Irish his Eminence Cardinal Logue, many of their Lordships and a wide circle of distinguished guests. He concluded his speech by noting the great sign of Irish unity it was to have gathered in Rome so many representatives of various institutions and various ways of thought, gathered in the name of Ireland to do honour to one of Ireland's martyred dead.

The Dáil was already seeking international support but this was slow in coming. Ireland was in the throes of birthing a new nation; its birth was not going to be easy and it was widely recognised that propaganda would play a key role on the international stage. Seán T O'Ceallaigh had sent a memorandum to the Pope: 'As practicing Catholics we have never allowed our national movement for independence to be contaminated by anti-religious or other dangerous movements condemned by the Church; yet we find that the continental press reproduces the calumnies fabricated in England, painting our struggle for bare liberty as a movement of anarchists... The Irish Hierarchy has endorsed the demand of the Irish people to choose its own form of government and again renewed that demand in their declaration of January 27th. of this year'.

Unfortunately, civil disobedience in Ireland was descending into anarchy as out of control hotheads on both sides, began taking independent action by committing atrocities and reprisals. The Irish Hierarchy rightly condemned all such actions while all the while supporting the right of the Irish people to self-determination. By this time, the possibility of a border was also complicating matters on all sides. Daniel Mannix, Archbishop of Melbourne was much more forthright in supporting the republican cause in Ireland and within three months of the beatification ceremony in Rome, he was refused entry into Ireland. He was taken off a liner by British military as it approached Cobh in his native county of Cork, and dropped off in England, before returning to Australia. The Dáil delegates while in Rome continued to promote the case for Irish freedom, against many prejudices of the day. Thirty years later, Sean T O'Ceallaigh would be widely welcomed on a visit to Rome as Uachtarán na hÉireann.

In Ireland, the beatification of Blessed Oliver Plunkett in 1920 was marked and celebrated in nearly every Catholic church and chapel in the land. In the Archdiocese of Armagh, Cardinal Michael Logue had instructed all parishes in the Archdiocese to organise a Triduum of Prayer in thanksgiving. This was to give thanks to God for the beatification, to pray for Blessed Oliver's intercession for a strengthening of faith, to pray for Ireland and to pray for schools. He also directed that at the end of each triduum, a solemn Te Deum was to be sung in thanksgiving.

At Ballybarrack just outside Dundalk, the site of Archbishop Oliver's church where he ordained priests, administered the sacraments and also lived during the early years of his ministry as Archbishop of Armagh, a large celebration was held on the day of the beatification. It was estimated that several thousand people attended the ceremony, many of whom were spread out into the neighbouring fields. A chalice used by Archbishop Oliver was used at the Mass, lent for the occasion by the authorities of Clonliffe College. The top of a brass thurible, found during clean-up excavations only a short time before the celebration in Ballybarrack, was placed on the altar for the celebration.

In London, many thousands took part in the procession from the old site of Newgate Jail to Tyburn. Republican prisoners, who had been released from prison shortly beforehand, joined the procession as a group. Some of these had been on a prison hunger strike and had been sent to hospital for observation and treatment; they had left hospital to join the procession and were literally feted by the thousands of Irish in attendance on the day. When the procession reached Tyburn, Benediction of the Blessed Sacrament was given from the balcony of Tyburn Convent. It was later reported that six thousand people received the blessing at Tyburn Convent, barely a stone's throw away from the site of Tyburn Gallows.

In Germany, the Diocese of Hildesheim also marked the occasion of Blessed Oliver's beatification in celebratory mood. The substantial relic of Blessed Oliver which was in their possession in Lamspringe, and had been left to them in 1883 when the rest of his body was translated to Downside, could now be displayed prominently and venerated more publicly. The procession in Lamspringe on Pentecost Sunday 1920 was a fervent one. The large reliquary of Blessed Oliver housed in the local church was carried in the procession and can be clearly seen in the picture on p.33. The parish of Lamspringe are faithful devotees of St. Oliver and have held a well organised celebration in his honour every year since, including during the war years.

The main Drogheda celebrations took place on the following Sunday, so as to allow time for those pilgrims who had travelled to Rome to return home. It was estimated that ten-thousand people knelt for the Blessing of the Blessed Sacrament that day in West Street after a solemn procession of the Blessed Sacrament had taken place around the town. The celebrations in Drogheda began on Pentecost Sunday with solemn high Mass at 12 noon in St. Peters' Church, the Memorial Church of Blessed Oliver Plunkett.

Monsignor Patrick Segrave PP oversaw the planning and organisation of the celebrations. At a meeting in the Presentation Convent in Fair Street to organise events for the week, it was stated that one hundred pounds had been collected for flags, bunting and other expenses. Fr. Sheehy, a teaching professor in All Hallows College, Dublin preached at the Mass in Drogheda, on the theme: 'This is the victory that overcomes the world'.

The Triduum was organised in St. Peter's parish for the following weekend, culminating in a procession of the Blessed Sacrament through the streets of the town on Sunday 30th May. The town was en- fête throughout the week and businesses and shops made an immense effort to decorate their premises, as did the residents of streets and houses in all quarters of the town. The Relic of the Head of St. Oliver was still under the care of the Siena community in the Chord Road at the time. A picture of the Shrine decorated for the beatification and incorporating the seventeenth century black ebony box reliquary may be seen on p.239 with a description of the reliquary on p.276. The Siena Convent was literally besieged by a continuous stream of people throughout the week, all of whom wished to visit and to venerate with joy, Ireland's new beatus. Before joining the procession in the town, the Mayor and members of Drogheda Corporation dressed in ceremonial attire, visited the Siena Convent and venerated the Relic. Along with the nuns of the community and boarders of the convent school, they recited the Rosary 'as Gaeilge' led by Dr. Keane O.P.

Along the procession route, poles had been erected twenty yards apart on both sides of the street and these were suitably draped with flags and bunting. The streets of Drogheda had never before seen such displays of public decoration. These can be clearly seen in the picture on p.78 which

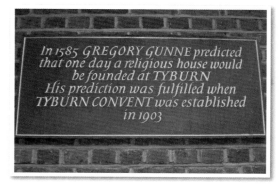

Plaque outside Tyburn Convent

was taken of the solemn procession as it passes the Tholsel in the town centre. Taking part in the procession were the members of the Drogheda Brass Band who provided music for the hymn singing throughout the proceedings. Walking under their respective banners were the members of all the religious organisations, sodalities and confraternities in the town. The St. Vincent de Paul Society had the honour of providing a guard of honour walking alongside the Blessed Sacrament. A group of young girls, all dressed in white, threw flower petals on the ground in front of the Blessed Sacrament upon each ringing of a hand bell. The procession began outside St. Peter's Church and traversed along West Street, Laurence Street, Palace Street, William Street, Fair Street, then proceeding into the grounds of the Sisters of Charity where an elaborate altar had been erected for a Benediction ceremony. Over the entrance gates to the convent grounds a giant banner was displayed with the words 'Céad Míle Fáilte'. The procession then proceeded across Fair Street, Georges Square and back into West Street. Bishop Sheils of Rockhampton Diocese, Australia then gave a blessing of the Blessed Sacrament from Our Lady's Grotto outside St. Peter's Church. It is recorded that the crowd kneeling for the blessing that afternoon stretched from the Tholsel, right across West Street to the top of Dominic Street.

The Church in Ireland and the Irish diaspora abroad celebrated with joy, the recognition given to Blessed Oliver, one of their own. Those Irish who were lucky enough to be present in Rome, celebrated with particular joy and they never forgot the scenes of jubilation in the Piazza of St. Peter's, at the Irish College or wherever else they gathered in Rome including at the tombs of the exiled earls on Montorio.

Pope Benedict XV told the Irish nation in 1920 at the time of the beatification and during a time of great strife in Ireland, that it was opportune that they had at that juncture, acquired a powerful patron in the Court of Heaven. The following year, Blessed Oliver's intercession for Ireland must indeed have been powerful as recounted many years later by Cardinal Tomás Ó Fiaich in his biography of St. Oliver, when he wrote: "It is worthy of note that the Truce, which brought to an end the War of Independence, came into force on the Feast of Blessed Oliver in 1921." Catholics in England must also have recognised the role of Blessed Oliver in this event, as the inscription on a reliquary containing a Relic of the Martyr Primate in Westminster Cathedral, states: 'From Irish English Clients of Blessed Oliver in the year of the Truce 1921'

After his beatification, the Feast of Blessed Oliver was celebrated on 11th July each year for the following fifty-five years. A saint is venerated by the Church worldwide, whereas the veneration due a beatus would usually be confined to a country or a region of the world. Shortly before St. Oliver's canonisation in 1975 a new date to celebrate his feast was debated as the 11th of July was already taken on the international calendar of saints, it being the Feast of St. Benedict, now a patron of Europe. The Irish Hierarchy were given a choice of dates on which the Feast of St. Oliver might be celebrated and July 1st was chosen. It was also a suitable date as it was the day of his martyrdom on the old style calendar of his day. On the written copy of his last speech he added his signature and date 1st July. The canonisation of St. Oliver is detailed in Chapter 99 p.249.

In 1975 at the time of St. Oliver's canonisation in Rome, Cardinal Manning of Los Angeles preached in a sermon: 'When saints are canonised, they are often felt to have a particular relevance to the era of their canonisation; they can serve as a means to overcome crises and to heal wounds in the Church. So it is with Oliver Plunkett...The martyr's dedication to duty, his courage in the face of death, his efforts to restore peace in his country at a time of troubles, all these have a special relevance to Ireland at the present time." Before preaching his great sermon for peace during his visit to Drogheda, Pope St. John Paul first venerated the Relic of the Head of St. Oliver Plunkett, widely recognised as Patron for Peace and Reconciliation in Ireland. With his solemn and prayerful words, St. John Paul's earnest appeal to the men and women of violence that afternoon, left a lasting impression on all present and were carried far and wide across the land: "On my knees I beg you to turn away from the path of violence and return to the ways of peace" In the modern era, St. Oliver is still interceding for us and it has been noted and is certainly more than coincidence, that the momentous first meeting of the new Northern Ireland Assembly took place on the 1st July 1998, the Feast of St. Oliver.

We would do well to pray more often to St. Oliver for his intercession, for in those words of Pope Benedict XV: "We have acquired a powerful Patron in the Court of Heaven".

St. Oliver's Well,
Doctors Quarters, Mullaghbawn

Deo Gratias for the life, example and intercession of St. Oliver Plunkett

Stained Glass Window
St. Patrick's Cathedral, Armagh

Tyburn Scene, St. Patrick's Church, Dundalk

Tyburn Scene

APPENDIX IX

THE LAST SPEECH OF ST. OLIVER PLUNKETT

St. Oliver wrote the speech during his final days in Newgate Prison, London, with the endorsement of Fr. Maurus Corker a fellow prisoner. He delivered it from the scaffold at Tyburn, immediately before his execution and it was printed shortly afterwards for distribution. The original manuscript, which is written in St. Oliver's own hand, is preserved in Downside Abbey, along with his final letters to Fr. Corker. The speech was apparently well received, as the large crowd listened to him deliver it to its very conclusion and it is probable that many people may have already sensed a great injustice was taking place.

It is a well-structured speech and was obviously crafted with the benefit of a trained legal mind. It answered his detractors on a point for point basis, showing forgiveness even to his enemies and it must have convinced many more people of his innocence. Indeed, the tide of the wicked Popish Plot turned immediately and Lord Shaftesbury its principle promoter was arrested on the following day. The Lord answered the Archbishop of Armagh's prayer and so St. Oliver Plunkett became the last of the one hundred and five Catholic martyrs of Tyburn who had given their lives over the previous one hundred and fifty years. Moreover it must be highly significant, that he is also the very last of the Catholic martyrs condemned by the state in these islands. Deo Gratias.

St. Oliver on the Gallows at Tyburn – Painting in Synod Hall, Armagh

Speech from Gallows at Tyburn 1st July 1681

I have, some few days past, abided my trial at the King's Bench and now very soon, I must hold up my hand at the King of Kings' bench, and appear before a Judge who cannot be deceived by false witnesses or corrupted allegations, for he knoweth the secrets of hearts. Neither can he deceive any or give an unjust sentence, or be misled by respect of persons; he being all goodness, and a most just Judge, will infallibly decree an eternal reward for all good works, and condign punishment for the smallest transgression against his commandments. Which being a most certain and an undoubted truth, it would be a wicked act and contrary to my perpetual welfare, that I should now, by declaring anything contrary to truth commit a detestable sin, for which, within a very short time I must receive sentence of everlasting damnation after which, there is no reprieve, or hope of pardon. I will therefore confess the truth, without any equivocation, and make use of the words according to their accustomed signification. Assuring you, moreover that I am of that certain persuasion, that no power not only upon earth, but also in heaven, can dispense with me, or give me leave to make a false protestation. And I protest upon the word of a dying man, and as I hope for salvation, at the hands of the Supreme Judge, that I will declare the naked truth, with all candour and sincerity and that my affairs may be the better known to all the world.

Painting of St. Oliver after Nineteen Months spent in Prison

It is to be observed that I have been accused in Ireland of treason and premunire and that there, I was arraigned and brought to my trial but the prosecutors men of flagitious and infamous lives perceiving that I had records and witnesses, who would evidently convince them and clearly show my innocence and their wickedness. They voluntarily absented themselves

Location of Tyburn Gallows, near Marble Arch, London. Otherwise known as Tyburn Tree. Marked now by Three Trees, Symbolising the Three Legged Gallows as depicted on p.221.

and came to this city to procure that I should be brought hither to my trial, where the crimes objected were not committed, where the jury did not know me, or the qualities of my accusers, and were not informed of several other circumstances conducive to a fair trial. Here, after six months close imprisonment, or thereabouts, I was brought to the bar, the third of May and arraigned for a crime, for which I was before arraigned in Ireland. A strange resolution, a rare fact, of which you will hardly find a precedent these five-hundred years past. But whereas my witnesses and records were in Ireland, the Lord Chief Justice gave me five weeks' time, to get them brought hither. But by reason of the uncertainty of the seas, of wind and weather and of the difficulty of getting copies of records and bringing many witnesses from several counties in Ireland and for many other impediments of which affidavit was made, I could not at the end of the five weeks, get the records and witnesses brought hither. I therefore begged for twelve days more, that I might be in a readiness for my trial, which the Lord Chief Justice denied and so I was brought to my trial and exposed, as it were with my hands tied, to those merciless perjurers, who did aim at my life, by accusing me of these following points:

First, that I have sent letters by one Nial O'Neale, who was my page, to Monsieur Baldeschi, the pope's secretary; to the Bishop of Aix, and to Principe Colonna, that they might solicit foreign powers to invade Ireland; and also to have sent letters to Cardinal Bouillion to the same effect.

Secondly, to have employed Captain Con O'Neale, to the French King, for succour.

Thirdly, To have levied and exacted monies from the clergy of Ireland, to bring in the French and to maintain seventy-thousand men.

Fourthly, to have had in a readiness seventy-thousand men, and lists made of them and to have given directions to one friar Duffy to make a list of two-hundred and fifty men, in the parish of Faughart, in the County of Louth.

Relic of St. Oliver's Arm in Poor Clare Convent, Arundel, West Sussex

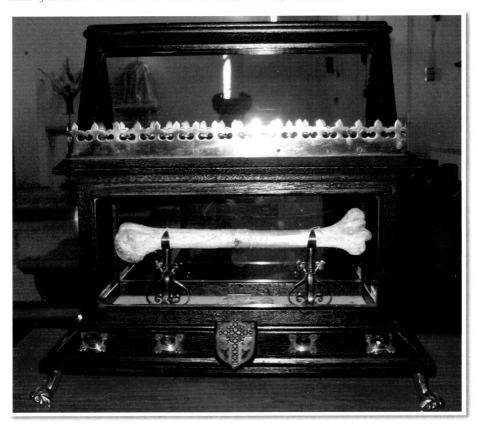

Fifthly, to have surrounded all the forts and harbours of Ireland, and to have fixed upon Carlingford, as a fit harbour, for the French's landing.

Sixthly, to have had several councils and meetings, where there was money allotted for introducing the French.

Seventhly, that I had a meeting, in the County of Monaghan, some ten or twelve years past, where there were three-hundred gentlemen of three counties; to wit, Monaghan, Cavan, and Armagh; whom I did exhort to take arms to recover their estates.

To the first, I answer, that Nial O'Neale was never my servant or page; and that I never sent letter or letters by him either to Monsieur Baldeschi, or to the Bishop of Aix, or to Principe Colonna. And I say that the English translation of that pretended letter, produced by the Friar MacMoyer, is a mere invention of his and never penned by me, or its original, either in English, Latin, Italian, or any other language. I affirm moreover, that I never wrote letter or letters to Cardinal Bullion, or any of the French King's ministers. Neither did any, who was in that court, either speak or write to me, directly or indirectly, of any plot or conspiracy against my King or my country. Further, I vow that I never sent agent or agents to Rome, or to any other court, about any civil or temporal affair. And it is well known, for it is a precept publicly printed, that clergymen living in countries, where the government is not of Roman-Catholics are commanded by Rome, not to write to Rome, concerning any civil or temporal affair. And I do aver, that I never received letter or letters from the Pope, or from any other of his ministers, making the least mention of any such matters: so that the Friar MacMoyer and Duffy swore most falsely, as to such letter or letters, agent or agents.

To the second, I say, that I never employed Captain Con O'Neale to the French King or to any of his ministers, and that I never wrote to him or received letters from him, and that I never saw him but once, nor ever spoke to him, to the best of my remembrance ten words; and as for his being at Dungannon or Charlemount, I never saw him in those towns or knew of his being in those places. So that as to Con O'Neale, Friar MacMoyer's depositions, they are most false.

To the third, I say, that I never levied any money for a plot or conspiracy, for bringing in French or Spaniards. Neither did I ever receive any, upon that account, from priest or friar; as Priest MacClave and Friar Duffy most untruly asserted. I assure you that I never received from any clergyman in Ireland, but what was due to me by ancient custom for my maintenance, and what my predecessors these hundred years past, were used to receive. Nay, I received less than many of them and if all that the Catholic clergy

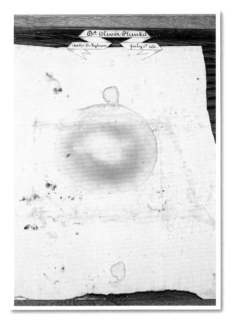

Linen Cloth stained with St. Oliver's Blood - Poor Clare Convent, Arundel, West Sussex

of Ireland get in the year, were put in one purse, it would signify little or nothing to introduce the French, or to raise an army of seventy-thousand men, which I had enlisted and ready as Friar MacMoyer most falsely deposed.

To the fourth, neither is it less untrue, what Friar Duffy attested, viz that I directed him to make a list of two-hundred and fifty men in the parish of Faughart, in the County of Louth.

To the fifth, I answer, that I never surrounded all the forts and harbours of Ireland and that I was never at Kinsale, Cork, Bantry, Youghal, Dungarvan, Youghal or Knockfergus, these thirty-six years past, I was not at Limerick, Duncannon, or Wexford. As for Carlingford I was never in it but once and stayed not in it, above half an hour. Neither did I consider the fort or haven. Neither had I it in my thoughts or imagination to fix upon it, or upon any other fort or haven, for landing of the French or Spaniards. And whilst I was at Carlingford by mere chance, passing that way, Friar Duffy was not in my company as he most falsely swore.

To the sixth, I answer, that I was never at any meeting or council, where there was mention made of allotting or collecting of monies, for a plot or conspiracy. And it is well known that the Catholic clergy of Ireland, who have neither lands nor revenues, and hardly are able to keep decent clothes upon their backs, and life and soul together, can raise no considerable sum; nay cannot spare as much as would maintain half a regiment.

To the seventh, I answer, that I was never at any meeting of three-hundred gentlemen in the county of Monaghan, Armagh, Cavan, nor of one county nor of one Barony. And that I never exhorted gentleman or gentlemen either there, or in any other part of Ireland to take arms for the recovering their estates. And it is well known that there are not even in all the Province of Ulster, three hundred Irish Roman Catholics, who had estates, or lost estates by the late rebellion and it is as well known, all my endeavours were for the quiet of my country, and especially of that province.

Now, to be brief, as I hope for salvation, I never sent letter or letters, agent or agents, to Pope, King, Prince, or Prelate, concerning any plot or conspiracy against my King or country: I never raised sum or sums of money, great or small, to maintain a soldier or soldiers, all the days of my life. I never knew nor heard, neither did it come to my thoughts or imagination, that the French were to land at Carlingford, and I believe there is none who saw Ireland even in a map, but will think it a mere romance. I never knew of any plotters or conspirators in Ireland but such as were notorious and proclaimed, commonly called Tories, whom I did endeavour to suppress; and as I hope for salvation, I am and I was all the days of my life, wholy and entirely innocent of the treasons laid to my charge, and of any other whatsoever. And though I be not guilty of the crimes, deposed against me, yet I believe no man ever came to this place, who is in such a condition as I am; for if I should even acknowledge (which in conscience I cannot do, because I should belie myself,) the chief crimes of which I am accused, no wise or prudent man who knows Ireland, would believe me. If I should confess that I was able

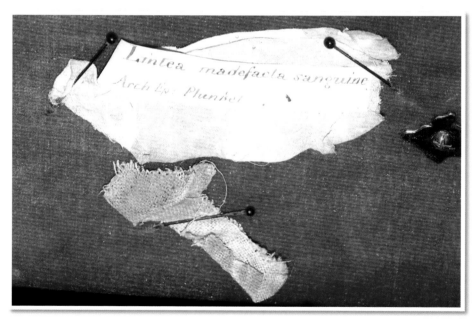

Linen Cloth stained with St. Oliver's Blood - Poor Clare Convent, Arundel, West Sussex

to raise seventy-thousand men, in the districts of which I had care; to wit, in Ulster; nay, even in all Ireland, and to have levied and exacted monies for the maintenance of the said army, from the Roman Catholic clergy and to have prepared Carlingford, for the landing of the French; all would but laugh, laugh at me. It being well known, that all the revenues spiritual and temporal of Ireland possessed by his Majesty's subjects are scarce able to raise and maintain an army of seventy-thousand men. If I will deny all those crimes, (as I did, and do,) yet it may be, that some, who are not acquainted with the affairs of Ireland, will not believe, that my denial is grounded upon truth, though I assert it, with my last breath. I dare venture further and affirm, that if these points of seventy-thousand men, etc. had been sworn before any protestant jury in Ireland, and had been even acknowledged by me at the bar, they would not believe me, no more than if it had been deposed, and confessed by me, that I had flown in the air from Dublin to Holyhead.

Relic of St. Oliver in Tyburn Convent, close to the Martyr's Altar

You see, therefore, what a condition I am in, and you have heard what protestations I have made of my innocence, and I hope you believe the words of a dying man and that you may be the more induced to give me credit. I assure you that a great peer sent me notice, that he would save my life, if I would accuse others. But I answered, that I never knew of any conspirators in Ireland but such as I said before, were notoriously known and proclaimed outlaws, and that to save my life, I would not falsely accuse any and thereby prejudice my one soul. *Quid prodest homini...etc* (**note 1**) To take away any man's life or goods wrongfully, ill becometh any Christian and especially a person of my calling; being a clergyman of the Roman Catholic Church, and an unworthy prelate. Neither will I deny, to have exercised, in Ireland, the functions of a Roman Catholic prelate, as long as there was any kind of toleration, and by preaching, teaching, and statutes, to have endeavoured to bring the clergy, of which I had a care, to a due comportment, according to their calling; but some of them would not amend and had a prejudice for me, and especially my accusers, to whom I did endeavour to do good; I mean the clergymen: who did accuse me, (as for the four laymen, viz. Florence Mac-Mover, the two Neals, and Hanlon, I was never acquainted with them). But you see how I am requited, and how by false oaths they brought me to this untimely death: which wicked act, being a defect of persons, ought not to reflect upon the order of St. Francis, or upon the Roman Catholic clergy. It being well known, that there was a Judas among the twelve Apostles, and that among the deacons there was a wicked man called Nicholas. And even, as one of the said deacons to wit, holy Stephen did pray for those who stoned him to death; so do I, for those who, with false oaths spill my blood; saying, as St. Stephen did, "O Lord! lay not this sin to them." And I beg of my Saviour to grant them true repentance and the grace never to sin any more. I do forgive them with all my heart, and also the judges, who by denying me sufficient time to bring my records and witnesses from Ireland, did expose my life to evident danger. I moreover forgive all those who had a hand in bringing me from Ireland, to be tried here, where it was morally impossible for me to have a fair trial. I do finally forgive all who did directly or indirectly concur, to take away my life, and I ask forgiveness of all those whom I ever offended by thought, word, or deed.

I beseech the All-powerful, that his Divine Majesty grant our King, Queen, and the Duke of York, and all the Royal family, health, long life, and all prosperity in this world and in the next, everlasting happiness. Now, that I have (as I think) showed sufficiently how innocent I am of any plot or conspiracy. I would I were able, with the like truth, to clear myself of high crimes committed against the Divine Majesty's commandments, often transgressed by me, for which, I am sorry from the bottom of my heart; and if I should or could live a thousand years, I have a firm resolution, and a strong purpose, by your grace, My God, never to offend you; and I beseech your Divine Majesty, by the merits of Christ, and by the intercession of his Blessed Mother, and all the holy Angels and Saints, to forgive me my sins, and to grant my soul eternal rest. *Miserere mei Deus…etc. Parce animae peccatrici meae; In manus tuas Domine commendospiritu meum.* (**note 2**)

For a final satisfaction of all persons, that have the charity to believe the words of a dying man, I again declare before God, as I hope for salvation, what is contained in this paper, is the plain and naked truth, without any equivocation, mental reservation, or secret evasion whatsoever, taking the words in their usual sense and meaning, as Protestants do, when they discourse with all candour and sincerity. To all which, I have here subscribed my hand the first of July.

Letters promoting Peace and Reconciliation in Ireland, ready for posting to every Parish and Religious Community in the Country for the Feast of St. Oliver

Jubilee Year of Mercy 2016 - St. Oliver Pilgrimage to Rome led by Archbishop Eamon Martin - Following the Way of the Seven Churches in Rome as recorded by St. Oliver

*50th International Eucharistic Congress 2012 - Bringing the Congress Bell up Slieve Gullion
to the location where St. Oliver is reputed to have hidden*

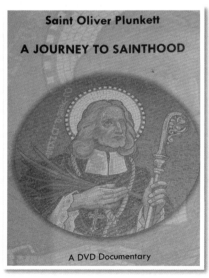

*The Church at St. Oliver's Home, Loughcrew,
where he attended or served Holy Mass*

*A DvD about the Life and Times of St. Oliver,
available at the National Shrine, Drogheda*

299

Stone Sarcophagus under St. Oliver's Tomb in Downside Abbey - His Body rested in this Box in the Church at Lamspringe for Two Hundred Years until it was brought to Downside in 1883

Bishop Norbert Trelle of Hildesheim alongside Cardinal Seán Brady of Armagh, giving a Blessing of St. Oliver Relic in Lamspringe

*St. Oliver Altar, Downside Abbey,
Consecrated in 1935 by Cardinal
Joseph MacRory of Armagh*

*Plaque in Downside Abbey -
Commemorating the visit in
1935 of Cardinal Joseph
MacRory of Armagh to
Consecrate the St. Oliver Altar*

'St. Oliver Plunkett - The Final Days'
A Drama performed by Duleek Drama Society on the Steps of St. Peter's Church, Drogheda -
Produced by Michael Ferguson

Cardinal Seán Brady with Concelebrants in St. Peter's Church, Drogheda - Mass of Thanks-
giving for Peace Process in Northern Ireland, October 12th 2007

St. Oliver Mosaic and Plaque outside Church in Clapham, London

National Shrine of St. Oliver, Drogheda - Showing a replica of Lamspringe Banner gifted to Drogheda 2017

APPENDIX X

PRAYERS TO ST. OLIVER

Despite the huge scientific and cultural changes since the days of St Oliver, his steadfast courage remains an admirable example in these challenging times. Pope Francis in Lumen Fidei, notes that 'Faith is no refuge for the faint-hearted.' We are constantly reminded of this in the bits and pieces of our own lives. So it comes as no surprise that the Archdiocese of Armagh has adopted the Martyr-Archbishop, Oliver Plunkett, as a guide and patron of renewal. Over the past ten years, Cardinal Brady has encouraged and sponsored a Pastoral Plan based on a consultative and participative model which challenges us all to be co-responsible for faith and mission. It is work that happens slowly and needs to be centred on prayer and nurtured by prayer.

Diocesan Prayer to St Oliver Plunkett

Oliver, Saint and hero,

You followed the way of Jesus

and stood up for what you believed in.

We honour your memory.

Guide our Diocese

as we engage with the challenges of our time.

Direct our energies in ways that nurture faith in

Father, Son and Holy Spirit.

Walk with us on the pilgrim path,

Which involves renewal and change.

Help us to trust in Jesus as leader and teacher.

May we value all that is sacred

and embrace courageously ways of peace

and reconciliation. Amen.

St Oliver Plunkett pray for us.

NOVENA PRAYERS TO ST. OLIVER

DAY 1 - MAN OF FAITH

Glorious Martyr, Saint Oliver, who willingly gave your life for your faith, help us also to be strong in faith. May we be loyal like you to the see of Peter. By your intercession and example may all hatred and bitterness be banished from the hearts of Irish men and women. May the peace of Christ reign in our hearts, as it did in your heart, even at the moment of your death. Pray for us and for Ireland. Amen.

Conclude each day with the following prayers

O Holy Saint Oliver, Bishop and Martyr, defender of the Faith and glory of our country, full of confidence we beg you to obtain our petitions, and pray for us to the God you loved and served heroically unto death. Amen.

Our Father... Hail Mary... Glory be...

DAY 2 - FOUNDER OF SCHOOLS

We thank you and we bless you, Lord our God. In times past you taught us in many and varied ways through the prophets, but in this, the final age, you have taught us through your Son. After his great example St Oliver founded schools for the education of the young. May they be filled with knowledge of your will in all wisdom and spiritual understanding, and bear fruit in every good work. Amen. Concluding prayers...

DAY 3 - PROMOTER OF PEACE AND RECONCILIATION

God our Father, you instruct us through the scriptures that we have been wonderfully made. We know that you have created us in love and to be loved; but we more often see that the life you regard as sacred is taken for granted, used and discarded, and treated as having no value. Through the intercession of St Oliver we ask you to banish violence and intimidation, to promote peace and stability, and protect our homes, our streets, our parish and diocese. Amen. Concluding prayers...

DAY 4 - LOYAL AND OBEDIENT

God our Father you have given us shepherds on earth to guide and care for your people. We pray for *N* our Pope and *N* our Bishop. We understand that the devil refused to serve an Incarnate God, and that his pride is also a great temptation in our hearts too. Help us, through the intercession of Archbishop Plunkett to remain faithful to our shepherds and follow their instruction with true Christian humility. Amen. Concluding prayers...

DAY 5 - HE LIVED THE BEATITUDES

God our Father, through your Son's preaching you have revealed to us that your ways are different from our ways. What our society considers lowly and contemptible you elevate, and what is exalted here on earth, you bring to obeisance. May we follow the example of St Oliver, a true man of the Beatitudes and listen first to the Word of God as our model for right living. Amen. Concluding prayers...

DAY 6 - BROUGHT HOPE TO HIS PEOPLE

Heavenly father, we come before you today in need of hope. There are times when we feel helpless, weak, and overwhelmed. Our daily routine becomes heavy and cumbersome when accompanied by so much useless worry. St Oliver worked tirelessly against great obstacles and anxiety and never lost hope. Help us in our perseverance too, that during our greatest trials the hope that was gifted to us by your Son may continue to burn brightly. Amen. Concluding prayers...

DAY 7 - MAN OF COURAGE

God our Father, you raised up St. Oliver to be a shepherd of your people in troubled times; we thank you for his example of love, faithful even unto death. May the memory of his life and sufferings confirm our faith, deepen our hope and inflame our own poor love for you. We ask this through Christ our Lord. Amen. Concluding prayers...

DAY 8 - A MAN OF FORGIVENESS AND MERCY

Almighty God, our heavenly Father: We have sinned against you, through our own fault, in thought, word, and deed, and in what we have left undone. For the sake of your Son our Lord Jesus Christ, forgive us all our offences. Through the intercession of St Oliver may we who have experienced your forgiveness and mercy willingly extend it to those who have offended us, and grant that we may serve you in newness of life, to the glory of your Name. Amen. Concluding prayers...

DAY 9 - A MARTYR AND A SAINT

God Our Father in every age the seeds of the Church are watered in the blood of the martyrs. St Oliver bravely counted his fidelity to you as infinitely more important than his own life and comfort. As persecutions against Christian faithful rises across the world, we pray that you will give your grace and strength to all who may be asked to witness for their love for you with their very lives. Amen. Concluding prayers...

NATIONAL PRAYER TO ST. OLIVER

Glorious Martyr, St. Oliver,

who willingly gave your life for your faith,

help us also to be strong in faith.

May we be loyal like you to the see of Peter.

By your intercession and example, may all hatred and bitterness

be banished from the hearts of Irish men and women.

May the peace of Christ reign in our hearts,

as it did in your heart, even at the moment of your death.

Pray for us and for Ireland. Amen.

The above prayer has been promoted widely in recent years.
Many recite it daily for the intention of Peace and Reconciliation in Ireland.